George Humphrey,
Charles Wilson
and Eisenhower's War
on Spending

ALSO BY JAMES WORTHEN

*The Young Nixon and His Rivals:
Four California Republicans Eye
the White House, 1946–1958* (McFarland, 2010)

*Governor James Rolph and the Great Depression
in California* (McFarland, 2006)

George Humphrey, Charles Wilson and Eisenhower's War on Spending

JAMES WORTHEN

McFarland & Company, Inc., Publishers
Jefferson, North Carolina

LIBRARY OF CONGRESS CATALOGUING-IN-PUBLICATION DATA

Names: Worthen, James, author.
Title: George Humphrey, Charles Wilson and Eisenhower's war on spending / James Worthen.
Description: Jefferson, North Carolina : McFarland & Company, Inc., Publishers, 2019 | Includes bibliographical references and index.
Identifiers: LCCN 2019029063 | ISBN 9781476677859 (paperback : acid free paper) ∞ | ISBN 9781476637709 (ebook)
Subjects: LCSH: United States—Politics and government—1953–1961. | Humphrey, George M. (George Magoffin), 1890–1970. | Wilson, Charles Erwin, 1890–1961. | Budget—United States—History—20th century. | Government spending policy—United States—History—20th century. | Cabinet officers—United States—History—20th century. | Statesmen—United States—History—20th century. | Eisenhower, Dwight D. (Dwight David), 1890–1969.
Classification: LCC E835 .W67 2019 | DDC 973.921092—dc23
LC record available at https://lccn.loc.gov/2019029063

BRITISH LIBRARY CATALOGUING DATA ARE AVAILABLE

ISBN (print) 978-1-4766-7785-9
ISBN (ebook) 978-1-4766-3770-9

© 2019 James Worthen. All rights reserved

No part of this book may be reproduced or transmitted in any form or by any means, electronic or mechanical, including photocopying or recording, or by any information storage and retrieval system, without permission in writing from the publisher.

Front cover image *left to right*: George Humphrey and Charles Wilson at NATO Council Meeting, April 1953 (National Archives)

Printed in the United States of America

McFarland & Company, Inc., Publishers
  Box 611, Jefferson, North Carolina 28640
    www.mcfarlandpub.com

Table of Contents

Introduction: Republicans at Sea	1
Prologue: Eisenhower to the Rescue	5
1. Recruiting a Team	9
2. Eisenhower's Businessmen	14
3. Paths to Public Service	21
4. Sizing Up the Newcomers	41
5. Eisenhower the President	54
6. Eisenhower's Economists	67
7. Humphrey Goes to Work	75
8. Wilson in the Maelstrom	94
9. Humphrey and the 1953–54 Recession	110
10. Humphrey and His Critics	129
11. "A banker's mentality": Humphrey and Foreign Aid	139
12. Wilson, Humphrey and the "New Look"	146
13. 1956: Wilson's Troubles Worsen	165
14. The Price of Prosperity	185
15. Humphrey for President?	199
16. The "Battle of the Budget" and Its Aftermath	204
17. Ike, Humphrey and Wilson in Retrospect	218
Chapter Notes	237
Bibliography	253
Index	259

Introduction:
Republicans at Sea

On a warm and humid day in early December 1952, a military transport landed at Wake Island in the central Pacific. Instead of troops or cargo, the plane carried several prominent civilians whose heavy coats revealed that they had traveled a great distance. Agents of the United States Secret Service had spirited them away from Washington, D.C., in the dead of night in a "hush-hush, cloak-and-dagger manner" and dispatched them on a secret 10,000-mile journey westward.[1] Cover stories were deployed to conceal their whereabouts. Even their families did not know where they were going.

Among those disembarking on Wake were two of the richest men in America. One of them, 62-year-old George Magoffin Humphrey, was a solidly built man with an easy smile and an outdoor look. He had a "faintly Bourbon cast of countenance—a long nose and a slightly protuberant lower lip."[2] The other arrival, Charles Erwin Wilson, also 62, was handsome, blue-eyed, silver-haired, and stocky. He walked with a slight stoop, "as if bucking a breeze"—one journalist called it the "Wilson sidle."[3]

Though neither man had a single day of experience in a state or federal bureaucracy, they had recently been recruited, to their complete surprise, for two of the country's most important public offices. Their flight to Wake was for the purpose of conferring with their new boss, the recently elected president of the United States, who would soon be arriving from Korea.

The election of Dwight Eisenhower a month earlier had ended a generation in the wilderness for the Republican party. Partisans celebrated the end of the Roosevelt and Truman years and eagerly looked forward to a more conservative administration in Washington. But just how conservative it would be was far from clear. The new president had no track record in public office and no strong identification with either political party.

As the Eisenhower administration began to take shape, political Washington sought clues to its agenda in an examination of Cabinet appointments. The recruitment of two Midwestern businessmen, George Humphrey and Charles Wilson, as treasury and defense secretary, respectively, seemed especially significant. Humphrey and Wilson, the chief executive officers of two mighty corporations, appeared to be typical of their class—men who favored a less expensive, less intrusive, business-friendly government.

After only a few weeks in office, it became apparent that one of Eisenhower's primary domestic goals was to stop the growth of federal spending. The Great Depression of the 1930s had led to a vast expansion of the government in Washington, and fighting World War II had cost a staggering amount of money. Now the country was involved in a new war in Korea, the financing of which had built a large budget deficit. Eisenhower was convinced that continued deficits would weaken the economy and thereby endanger national security. Thus, his priorities were to end the war and then pare federal expenditures to their essentials, with the goal of balancing the national budget within a year or two.

George Humphrey would necessarily be at the center of this effort. He arrived in Washington determined to challenge every penny spent by the government. His obsession with frugality reinforced Eisenhower's instinctive economic views, and his calm confidence and personal magnetism gave him entrée into the president's small circle of close friends. For several years, these assets rendered him nearly unassailable in Cabinet deliberations. Even in the face of recession in 1953–54, he torpedoed arguments for increased federal spending to revive the economy, not only from other presidential advisers but from the president himself. In time, he proved to be one of the most influential Cabinet members in the history of the presidency.

Because national security needs accounted for most discretionary government spending, Charles Wilson's Defense Department was the main target of Humphrey's belt-tightening crusade. Hindered by a management style at odds with the Pentagon's top-down culture and a penchant for blunders, Wilson struggled to find a balance between maintaining military readiness and acceding to the draconian cuts being forced on him. The relentless pressure for reductions caused an uproar in the uniformed services and in Congress, and ultimately undermined Eisenhower's credibility as a military leader.

Looking back from the twenty-first century, the administration's preoccupation with budget balancing can seem misguided. The United States budget deficit in 2015 was over $400 billion, yet Ike and Humphrey would agonize about being a few million dollars in the red—a rounding error by today's standards. The cuts in defense resulting from their constant exhortations against spending were so steep that they required the development of a new, less expensive military posture—one that increased American reliance on nuclear weapons and de-emphasized the need for conventional forces. It can be argued that this policy was short-sighted, given the ensuing half century of small-scale conflicts.

Most important to the Republican party, the tight limit on spending was in many ways politically counterproductive. It contributed to the perceptions that the president's men favored the interests of big business over those of average Americans and that the country's military capability was falling behind that of the Soviet Union. In time, these beliefs gave Democrats potent ammunition in national elections. The congressional contests of 1958 were a disaster for the Republicans. Two years later, as Vice President Richard Nixon fumed about Eisenhower's refusal to stimulate the economy in a presidential election year, he lost his 1960 White House bid by a whisker to Democrat John F. Kennedy.

George Humphrey and Charles Wilson were key players in the economic and defense debates of the mid-1950s. Long-time captains of industry, as well as good friends, they were nearing retirement and looking forward to lives of leisure on their country estates when Eisenhower made them offers they could not in good conscience refuse. Neither of them saw his Cabinet position as the crowning achievement in a long and successful career but instead regarded it as an obligation, undertaken with great reluctance. Each viewed his service as temporary and would have been surprised if told that his new responsibilities would keep him in Washington well into Eisenhower's second term.

This book charts their unlikely journey from the corporate world to the highest levels of government and assesses their contributions to Eisenhower administration goals. It also examines the validity of widespread skepticism that their business experience would be of any value in running federal bureaucracies. Telling the full story of their relationships with Eisenhower and with each other promises to shed new light on how the president used his subordinates and made decisions. Finally, by probing the connection between their radically different styles and their success or failure, the book illustrates how personality can affect political behavior.

By focusing on only two individuals in the larger context of Eisenhower's "war on spending," I have necessarily simplified a complex policy environment. The administration's early years were devoted to a top-to-bottom reevaluation of America's international, defense and economic postures. The policies developed from this process then had to take into account the views of key congressmen and the political balance of power on Capitol Hill, as well as public opinion. I have summarized many of the details of this larger story in the interests of clarity and brevity.

Humphrey and Wilson were the only major Cabinet figures who did not write recollections about their government experiences and who were not later the subject of biographies. With minor exceptions, neither sat for the many detailed oral history interviews that were later conducted with major administration figures. Much of the source material for this project was gathered from three archival collections—the George M. Humphrey Papers at the Western Reserve Historical Society in Cleveland, Ohio; the Charles E. Wilson Papers at Anderson University in Anderson, Indiana; and the Dwight D. Eisenhower Library in Abilene, Kansas. I am indebted to the archivists in each institution for their valuable assistance in locating and assessing relevant documents and photographs. Special thanks go to Heather Robinson-Mooney in Cleveland, Nicholas Stanton-Roark in Anderson, and Valoise Armstrong and Kathy Struss in Abilene.

The deliberations of Eisenhower's Cabinet and National Security Council, as recounted in Eisenhower library files, were important sources of information. The give-and-take among participants in these sessions was documented in summaries prepared by Eisenhower's staff. I have put many of the reported remarks in quotes, even though the summaries may not always contain the exact words spoken. All other quotes are sourced, but widely available background material is not.

Prologue:
Eisenhower to the Rescue

In the early 1950s, the Republican party was in crisis. The last Republican administration, that of Herbert Hoover, had been voted out of power in 1932 after failing to arrest the economic collapse that followed the stock market crash of 1929. During the subsequent five presidential terms of office, Democrats Franklin Roosevelt and Harry Truman guided America through depression and world war into a precarious postwar peace. As the election of 1952 approached, frustrated G.O.P. leaders sought a winning presidential candidate—someone who would end twenty years of electoral futility.

Republicans had their first real chance at returning to the White House in 1948. Though Truman would be remembered decades later for his toughness and courage, the Missourian who assumed the presidency following Roosevelt's death in 1945 was not a popular chief executive and seemed particularly vulnerable as he sought to be elected in his own right. New York governor Thomas Dewey, who had lost to Roosevelt in 1944, was again chosen as the Republican standard bearer.

Once more, victory eluded the G.O.P. Dewey's woodenness and overly cautious campaign inspired little enthusiasm and gave Americans insufficient reason to vote for change. Far behind in the polls, Truman mounted a stirring comeback during the fall and was returned to office in November. Republican leaders could stomach the loss of four consecutive presidential elections to a man as popular as Roosevelt, but Dewey's defeat at the hands of Truman was bitter medicine.

A soul-searching debate among Republicans followed the 1948 election. One of the main issues facing the party was how to respond politically to the unprecedented growth of the federal government during the long years of Democratic political control. Restive conservatives concluded that Dewey had not offered the electorate a clear choice between continued big government programs and a return to fiscal orthodoxy and small-town values. They wanted a candidate who would make a serious effort to roll back the Roosevelt revolution.

But the party's moderate wing, still headed by Dewey, believed that the conservatives were nostalgic for an America that was fast disappearing. The popularity of federal programs easing the financial burdens of old age and reining in the worst excesses of the free market had made the Democrats the majority party. Sticking with principles might be personally satisfying, but the moderates recognized that Republicans could not win a national election any longer without Democratic votes.

Turning to Ike

The presidential candidacy of Dwight Eisenhower in 1952 was made possible by Republican desperation. A sixth consecutive defeat would be catastrophic. The party badly needed "the sobering experience of responsibility."[1] In order to win, it required a candidate with broad appeal, someone who would capture the national imagination. The party's moderates believed that electability should trump both doctrinal purity and political experience in nominating a president. As the television age dawned, candidates could now be evaluated by their human qualities—personality, sincerity and charisma—rather than merely by their resumes and public statements.

His leading role in victory over Germany in World War II had made Dwight Eisenhower a national hero. The commander of allied forces in Europe returned home in 1945 as the most popular living American. Along with his skills as a military tactician, he had proved his ability to persuade men with different agendas to work together toward common goals. People were encouraging him to run for president even before the war ended.

Most aspirants to the presidency identify with an ideology of governing, whether liberal or conservative. In the late 1940s, no one even knew what political party Eisenhower favored, because he had never held elective office. But that did not seem to matter. President Truman recognized his potential as a civilian leader in 1948, offering to stand aside in the November elections if Ike wanted to run as a Democrat. He declined. Instead, he accepted the post of president of Columbia University. Periodically he spoke out on national issues, but for the most part his public remarks lacked policy content.

In time it became clear that Eisenhower was not really a political partisan at all. As a military officer, he had loyally served Democratic administrations for more than a decade. The national interest—his view of it—took precedence over the parochial interests of politicians. He would always reject advice urging actions aimed at gaining narrow political advantage.

The only cause in which he appeared fully invested was American participation in rebuilding and defending Western Europe and assuring the success of the North Atlantic Treaty Organization. Too much blood had been shed defeating Germany to allow Europe to go its own way again. He was a fervent backer of the Marshall Plan, which bore the name of his long-time mentor and boss, George Marshall. In a concrete demonstration of his commitment to the new postwar order on the continent, he accepted the post of NATO supreme commander in 1950.

In early 1952, Eisenhower was not a candidate for president and would have been far behind if he was. The Dewey wing of the Republican party, which had recently been so hopeful about the upcoming election, was reassessing the political balance of forces. What these men saw coming was another train wreck.

The clear front-runner was Ohio's veteran senator, Robert Taft. He was the choice of Republicans with an orthodox bent, especially those from rural, small-town America. The son of a former president, he had both experience and integrity. The Ohioan had sought the party's nomination in both 1940 and 1948 and had lost each time. But it was not clear to the party's moderates that Taft had a better chance to win than Dewey had in 1948. Taft lacked charisma, did not suffer fools gladly, and refused to shade his opinions to spare feelings.

In addition, he embodied a Midwestern mindset that had little appeal in the nation's great urban centers or among Democrats who might be ready for change. Granting his impeccable political resume, Republican moderates believed that Taft's flaws put victory in doubt. As Taft's nomination seemed more and more inevitable, they began urgent talks with Eisenhower, appealing to his sense of duty. California senator Richard Nixon, for one, was solidly in his camp: "I don't say Taft can't win," said Nixon carefully, "but I do say that I'm not *sure* he can win. And I'm sure Ike *can* win."[2]

The 1952 Election

After months of soul-searching, Eisenhower agreed to run. In a dramatic and bitter convention struggle, he narrowly prevailed over Taft. His selection amounted to a leap of faith, and it accentuated divisions within the party. His campaign that fall was based on his unimpeachable authority as a wartime leader. With the Korean War in full swing, an aggressive Soviet Union building an Iron Curtain across Eastern Europe, and the future of the West hanging in the balance, the times seemed to call for national security experience.

Advisers saw no need for him to venture beyond vague generalities on domestic issues. People will vote for you, they assured him, because they believe you will keep the country safe. Ike was not entirely happy with their reassurance—in fact, he felt that Republican leaders were being condescending. After an early meeting with party professionals, he seemed upset. "All they talked about was how they would win with my popularity. Nobody said I had a brain in my head."[3]

Ike's campaign comments on domestic policy lacked specificity, but they revealed a conservative turn of mind. He promised to fight inflation and to work toward a balanced budget, lower taxes, and smaller government. He singled out the Defense Department for budget reduction, in view of enormous recent increases in national security spending made necessary by the Korean War. But he also reassured a large segment of the population by not joining calls for the repeal of major New Deal social and economic programs. In fact, he pledged to improve and extend Social Security.

Taft Republicans put aside their apprehensions about the nominee's ideological bona fides and joined other party members and an enthusiastic public in giving Eisenhower a resounding victory over Adlai Stevenson in November. The election ended the Roosevelt-Truman era and broke the Democrats' twenty-year lock on the presidency. Among the party faithful, it produced a long-delayed wave of relief and euphoria.

What Next?

The election of Eisenhower solved one Republican problem—that of returning to power—but instead of resolving their internal ideological struggle, his victory drove it underground. Republicans would ride the president's astonishing popularity through two full presidential terms, even as factions within the administration and in Congress sought to shape the party's post–Eisenhower future. The president would attempt to keep a lid on internal dissension and, if possible, build a consensus behind his brand of Republicanism that would keep the party in power for years to come.

How would he handle the challenge? He had little public policy experience, so he would need professional advice on many subjects. He seemed to be well prepared to handle foreign affairs and defense—he already had a personal relationship with the most important world leaders. But his domestic policy was, to put it kindly, a work in progress. As the year drew to a close, his supporters began to wonder what kind of government this most nonpolitical of presidents would put together.

1

Recruiting a Team

A Time to Plan

Dwight Eisenhower's campaign promise, "I will go to Korea," probably clinched the 1952 election for him. American troops were mired in a stalemated and unpopular war in that divided country, and his dramatic pledge to assess the situation on the ground reminded the voters that he was the nation's most celebrated hero, the leader of allied forces in Europe during World War II. Though some of his advisers considered the pledge a risky idea, it turned out to be a masterstroke. After the election, they again raised objections to such a dangerous and perhaps unprofitable trip, but Ike insisted on going.

He also viewed the journey as an opportunity to get to know his new leadership team. On Wake Island, he was joined by several members of his Cabinet, including Humphrey, for the journey aboard the cruiser *Helena* to Hawaii. Wilson was met by Admiral Arthur Radford, who had been with Eisenhower in Korea. Instead of joining Ike's party aboard ship, the two men flew directly to Hawaii.

The three-day voyage aboard the *Helena* turned out to be more useful to the president-elect than his mostly symbolic visit to Korea. The Wake Island summiteers included the incoming secretary of state John Foster Dulles, the new head of the Bureau of the Budget Joseph Dodge, and Eisenhower confidant Lucius Clay. Ike engaged his new advisers on a wide range of problems, while forming impressions of their abilities and personalities. The group took stock of the challenges before them and made several tentative decisions about priorities—one of them being to find a way to end the war.

The proceedings could easily have been aimless and inconclusive, but that would not have mattered much to Ike. The president-elect was more concerned with group chemistry. To his satisfaction, he found his new colleagues a congenial bunch. They were confident, successful men, and they looked ahead with optimism to being part of the first Republican administration in a generation.

The Challenge of the 1950s

The 1950s have a reputation today as a "placid decade,"[1] but Eisenhower assumed leadership of the country during a period of great uncertainty and apprehension. Victory in World War II, instead of ushering in a benign and cooperative world order, was followed by a new challenge from a wartime ally, the Soviet Union, and the spread of Communism in Europe and Asia. In 1949, the victory of the Chinese Communists over the U.S.-backed Nationalists shocked Americans. The competitive relationship with the U.S.S.R. and Communist China was soon being called a cold war. A year later, the Truman administration sent thousands of troops to Korea to oppose an invasion from the north. As voters went to the polls in November 1952, the United States was still mired in Korea and the international environment seemed threatening and unpredictable.

Even more unsettling was the realization that the Soviet Union was developing and testing atomic weapons. Though Americans knew that their nuclear monopoly could not continue indefinitely, the news caught them by surprise and unleashed a wave of anxiety. For the first time in its history, the United States could be destroyed by an attack it was powerless to prevent. Would nuclear weapons actually be used? The rules of the game were yet to be written. The situation required the new president to address two crucial questions: What constituted an effective defense against the new threat? How much defense could the country afford?

Eisenhower was on firm ground when it came to the first question. After a career in the army, he understood the country's defense posture at least as well as any other American. His foreign policy team, headed by Secretary of State Dulles, was experienced and skilled. Dulles would find reason to consult with the president at least once a day during the next eight years, far more often than any other Cabinet official.

But the second question led into the complexities of economic policy. This was not a subject on which Republicans had distinguished themselves in the past. Memories of Herbert Hoover's failure to arrest the country's descent into the trauma of the Great Depression lingered. Many Americans feared that a Republican-led government would fail the country again during an economic crisis. Consequently, many party leaders regarded good economic management as the administration's highest priority. They believed that it needed to avoid the kind of cataclysm that would remind voters of the Hoover years and once again cast the party into the political wilderness.

Delegating the Talent Search

A crucial task for Eisenhower was to shore up his perceived weaknesses by choosing a capable Cabinet and White House staff. His leadership style had always depended heavily on delegation, teamwork, and group decision making. During the war, he had managed contentious meetings with assertive, head-strong army subordinates and egotistical British generals. As president, however, he would be surrounded by specialists in many subjects he knew little about. Staying in control of national policy discussions would be more difficult.

He was a man with a slim Rolodex. His closest associates were current or former military officers and a group of liberal Republicans, mostly New Yorkers, who had organized and conducted his successful presidential campaign. Identifying good Republican Cabinet candidates was going to be difficult in any event. The party had been out of power for so long that few of its leading members had significant experience in national government. According to an aide, the new president "had to overcome a feeling that he was in a world he didn't know very well."[2]

One of Ike's campaign advisers, the economist Gabriel Hauge, reminded him of the importance of his treasury secretary selection and the breadth of experience the eventual nominee would need. State and Defense, he conceded, are more in the news, "but Treasury is basic to everything." This was especially true in view of the administration's promised emphasis on balanced budgets, tax reduction, and inflation fighting. The new secretary had to understand how the overall economy worked, how spending, taxes, and debt management interacted, and how fiscal and monetary policy complemented each other. Hauge admitted that "there aren't many Americans of prestige and background who qualify."[3]

Eisenhower did not act as though he considered these decisions crucial. He was humble enough to realize he had much to learn, but too self-confident to be troubled by it. In fact, he was remarkably disengaged from the search for Cabinet-level talent he launched shortly after the election. He turned over that task to an old friend, General Lucius Clay, and to Herbert Brownell, a political strategist whose campaign management skills helped win the 1952 election.

Clay's Mission

A long history with the president-elect made Clay the more influential of the two. He was a blunt-spoken former army officer who had served with

Eisenhower under Douglas MacArthur in the Philippines during the 1930s. Ike considered him a "walking dictionary"—the person "best acquainted with me and my methods, and who also had a wide acquaintance with people of substance" in the country.[4]

Clay had a well-earned reputation as a man who did not suffer fools gladly. A business associate spoke for many of Clay's acquaintances and co-workers over the years in describing him as the "most arrogant, stubborn, opinionated man I ever met." His views of other people bordered on the dogmatic—positive or negative but rarely nuanced. He never seemed to second-guess himself. "He was quite sure that his judgment was correct ... and rather insisted on it, sometimes to the embarrassment of the people around him," recalled Truman's defense secretary Robert Lovett.[5]

Henry Cabot Lodge, who played a key role in Eisenhower's presidential campaign, considered Clay a real asset to the politically inexperienced candidate. "Lucius is terrifically blunt," said Lodge. "A man like Clay is extremely useful. He scared some people to death."[6] He was also prone to the occasional snap judgment. Any self-doubt, it seemed, had been filtered out by fifty years of army command.

Giving such a man the responsibility of identifying key officials in the first Republican administration in a generation carried obvious risks—all the more so because Eisenhower had only a general idea of what or who he was looking for. He departed for a vacation after the election, leaving Clay and Brownell to put together an administration. "He didn't give me any instructions," Clay later recalled. "I think he had enough confidence in our judgment to know that we were going to try to find men of high caliber."[7] Brownell agreed that he and Clay had a "remarkably free hand."[8] Ike did have one stipulation—that they consult first with Dewey and Taft. It is not clear what advice, if any, Dewey gave them. Clay later noted that Taft showed little interest in the process.

By this time, Clay had abandoned the dull life of a retired military officer to run the Continental Can Company. Both in military and civilian life, he had a reputation as a "chaos-into-order man of global standing."[9] He was someone who could come into an organization with no knowledge of its operations or product and stiffen its spine.

Eisenhower knew something else important about Clay—that despite his strong opinions, he was, like Ike, essentially apolitical. He had spent the war years working for Franklin Roosevelt as deputy director of the Office of War Mobilization and Reconversion, second only to Democrat James Byrnes in running the U.S. economy. He was a great admirer of Byrnes, who went on to become secretary of state under President Truman. Clay also regarded

Roosevelt as a "diplomatic genius," and he had the "highest respect" for Truman.[10] Holding such heretical views, Clay would have had little credibility with any other incoming Republican administration.

Clay's lack of strong identification with either party meant that Ike could trust him to recommend good people for Cabinet posts, regardless of their specific policy preferences. Clay understood that the president-elect put a premium on character, decisiveness, and the ability to be a team player. Given advisers with those strengths, Ike believed, good policy would emerge.

It did not even matter to Clay if the appointees had no previous connection with the president or with the Republican party. "In the Army you rarely know the people you're assigned to work with beforehand," Clay pointed out. "General Eisenhower was remarkably gifted in bringing people from a variety of backgrounds together and forging them into a successful team." He continued: "What he wanted were people who were exceedingly competent and on whom he could rely to run their departments.... We didn't go into this extended search in which you have elaborate committees and staff people play such an important role. Brownell and I knew most of these people first-hand."[11]

Eisenhower also favored subordinates who were psychologically suited to working in groups and who would contribute to good overall chemistry. He considered personality just as important as ability. The need to recruit senior officials who were compatible as well as competent placed an additional burden on Clay and Brownell.

Armed with little more than the confidence of the president-elect, they began their search for Cabinet candidates—a job that would consume nearly all of their energy and waking hours until inauguration day.

2

Eisenhower's Businessmen

Clay and the president-elect had agreed at the outset that representatives of the business world would play a prominent role in the new administration. In fact, Ike had promised voters that he would find "the best kind of business management this nation can produce to help us run this government."[1]

Ike respected and admired the nation's corporate leaders, viewing them as exemplars of American success. He appreciated their optimism, self-confidence, and ability to manage complex organizations. The attraction was mutual. Business groups, in particular, were eager to hear him expound on international political and military affairs. Soon after returning from the war, he became acquainted with many of the country's wealthiest and most powerful corporate executives, who were thrilled to be in the company of an authentic national hero.

The best example of Ike's affinity for the rich and successful was his "gang" of good friends, which included the vice president of the *New York Herald Tribune*, a New York investment banker, the chairman of the board of the Coca-Cola Company, the president of the Cities Service Company, and the president of a distillery. He shared with these men a love of golf, hunting, bridge, and relaxed banter. He could be himself around them and forget for a while the problems that burdened him. Though all members of the group except one were dyed-in-the-wool Republicans, the glue that held it together was fellowship rather than ideology. After he was elected president, Ike convened the gang and their wives for a few days of fun whenever he saw a gap in his schedule. Sometimes they would fly in on just a few hours' notice.

Many prominent businessmen had sought to convince Ike to run for president in 1952. One of these men was Paul Hoffman of Studebaker Motors, a long-time political activist and head of the Committee for Economic Development during the war. Hoffman was also a leading member of the Business Advisory Council, which worked closely with the U.S. Commerce Department.

Founded during the depths of the Great Depression, the Business Advisory Council was a reservoir of business talent with a relatively progressive bent. Its executives differed with their more conservative colleagues in coming to terms with the major social and economic accomplishments of the New Deal. In return, the Roosevelt and Truman administrations gave the council an important consultative role during the war and sought its help in shaping domestic legislation in the early postwar years. Hoffman and other members of the Council saw Eisenhower as a kindred spirit and strongly supported him for president.

What Manner of Men?

A survey conducted by a national magazine in 1953 found the nation's top capitalists to be a parochial bunch. It pointed out that C.E.O.s of the larger companies tended to be from small, conservative Midwestern towns. Their work experience was deep rather than broad—they generally climbed to the top in the same or a related business.[2] The most accurate collective description—that they were white males—was too obvious for the survey to mention.

They differed from their iconic predecessors, the founding giants of American industry. Men like Andrew Carnegie and Henry Ford had been intuitive visionaries who invented entire industries and imposed their personalities on their products. The newer generation of industrialists came of age during the prosperous 1920s. They were management specialists, concerned above all with efficiency and rational use of labor. Automotive executives like Alfred Sloan, the genius behind the rise of General Motors, and Paul Hoffman, who saved Studebaker from bankruptcy, took the lead in restructuring and rationalizing the American corporation. They regarded administration as a science, with universal principles that could be applied with equal success to any business. The sudden popularity of books on subjects such as personnel management, public relations, and long-term planning helped to spread the new gospel.

Though the Great Depression changed the country in many ways, most heartland businessmen remained socially and economically conservative, as well as anti–Roosevelt. They viewed the growth and intrusiveness of the federal government with alarm, certain that Roosevelt was moving the country toward socialism. If the majority were not outright isolationists, they tended toward a circumscribed view of America's role in the world. Their natural political hero was fellow Midwesterner Robert Taft.

While Roosevelt's New Dealers were busy trying to alleviate the widespread economic distress of ordinary Americans, many of the country's largest companies continued to earn sizeable profits. As the country moved toward war in the late 1930s, it became clear that a healthy private sector would be the key to victory. After Pearl Harbor, the importance of weapons production brought the prestige and importance of the U.S. business community to a new high. Dislike of the president did not prevent the country's industrial leaders from rallying to the cause of defeating Germany and Japan. The quickness with which civilian manufacturing plants were retooled after Pearl Harbor allowed airplanes, tanks, and ships to come off American assembly lines in astonishing numbers.

Like his counterparts in the Pacific campaign against Japan, General Eisenhower and his troops were dependent upon a steady flow of materiel. The prodigious armaments production—$12 billion worth—of General Motors, the enormous company headed by Charles Wilson, landed him on the cover of *Time* magazine. Companies like G.M. and General Electric were equal partners with the nation's political leadership and military forces in winning the war.

It is easy to understand why Eisenhower carried his appreciation for this successful cooperative effort and his admiration for the efficiency of the American corporation into civilian life.

Offers at Sea Island

Conveniently, by late 1952 Clay was a businessman himself. He was tasked with filling two of the three key Cabinet posts—treasury and defense. (Little serious debate surrounded the choice of John Foster Dulles as secretary of state.) Representing Continental Can, Clay attended a Business Advisory Council retreat at Sea Island, Georgia. He took the opportunity to confer with fellow executives about possible administration appointees. Not surprisingly, most of the C.E.O.s suggested other corporate leaders. Clay had in mind two men, both of whom were present at the gathering.

First, he approached Charles Wilson, the long-time president of the world's largest company, and offered him the Defense Department post. After swearing Wilson to secrecy, Clay then located Humphrey, a former chairman of the Council and the head of a sprawling conglomerate known as the M.A. Hanna Company. Humphrey, told by friends that Clay was in Sea Island, began to "smell a rat." When the job of treasury secretary was offered to him, he just laughed and said: "Lucius, why in the devil did you think of me?"[3] Both he and Wilson asked for time to think it over. A few hours later, Clay went to Wilson's hotel room to learn his decision and was surprised to find him sharing the news of the offer with his friend Humphrey.[4]

Humphrey was in a quandary. After almost thirty years running M.A. Hanna, all he wanted to do was "shoot some quail, raise some horses, and play with the grandchildren." But he and his wife, Pamela, went off to a favorite spot in the woods to decide. In the end, they bowed to a sense of duty. "Wouldn't we feel I'd let the president and the country down?" he recalled. "As I said to my wife, this sort of thing is kind of like the draft. If your number's up, you've got to go."[5] His sense of duty made it impossible to say no.

A Closer Look

One insider had the impression that Humphrey had been picked out of the "blue yonder,"[6] but that was not exactly true. Along with being a member of the Business Advisory Council, he had been finance director of the Republican party during the 1952 presidential campaign and had bankrolled several local Republican candidates in Ohio over the years. Some analysts saw his treasury appointment as a reward for this service to the party.[7] The fact that Humphrey was not a crony of the new president's and had not sought the position doubtless were positive factors in Ike's mind, given his distaste for greedy office-seekers.

Eisenhower's political advisers endorsed the idea of bringing Humphrey into the administration, assuming that doing so would please fellow Ohioan Bob Taft. Humphrey had supported Taft's presidential candidacy and had raised funds for his campaign. But the two men turned out not to be especially close,[8] and Taft's lukewarm response to the appointment must have disappointed the Eisenhower team.

Perhaps the main reason for Humphrey's emergence was his close ties to two men who had Clay's ear. One of these was Hoffman, and the other was Sidney Weinberg, the colorful chief executive of the investment firm Goldman, Sachs. Weinberg was legendary for his vast network of friends. He was so well connected to the nation's industrial leadership that one historian called him "an ambulatory quorum of American business."[9] Both he and Humphrey served on over a dozen corporate boards as part of the interlocking system that characterized American corporate life at the time.

Their similarities extended to their personalities—both men were known for their social gifts. Weinberg's influence was said to derive more from his winning and persuasive manner than from his substantive knowledge. Similarly, Humphrey's personal magnetism and deal-making skills were more important to his business success than his knowledge of steel production. In suggesting Humphrey to Clay, Weinberg was promoting a man with whom he had much in common.

Clay also knew that Humphrey had considerable experience in the world of industrial finance, mergers, and acquisitions. Humphrey's reputation as an able organizer and manager had gained him membership on government-affiliated commissions, formed to study the future of the American economy. After his brief acquaintanceship with Humphrey, Clay was impressed with his rare combination of "forward-looking imaginativeness" and "complete normalcy."[10]

Viewed from the standpoint of relevant experience and knowledge, however, the choice of Humphrey was unorthodox, even risky. His immediate predecessors had been well-connected men with national reputations. Henry Morgenthau, who served Roosevelt for over a decade, was an aristocrat from a famous family and a close friend of the president's. Truman's first treasury secretary, Fred Vinson, served in all three branches of government and ultimately became chief justice of the United States. His successor, John Snyder, a banker and Truman confidant, had led the country's transition to a peacetime economy as director of War Mobilization and Reconversion.

Humphrey had no such cachet. He did not have a personal or professional relationship with the president who selected him. He had no relevant experience in a Washington bureaucracy, or anywhere in the public sector. He had little opportunity to learn the intricacies and nuances of national economic issues. He had no role models or mentors in the field of economic policy making. He knew few members of the capital's political and media elite (though he had befriended a number of Republican congressmen) and had not been the target of the kind of intense scrutiny he was certain to receive from them.

Wilson was the better known of the two nominees, having overseen much of America's wartime defense production. Like Humphrey, he was regarded as a brilliant technocrat as well as a good Republican. Nearly everyone viewed Wilson as a good choice for the Defense Department, because his skill set seemed to match the assignment. Eisenhower wanted the department reorganized, and doing so would involve complexity on the same level as running a large corporation. Two weeks after his election, he told an old friend that the job needed an industrialist, "a man who is used to knocking heads together and is not easily fooled."[11]

There are two slightly different versions of who first brought up Wilson's name. According to Clay, Ike said he was considering appointing the chairman of the Chrysler Corporation to run the Pentagon. "If you are going to go to the business world for the Secretary of Defense," Clay claimed to have countered, "why not go to the biggest business we have?"—meaning G.M. But one of Eisenhower's "gang," Cliff Roberts, who said he was present at that meeting, recalled that when Ike suggested the head of Chrysler, Roberts quickly put forward Wilson's name as the better option. (He said he later regretted having done so.) Roberts professed surprise when Clay agreed.[12]

Right Men for the Job?

The corporate world was well represented in Eisenhower's full Cabinet, which critics described derisively as "eight millionaires and a plumber." Their appointments re-ignited an old argument about the wisdom of hiring businessmen for senior government posts. Leading Democrats tended to believe that the skills required to manage an enterprise concerned solely with the bottom line were irrelevant in Washington, where politics and policy were paramount. Republicans countered that former businessmen would bring much needed efficiency and economy to bloated government bureaucracy.[13]

One important dissenter from his party's view was Senator Taft himself, who shook his head when he learned of Ike's appointments. "I don't know of any reason why success in business should mean success in public service," he observed. "They're very different fields.... Anyone who thinks he can just transfer business methods to government is going to have to learn that it just isn't so."[14]

Recent history suggested that Taft's concerns were exaggerated, or perhaps an expression of personal pique. Former businessmen had held leading positions in government even during the Roosevelt and Truman administrations. Among them were James Forrestal, a Wall Street bond salesman who became secretary of defense; Robert Lovett, an international financier who also headed the Pentagon; Edward Stettinius, a former chairman of U.S. Steel who held high-level positions in the Roosevelt State Department; Charles Edward Wilson (often confused with Defense Secretary Charles Erwin Wilson), the president of General Electric and a prominent wartime official; and Paul Hoffman of Studebaker. The businessmen in Ike's Cabinet would have an advantage their predecessors did not enjoy—that of serving in a more ideologically congenial administration.

But the inexperience of Wilson and Humphrey carried obvious risks. Shared Midwestern backgrounds separated Humphrey and Wilson from the more liberal, cosmopolitan and internationally oriented Republicans, such as Tom Dewey, Herbert Brownell, and other leading lights of the 1952 campaign. Yet Humphrey and Wilson were invited into the Cabinet of a man who had been drafted by liberal Republicans for the express purpose of putting a more progressive face on their party.

This inconsistency mattered because Eisenhower was not much better prepared for his new job than the others. To his credit, he was not surrounding himself with old cronies. "You must get courageous men, men of strong views, and then let them debate and argue with each other," he emphasized.[15] To those he trusted the most, he was prepared to delegate considerable operational authority, because government had become "too big, too complex, and too pervasive in its influence on all our lives for one person to pretend to direct the details."[16]

The consequences of the Humphrey and Wilson appointments could hardly be anticipated. The two men came from the same milieu, had similar backgrounds and political views, and were expected to work in harmony to advance Eisenhower's agenda. In the end, however, what they had in common personally would matter less than their new institutional perspectives.

3

Paths to Public Service

The success stories of George Humphrey and Charles Wilson were alike in many respects. Both men had high achieving parents, grew up in prosperous circumstances, and developed a strong work ethic. Their long careers in business and their Midwestern provincialism fed their opposition to government interference in the private sector and limited their perspective on conditions in big cities or overseas. They saw the world through "business eyes."

The Man from Hanna

Humphrey was born in Cheboygan, Michigan, in 1890, into a family of privilege, if not great wealth, and spent his early years in Saginaw, a prosperous lumber-processing town.[1] The oldest of four children, he was a standout in high school, where he played football, earned good grades, and was twice elected class president. The gift of a pony at age eight began a life-long passion for horses and riding. His ability to handle animals was aided by his preternatural calm, a quality that contributed to his later success.

His self-confidence and social skills were nurtured in childhood by parents who were excellent role models. His father was a leading citizen of Saginaw—a prosecuting attorney by profession, who served for a time as president of the Michigan state bar association. He was active politically and ran unsuccessfully for Congress the year George was born. He led local pro–William Howard Taft forces against the Theodore Roosevelt Bull Moose insurgency in the presidential election of 1908. The younger Humphrey called his father "the most forceful, dynamic, positive man I ever knew."

His mother had an equally strong influence on his development. A schoolteacher, she was a gentle but firm taskmaster with a winning sense of humor. Her politics were conservative—when she wrote the name Roosevelt, it was always with a small "r."

The influence of both parents gave their son ambition and a sense of possibility. After graduation, he enrolled at the University of Michigan and, after a brief flirtation with engineering, wound up studying law as his father had. His college record attested to his high intelligence and self-discipline: he earned an L.L.B. degree, edited the *Michigan Law Review*, and was admitted to the state bar in 1913.

Humphrey's path to success was well lit by his father, whose corporate law firm hired him right out of school as a partner. The position provided contact with the region's business elite, and he quickly became known as a young man on the way up. According to one source, by 1913 he had already tried a case before the U.S. Supreme Court. The president of the local bank, who was planning on retiring, persuaded Humphrey to succeed him in a year or two, presumably in addition to his legal duties.

At about the same time, Humphrey married his childhood sweetheart, Pamela Stark. Her father, also a well-to-do local attorney, gave the couple a house as a wedding present. Only 23, Humphrey gave every indication of being launched on a successful and lucrative career in Saginaw.

For the next several years, he gained legal experience as a representative of the Michigan Central Railroad, defending damage and personal injury claims against the company. The young man was so effective in his early assignments that the Michigan Central offered him a position in Detroit as its principal lawyer, but he turned it down. The case work led to a personal revelation—that success in law enhanced his personal reputation but provided little tangible satisfaction. "I was much more interested in building something you could see or touch," he recalled.

Humphrey's big break was his relationship with one Richard Grant, the general counsel of the M.A. Hanna Company in Cleveland. Grant had married a Saginaw girl whose father was one of the elder Humphrey's best friends. His frequent presence in town soon led to a friendship with George and Pamela. It did not take Grant long to ask Humphrey to move to Cleveland as his assistant. He took the job with Hanna in 1917, later telling an interviewer, "why I'll never know." He confessed that he did not like big cities and that he was doing "plenty well" in Saginaw, but added that "these things have just happened in my life like fate."

The M.A. Hanna Company was named for a U.S. senator and financial backer of President William McKinley. It was in the mineral extraction business, but perhaps a better term was a hodge-podge. Originally focused on mining in the Great Lakes area, it grew in all directions—starting or acquiring companies related to its core business—until it owned ships, docks, coal and iron mines, blast furnaces, and warehouses, becoming at last a "mixture of industrial and financial odds and ends." It was, to say the least, a complex business. Humphrey began work at Hanna as its deputy general counsel during the height of a World War I boom, specializing in tax matters.

His move to Cleveland brought him into Ohio, one of the nation's Republican strongholds. With the election of William McKinley in 1896, five of the last seven presidents had been Ohio Republicans. Ohioan Robert Taft would later become the most important Republican member of the U.S. Senate. A resident of the state for the rest of his life, Humphrey was steeped in this conservative, pro-business environment.

A severe economic downturn at the war's end in 1918 forced American businesses into a challenging new environment but provided Humphrey with a golden opportunity. A decline in demand for raw materials like iron ore hit mining interests especially hard. At about the same time, leadership of the company passed to the last living member of the founding family, Howard Hanna. The Hanna and Humphrey families established a close personal relationship, based on shared recreational interests. (Humphrey's eldest daughter later married Howard Hanna's son.) When one of the six partners died in 1920, Humphrey assumed his portfolio, the management of iron ore mining operations.

But the hemorrhaging of money continued. When the company lost $2 million in 1924, the owners agreed that radical steps were needed. "Things were in a heap," Humphrey recalled. "There had to be a reorganization to satisfy the public and the stockholders. They came to me and wanted to know if I would do it"—that is, take over the company. He agreed to become executive vice president with wide powers and a mandate to act but also insisted that Howard Hanna remain formally in charge.

His first action was to propose a new business plan and reorganization aimed at jettisoning unprofitable activities. His scrutiny of company ledgers told him where the profit and loss centers were. In short order, and with little regard for any consideration save the bottom line, he reduced the company to its bare essentials. He wrote off millions of dollars worth of unprofitable companies, sold depleted coal mines and obsolescent blast furnaces, and cut payrolls. In the process, Humphrey showed that he could be ruthless, albeit with a human touch. "He'd fire his grandmother if she wasn't doing a good job ... but he'd put her on a pension," cracked a friend. When asked for the secret of his success, he had a stock answer—getting all the facts, and then "doing the obvious."

Once he had trimmed the fat, he began to reorganize and consolidate, based on his understanding of the direction in which the steel industry was headed. In addition, he looked around for partners. He bragged throughout his career about his ability to pick good business associates—a skill that was

George Humphrey (upper right) with his University of Michigan law school class. After a few years at his father's law firm, he went to work for the M.A. Hanna Company in Cleveland. Still in his early 30s, he was put in charge of developing a business plan that saved Hanna from bankruptcy (Western Reserve Historical Society, Cleveland, Ohio).

aided by his ability to make friends. He began negotiations that led to the formation of a new entity, called National Steel, which linked the companies with Hanna's ore and coal mines, blast furnaces, and lake freighters.

In the deal, Hanna secured a quarter of the new company's stock, becoming the conglomerate's biggest shareholder and retaining a controlling interest. His plan not only saved Hanna but positioned it for huge profits in the years ahead. The ascendancy of National Steel was said to have amazed American business during the Depression, and it became recognized as the largest operation of its kind in the Western Hemisphere.[2]

Humphrey was a great admirer of Herbert Hoover and supported his successful candidacy for president in 1928. He was attracted to Hoover's concept of scientific management, in which the business community regulated itself and strived to serve the public good. Later he recalled the 1920s nostalgically as an era in which a man could achieve financial success without high taxes and excessive government controls.[3]

In the late 1920s, Hanna still had a large investment in coal mining, and Humphrey began to reorganize its coal operations. He also started negotiations with firms owned by business titans John D. Rockefeller and Andrew Mellon about forming a partnership. These talks continued on and off for several years, all through the Great Depression, as he assembled his new organization piece by piece.

Fully realized by the end of World War II, the new giant became known as Pittsburgh Consolidated. "We took two busted coal companies," he later bragged, "and put them together to build the greatest coal company in the world." One Hanna executive said admiringly that Humphrey "could be abandoned in the middle of the Sahara Desert and soon would turn up with a newly organized company producing dividends."[4] Hanna assumed financial control of the coal company and Humphrey took over as chairman of the board.

While most of the country was mired in the Depression, Hanna sat at the center of a web of interrelated firms, from which it took stock in exchange for infusions of cash and management skills. Humphrey took a direct role in setting policies and priorities for each enterprise, yet he did so as unobtrusively as possible and refrained from interfering overtly in local operations. He moved, as *Forbes* magazine put it, "in the shadows of a silent partnership." Another journalist called his approach managing "from the sidelines."

Humphrey also sought ties with the financial sector, and with almost any business that looked as though it might be profitable. When banks were closing by the dozen during the panic of 1933, Hanna stepped in to buy stock in the reorganized National City Bank of Cleveland, of which he became a director. Later Hanna bought 8 percent of the common stock of another big Cleveland bank, the Union Bank of Commerce.

Along the way, Humphrey avoided publicity and was characteristically modest, but the results of his activities attested to his personal effectiveness and strategic vision. "In extraction industries," he later said, "you have to look ahead or you will find that you have got everything out of the ground that is to be had—and you're out of business."

Republican Roots

Unsurprisingly, Humphrey self-identified as a Republican from an early age and was particularly active as a fundraiser for local party candidates in the Saginaw area. He told an interviewer that he considered Republicans "just one step above good Christians."⁵ The Hanna Company, with its links to William McKinley, was intimately linked with Ohio Republican politics. The firm raised money for Herbert Hoover in 1928. After the election, according to one source, Humphrey and Hoover became friends.

As Humphrey's empire took shape in the 1930s, he viewed the Roosevelt administration with sharp disapproval. He took an uncompromising view of the New Deal, whose actions he believed had undermined the capitalist system and thus the American way of life. He remained convinced that Hoover, if retained in office, would have done a better job of fighting the Great Depression. Such a mind-set was bound to affect his later performance as treasury secretary.

Disappointed in Hoover's loss to Roosevelt in 1932, Humphrey supported the next Republican nominee, Kansan Alf Landon, for president in 1936. He worked at the Republican convention to raise money for the candidate, while promoting his view that Roosevelt's National Labor Relations Board was unconstitutional and opposing the unionization of the steel industry. After Roosevelt's landslide victory, Humphrey remained a behind-the-scenes financial backer of Ohio Republicans. He assisted Robert Taft in his run for the Senate in 1940 and in all three of Taft's presidential campaigns.⁶

Years of political activity, coupled with his business ventures and lobbying efforts, gave Humphrey a long list of valuable political contacts in the nation's capital. He cultivated senators and representatives from Midwestern states and often invited them to his estate in Georgia for weekend vacations. These associations provided useful insight into how Washington worked.

As his success grew, Humphrey kept exclusive company with other prominent businessmen and joined clubs whose memberships included the economic elite of eastern Ohio and western Pennsylvania. He entertained enthusiastically and lavishly. At leisure, he led a life similar to that of an English country squire. In 1937, he purchased a mansion in Thomasville, Georgia, where he relaxed, hunted, and fraternized with his neighbors in the region's "estate belt," including Wall Street executives and leading New York bankers. He remained an avid horseman, owning his own stables, attending important races such as the Kentucky Derby, and riding frequently despite having suffered many broken bones in falls.

A Parallel Life: Wilson at G.M.

While Humphrey was climbing into the ranks of Ohio's elite, another exemplary business career was taking shape not far away from Hanna headquarters in Cleveland. Like Humphrey, Charles Wilson was raised in an industrious Midwestern family.[7] He was born in 1890, the same year as Humphrey, in the Ohio town of Minerva, seventy miles southeast of Cleveland. His father was the principal of the local school, while his mother was a teacher there. Charles (called Erwin by his friends) was the first of four children.

The boy enjoyed a childhood similar to that of Humphrey—active and happy, with strong support from involved parents. As with Humphrey, a pet pony gave him a lifelong appreciation of horses. The typical chores of a nineteenth-century rural family, such as milking cows and filling oil lamps, nurtured a work ethic that would in adulthood come dangerously close to workaholism. His parents also taught him the importance of education and of making an extra effort to get along with people.

As it happened, the neighbors on both sides of the Wilson home in Mineral City were railroad engineers. These men became heroes to young Erwin. They gave him tours of the engine cabs on their trains and explained how the automatic couplings and the new Westinghouse air brakes functioned. Wilson also spent hours at the town's new power plant, trying to understand how electricity was conducted and controlled. Fascinated by both experiences, he decided he wanted ultimately to work with machinery.

Wilson's family moved to Pittsburgh in about 1905. Erwin attended high school there, skipped two grades and, despite a bout with typhoid fever that almost killed him, graduated at age 16. He then enrolled in an electrical engineering program at the recently established but already well regarded Carnegie Tech. He graduated with honors after three years. His reputed ability to do integral calculus in his head earned him the nickname "Wizard."

Some time after graduation from Carnegie, the Westinghouse Electric company recruited Wilson as an apprentice engineer. He was quickly identified as a young man with unusual promise. He had a special talent for simplifying processes and improving designs. In 1912, Wilson gained further recognition by designing Westinghouse's first automobile starting motor.[8] His work attracted the attention of the Remy Electric Company, which was a subsidiary of automotive giant General Motors.

After World War I, Wilson found his path to advancement at Westinghouse blocked by a glut of senior officers, whose death or retirement he would have to await. Though he was happy there, he followed the advice of a sympathetic company official and contacted G.M. chief executive Alfred Sloan. In 1919, two years after Humphrey had made his fateful decision to join M.A. Hanna in Cleveland, Sloan lured Wilson to a job interview and offered to triple his Westinghouse salary if he would move to Anderson, Indiana and join Remy Electric as chief engineer and sales manager. With some reluctance—the move would uproot Wilson's growing family—he said yes.

The Education of a Manager

At Remy, Wilson encountered a situation similar to Humphrey's at Hanna—a business in decline during the postwar recession and badly in need of new thinking. He found that though Remy's products were good, they were not well designed for mass production. Without a smooth flow of materials, inventories accumulated, wasting time and space. He set about reengineering the company's products and devising ways to improve productivity.

Neither Remy nor Anderson welcomed Wilson with open arms. Even after the recession ended and solvency returned, the city's establishment was often hostile to the now thriving plant in its midst. In a region that was still in many ways a traditional agrarian society, a social stigma attached to blue-collar workers and industrial labor. Wilson and his executives were denied admission to the local country club. With the continued expansion and profitability of Remy, however, they eventually succeeded in convincing the locals of their respectability.

G.M. executives, watching from afar, gave Wilson a free hand and promoted him to factory manager in 1925. A year later, the company merged with another engineering business in Dayton called Delco, and Wilson was named president of the combined Delco-Remy Company. He was now in charge of over 12,000 employees who manufactured shock absorbers, industrial refrigeration motors, automobile headlights, washing machines, batteries, and related products. His childhood wish to work with equipment had been more than fulfilled.

Delco-Remy's expansion created a need for more housing in Anderson. Wilson found that his responsibilities now extended beyond plant management and into the building and financing of homes and an apartment complex for his workforce. Again meeting resistance from local interests, Wilson's executives pooled their resources and formed their own real estate company. At significant personal risk, they sought financial backing for an entire housing subdivision. The venture was successful: five hundred homes were built. The success of G.M. and Delco-Remy thus had enormous consequences for the town of Anderson and made Wilson a key figure in its history.

Wilson continued to work hard to gain acceptance for Delco-Remy in the community. Colleagues were struck by his concern for human relations—not a quality common to supposedly hard-boiled factory managers. He instituted "visitors day" for local citizens to meet the staff and observe the pleasant working conditions. For the grand opening of one of the company's new facilities, he financed a two-day performance of a circus, at which Alfred Sloan and other G.M. executives were guests of honor. Downtown merchants closed their doors so that their employees could attend. The extravaganza was wildly successful—both in impressing G.M. management and promoting Anderson as a town on the move.

Wilson's propensity for overwork caught up with him during the go-go years of the late 1920s. He ended up at the Mayo Clinic with severe ulcers, brought on by stress, long hours, and physical inactivity. According to a contemporary account, he nearly died before getting help.

The 1920s and 1930s were the Alfred P. Sloan era at General Motors. From company headquarters in Detroit, the G.M. board chairman took notice of Wilson's accomplishments at Delco-Remy. In 1928, once his health problems resolved, he was appointed vice president in charge of a group of auto accessory companies, a responsibility that furthered his interest in organizational structures and problems. He later claimed to have learned from that and future management assignments that organizations should not follow rigid rules, but rather should be adapted to the abilities and personalities of the people who staff them. Like Humphrey, Wilson oversaw the acquisition of other businesses—in his case electrical engineering firms.

Through the Depression years, Wilson continued to serve as a vice president of G.M. The company's sales rose despite the fact that the automobile industry was among the hardest hit by the economic decline. By marshaling its superior resources and management, it doubled its profits between 1934 and 1937. It also benefited from the bankruptcy of dozens of smaller car manufacturers, which allowed it to increase its market share. During the late 1930s, the Roosevelt administration sought briefly to press anti-trust actions against large companies like G.M., but as war seemed increasingly likely, it worried more about damaging firms that would be the backbone of any future military effort.

Wilson moved up to executive vice president in 1939. The following year, with war having begun in Europe, the Roosevelt administration asked G.M. president William S. Knudsen to direct the government's Office of Production Management. His departure gave Wilson his big chance. He became head of G.M. in time to lead the company through World War II.

The Business Advisory Council

The economic emergency of the 1930s and the war that followed brought government and industry into an awkward embrace. The idea of a strong central government making national economic policy was obviously anathema to the business community. Many of the nation's corporate chieftains viewed themselves as just slightly less powerful and important as the president himself.[9] At General Motors, board chairman Alfred Sloan was virulently anti–Roosevelt. He was openly critical of FDR's moves to rearm America in the years before Pearl Harbor, and even insinuated that the biggest danger to the country was from New Deal policies rather than any foreign threat. Henry Ford was also an implacable Roosevelt opponent.

The idea that the American economy could always right itself without government help died hard—and among some conservatives did not die at all. But many leading businessmen began to see that the panic and decline of the Great Depression could not be arrested by market mechanisms or voluntary efforts. Increasingly they saw the assertive policies of the Roosevelt administration as essential to recovery.

The most important organizational reflection of this revisionist sentiment was the Business Advisory Council. In helping the government devise an industrial recovery strategy, it became, in effect, a "business cabinet," working closely with the U.S. Commerce Department in "marrying corporate expertise to federal power."[10] Commerce provided office space and learned from its deliberations but exercised no direct oversight over its activities.

From the beginning, this quasi-public undertaking gave the nation's corporate elite a sense of involvement in national policy. By entering into a cooperative relationship with a Democratic administration, the men on the Council showed themselves to be more progressive than conservatives such as Sloan, who "look[ed] upon trade unions as an adult form of juvenile delinquency and [thought] of Franklin D. Roosevelt as a closet communist."[11] The Council's awareness that FDR was trying to save capitalism rather than destroy it led to its acceptance of government's role as regulator, arbiter, and umpire in the national economy. Its leadership thus worked informally but closely with leading officials of the executive branch.

In fact, Business Advisory Council executives helped to shape the welfare legislation that emerged in 1935 as the Social Security Act. One of those most closely associated with its formulation was Marion Folsom, the president of Eastman Kodak, who would become George Humphrey's deputy at the Treasury Department eighteen years later. From a business point of view, the genius of the Social Security system was that it was self-financing—it relied on contributions from workers and their employers. (Folsom had created a similar retirement plan at Kodak.) Thus, a massive entitlement program came into being that had the support of much of the nation's business elite.

At the same time, many conservative C.E.O.s were unhappy with the Business Advisory Council's limited partnership with the Roosevelt administration. Well into the war years, they regarded Council members as "accomplices to New Deal criminality." More far-sighted business leaders—among them Gerard Swope, president of General Electric; Averill Harriman, the council's chairman;

and Folsom—realized that the federal government was inevitably going to play an essential role in their lives and that opposition was futile.

In 1938, four members of the Council, with the assistance of a young Harvard economist, John Kenneth Galbraith, drew up what they called a "constructive businessman's recovery program." This document, called *Toward Full Employment*, was notable for its early recognition of key principles propounded by British economist John Maynard Keynes. It declared that federal budgets did not need to be balanced at all times, that the purposeful running of deficits could aid recovery efforts, and that wealthier businesses should be taxed more than wage earners.[12] These views remained heretical among many businessmen well into the Eisenhower administration.

After Pearl Harbor, a spirit of national unity and a willingness to assist the war effort were required of all Americans. That meant saying yes when the federal government sought help from the private sector. G.M.'s William Knudsen, an emigrant from Denmark, responded instantly to Roosevelt's appeal for assistance. "This country has been good to me," he told his wife, "and I want to pay it back."[13] Wilson and Humphrey shared the anti–Roosevelt attitudes of most leading American business leaders, but they were patriots too. They decided—as they would eleven years later—that if the country needed their services, they were duty-bound to help out.

In 1942, George Humphrey's standing among the nation's business elite was ratified when he became a member of the Business Advisory Council. Working with the Roosevelt administration, the Council played a leading role in the massive defense mobilization of the next two years. Industrial leaders also banded together to form the Committee for Economic Development, which helped plan the expected transition from a wartime to a peacetime economy. The C.E.D. was led by the widely admired Studebaker president Paul Hoffman. While in Washington, Humphrey and Hoffman became well acquainted.

Business participation in national defense was not entirely about patriotism and sacrifice. The Roosevelt administration understood that in order to guarantee its maximum effort, industry also had to turn a profit. "If you are going to ... go to war ... in a capitalist country," said Secretary of War Henry L. Stimson, "you have to let business make money out of the process."[14] Special tax provisions, production subsidies, and credit guarantees sweetened the pot and virtually eliminated any risk companies took in converting from civilian to war production. As the most important supplier of the war effort, G.M. was best positioned to profit from these provisions.

As postwar conversion planning gained speed in 1943, the Committee for Economic Development, which included many Business Advisory Council members, drafted a statement that recognized new realities in government and society. It accepted labor's right to organize, the role of government in setting fiscal policy to prevent inflation, deflation and depression, and the legitimacy of social welfare services. This declaration was based on "the lessons of recent experience," and it seemed to accept key elements of the New Deal as a permanent reality.

Though it became clear in time that Humphrey was one of the more conservative members of the Council, his association with it set him apart from the nation's more reactionary C.E.O.s. He seemed to be a pragmatic executive who respected facts and accepted both an expanded role for government in the economy and the need to accommodate the interests of workers and unions. In 1946, he began brief service as Council chairman, which earned him an appearance on the cover of *Business Week* magazine. In the accompanying article, Humphrey was described as a "matter-of-fact, realistic businessman who recognizes that times are changing."[15]

By the end of the war, the Business Advisory Council had concluded that the growth of government had gone far enough. It now saw as its main role the blocking of further liberal initiatives undertaken by the new Truman administration. One of its main efforts was a well orchestrated attempt to water down a bill sponsored by former New Deal liberals designed to guarantee full employment. Its efforts, described by one historian as sophisticated political infighting, were entirely successful.[16] Business leaders were learning an important lesson: how to use the former enemy of corporate America— the federal government—as a tool in achieving its goals.

Another important issue for the Council was relations with labor. After the war and the national hardship it brought, trade unions were becoming more assertive in their long-suppressed demands for better wages and working conditions. In the face of this rising militancy, the Council worked pragmatically to limit the power of unions while accepting them as permanent fixtures in national life. Its strong lobbying efforts paid off in the Taft-Hartley legislation of 1947, which succeeded in binding unions in a net of legal restraints and was generally regarded as a victory for business.

Role in Postwar Settlement

Business activists also played an important role in the development of postwar American foreign policy. The task of helping to rebuild Western Europe as a bulwark against Soviet influence brought together many of America's best military and business minds. With conservatives in Congress suspicious of Secretary of State George Marshall's proposal of a large-scale aid program, Truman sought to convince the Business Advisory Council of the importance of Marshall Plan goals.

Speaking as an emissary for the administration, Averill Harriman, a former council chairman and wartime ambassador to the Soviet Union, had no difficulty bringing his former organization around. Council leaders, particularly Paul Hoffman, then assisted Harriman in formulating the Marshall Plan and guiding it through Congress, against the objections of conservative senators like Taft.

The adoption of the Marshall Plan required an organization to administer and coordinate aid. For this purpose, the Truman administration established the Economic Cooperation Administration and placed Paul Hoffman in charge. Hoffman then selected a team of fellow businessmen with a distinctly non-partisan cast. "We weren't interested in whether they were Republicans or Democrats," Hoffman recalled. "What we wanted to know was their record, what they had accomplished." Nor did Hoffman view the president with the distaste felt by most nationally prominent Republicans: "I learned to have not only great regard, but deep affection for him," he later said. "History will, I'm sure, accord him a great place because of many qualities, but among them, courage and never failing common sense."[17]

Inasmuch as George Humphrey was to that point a provincial corporate titan with little interest in American foreign policy, it was ironic that the issue of how to treat the defeated German nation brought together Clay, Hoffman and Humphrey and ultimately led Humphrey into Eisenhower's service.

Two of Hoffman's primary concerns were what to do with the German industrial sector and how to handle the problem of German reparations—subjects on which there was no shortage of opinions in official Washington. Hoffman had worked with Humphrey on the Business Advisory Council and regarded him as a man with "a very rare combination of tough-mindedness and tact."[18] He was also impressed with the Ohioan's ability to reduce complicated problems to their essentials. Hoffman called upon Humphrey to assist him in devising a sensible policy on the dismantling of German industry. Humphrey, in turn, put together a committee of corporate leaders that included Charles Wilson of General Motors.

The dismantling issue was immensely complicated. American disagreements with Britain and France on the dismantling or relocating of German industrial enterprises reflected the different postwar aims of the allies. Political concerns were overlaid with economic and psychological ones, providing a negotiating challenge of the highest order. Humphrey now headed an advisory committee charged with formulating a compromise that would be acceptable to all the parties.

Once this group had decided on a proposal, it faced the difficult job of selling it to Lucius Clay, who was the allied military governor of occupied Germany and a close friend of General Eisenhower. A formidable person in any circumstance, Clay was leery of interference from Washington and had little use for "junketing committees." The situation called for smooth persuasiveness, and Humphrey was the man to provide it. "The wrong phrase or even the wrong look might have upset the whole situation," Hoffman later recalled. "But Humphrey avoided both."[19]

Agreeing on an American position, difficult though that was, was just the beginning. A consensus on the issue with the British and French, who above all feared eventual German industrial resurgence, had to be forged, and congressional support at home had to be secured. In addition, a plant-by-plant investigation had to be conducted. By the time Humphrey became involved, the U.S. stance had already changed several times in response to domestic pressures. Though it was in many ways a straightforward job of economic analysis, *Fortune* magazine summed up the situation as "loaded with political and diplomatic dynamite."

British foreign secretary Ernest Bevin had become increasingly impatient and ill-tempered about what he considered American delaying tactics. Still new to the problem, Humphrey accompanied Hoffman to a meeting with Bevin. Hoffman later recalled, "We were in a difficult position. It was the third time the Americans had changed their minds on the dismantling problems. [Foreign Secretary] Bevin was anxious for us to make up our minds, and Humphrey was new on the job. When we met, Bevin glared at Humphrey and me. He got red in the face and I thought he was ready to explode. I was afraid he might get ill on our hands, but by the time Humphrey got through, Bevin was offering him one of his special brand of cigars."[20]

The Humphrey committee finished its work and submitted it to the State Department in January 1949. Hoffman was so pleased with its realistic and sound recommendations and with the confident and convincing manner in which Humphrey had run the committee that he invited him to attend the allied foreign ministers meeting that would vote up or down on the report. With only minor changes, the report was adopted.

The report's thoroughness, a Humphrey hallmark, proved a solid beginning to Europe's eventual economic union, while aiding major goals of Clay's—the creation of a West German constitution and government and Bonn's integration into the Western alliance. Both Clay and Hoffman sized up Humphrey as a man with vision, energy, diplomatic skill, and an ability to solve large problems. They filed away their impressions for later use.

Wilson Retools G.M.

Charles Wilson's wartime experience was more circumscribed than Humphrey's. Though also a member of the Business Advisory Council, he was busy full-time with one of the most challenging civilian assignments undertaken by anyone on the home front. As Pearl Harbor drew the United States into the conflict, Wilson oversaw a massive effort to convert the automobile plants of General Motors and its affiliates into weapons factories. Hundreds of workers had to be retrained, and dozens of plants had to be retooled. As Wilson explained: "When you convert one of our factories, you move everything out and start with a blank space. Out of a long row of intricate machines on the production line, a certain percentage can be used in the manufacture of a war product. But the production line will necessarily consist mainly of new, special purpose machines."[21]

Those special purpose machines would require months to design and build. Once again, Wilson found himself working endlessly, under constant deadlines and a crushing burden of managerial responsibilities. In order to save time, he often spent the night in the corporate suites and made the twenty-minute drive home only two or three nights a week.[22] At one point, the constant strain became too much for him, and he found it necessary to take three months off. He managed to make a complete recovery, but for the rest of his life, he suffered from headaches and circulatory problems.

The war, with its pressure to produce vast amounts of armaments, was more successful than a decade of New Deal policies in lifting the country out of the Great Depression. General Motors, in particular, produced a large percentage of all the guns, tanks, and planes used in the war. Its contribution to the cause was so extensive that Wilson became a public figure. He also learned a considerable amount about military equipment, which enhanced his qualifications for defense secretary.

Labor Conciliators

Both Humphrey and Wilson shared with Studebaker chief Paul Hoffman a far-sighted view of business relations with labor. They understood the importance of a motivated and cooperative workforce and were willing to pay a price to secure one.

Returning full time to the business of mineral extraction in the late 1940s,[23] Humphrey faced the rising power and militancy of the United Mine Workers and its leader John L. Lewis. Lewis was a controversial figure whose frequent violation of a no-strike agreement with the Roosevelt administration during the height of the war had caused public outrage. With men dying by the thousands in Europe and the Pacific, many Americans considered strikes in industries vital to the war effort treasonous.

A threatened coal strike in 1947 led to a "summit" meeting between Lewis, Humphrey, and the head of U.S. Steel. Much to the surprise and dismay of Lewis' many detractors, who included several congressmen with long memories, the two industrialists agreed in full to U.M.W. wage demands. In defense of the settlement, Humphrey characterized the union's stand as reasonable and even beneficial for the coal industry as a whole. The agreement, he felt, would lead to increased output and higher worker morale. However, many congressmen and other industrialists viewed the settlement as a "sell-out" to Lewis that would feed a wage-price spiral in the coal industry.[24]

In his assessment of the situation, Humphrey was likely motivated less by sympathy for labor demands than by his calculation of the economic damage that would be caused by a work stoppage.[25] His negotiations with Lewis were so amicable that the labor leader later said he would back Humphrey for president if he ever ran.[26] The episode added to his reputation as a man who saw things as they were rather than as he would like them to be.

A large part of Charles Wilson's postwar fame similarly derived from his innovative and conciliatory policies toward the powerful trade unions associated with his industry. G.M. had labor difficulties similar to those experienced by Humphrey's enterprises at the time. Instead of John L. Lewis, Wilson's labor adversary was Walter Reuther, head of the United Auto Workers, whose drive to unionize automobile production had led to strikes and unrest, punctuated by uneasy truces.

Labor problems at G.M. were hardly new—they had plagued the company since the late 1930s. Sit-down strikes and other aggressive actions had so angered company president Bill Knudsen that he had deputized Wilson back then to handle union negotiations. "You take care of this labor business," he told Wilson. "You've got more patience than I have, and you talk more."[27] The usefulness of Wilson's Quaker mother's long-ago admonition—that he make a special effort to get along with people—became apparent. As Knudsen noted, he enjoyed talking, and he would talk and negotiate as long as necessary to reach an agreement.

Wilson's ability to understand and even sympathize with union aspirations turned out to have been rooted in an unlikely family affinity for socialist ideals. His father had been a toolmaker before becoming an educator, and he had organized a union local in Pittsburgh. The younger Wilson supported the presidential candidacy of Eugene Debs, one of America's most noted

Charles Wilson (second from right), the head of General Motors, oversaw the production of $12 billion worth of materiel for American troops during World War II. Others in the photograph are K.T. Keller (left), president of the Chrysler Corporation, and Edsel Ford, president of the Ford Motor Company (courtesy Anderson University & Church of God Archives).

socialist leaders. Backing Debs, he said, prevented him from getting a job in engineering when he graduated from Carnegie Tech. Instead he worked as a patternmaker and became business agent for the patternmaker's local. As G.M. president, he kept a framed copy of his union card on his desk.[28]

Shortly after Pearl Harbor, Wilson had accepted a challenge to debate the more dynamic Reuther. The debate, on the subject of how American industry could have better prepared for the war, lasted almost six hours and attracted media attention from all over the country. Everyone agreed that Wilson held his own.[29] The public relations success of the encounter reinforced in his own mind the importance of treating labor and its representatives with respect. Though not much progress was made during the early 1940s in reaching an overall settlement of union grievances, Wilson gained agreement to end "wildcat" strikes, in return for a promise of fair treatment and no bullying from company managers.

Soon after Wilson became president of G.M., a fractured hip caused by a fall on the ice gave him time to think through an idea that could reduce conflict with the unions in the future. He concluded that a long-term agreement was key—one that would include an "escalator clause" tying wages to the cost of living and thus protecting workers against inflation. Though most G.M. executives opposed the idea, Wilson saw—as Humphrey was also recognizing—that labor peace, even at a high cost, would lead to better worker morale and greater productivity and profits. He tried to convince his colleagues to go along.

As difficult for the rest of G.M. management to stomach as the escalator clause was, it was not the most liberal of Wilson's proposed concessions. He also developed a concept that he called an "improvement factor." As new technology and more streamlined processes increased the company's productivity, worker salaries would be adjusted upward accordingly. Resistance to this idea was immediate, because no one, including Wilson, knew how to measure productivity increases with any precision. He also proposed the industry's first pension plan for retired workers, an idea far ahead of its time.

In 1950. G.M. reached an agreement with the U.A.W. incorporating the escalator clause. Within a few years, the G.M.-U.A.W. pact came to be recognized as industrial statesmanship of the highest order, and it led to the company's dominance of the automobile market for a decade. Like Lewis and Humphrey, Reuther and Wilson took to calling each other friends. Some fellow industrialists who had opposed the generous terms called Wilson a "near New Dealer" and insisted that the C.E. in his name meant "compromise everything."[30] He responded by labeling them "classic reactionaries."[31]

Profits and production were not the only things on Wilson's mind. He bred cattle and had the largest private herd in Michigan. On his farm, he experimented with cross-breeding techniques aimed at a breakthrough in milk production. He enjoyed outdoor activities, but some of his efforts to take part in active sports ended in serious injury. He gave up riding after breaking his shoulder in a fall from a horse. Then he took up ice skating, only to fracture a hip in a fall. Hunting and fishing became his primary outdoor pursuits.

Wilson also took part in the fund-raising work of numerous charitable groups, including the Michigan Heart Association, the American Red Cross, and the United Fund. For a man who spent nearly five days and nights a week at the office, finding the additional time could not have been easy, but it marked him as an executive with a social conscience.

Humphrey's Labrador Venture

In the early 1950s, with his labor force secured, Humphrey embarked upon a risky project that again showed his ability to think strategically and move quickly. Long worried about the depletion of iron-ore reserves in the Great Lakes area, he decided to attempt to exploit the discovery of millions of tons of ore in far-off Labrador, in eastern Canada. More cautious businessmen doubted the profitability of such an enterprise: the ore would have to be mined and then transported by both ship and rail over tundra, mountains, lakes, rivers and bogs in an inhospitable climate a distance of more than 1000 miles before it could be processed.

To secure mining rights in the area, Humphrey buttonholed the Canadian owner of the land, who had been searching for gold and instead found "only" iron ore. Soon the two men had formed a mining partnership. Next he launched a search for investment partners. In typical Humphrey fashion, he managed to enlist five American steel companies and three Canadian mining and exploration companies in a huge joint effort that *Life* magazine described as "the product of cold logic and bold imagination."[32] A Humphrey friend noted that "nobody else in the United States could have raised so much capital so fast for a project in Labrador." The result was a new entity, the Iron Ore Company of Canada.

Contemporary sources believed that ore deposits in the Great Lakes area were in no immediate danger of depletion, and it would have been easy to pass on the Labrador venture in the face of the formidable geographic obstacles. Yet Humphrey never hesitated once the ore discoveries were confirmed. His aggressiveness was typical. "George rides hell for leather up to a jump," observed a banker friend, aptly using a horsemanship metaphor. "[But] before he makes the jump, he knows damn well what's on the other side."[33]

The project also showed his fondness for partnering and his energetic and peripatetic work style. Though he often delegated operational details to other companies, he flew thousands of miles each year in a Hanna plane to inspect, consult and exhort. (Uncommonly in an era of much slower transport, Humphrey often attended meetings in three different cities on the same day and returned home in time for an evening social event.) He recognized that effective oversight required detailed technical knowledge of each business in which Hanna had a stake. No one failed to be impressed with his mastery of every detail.

At the time Humphrey joined the Eisenhower administration, the Labrador project was still years away from completion. The iron mines, a 360-mile railroad, and a terminal had yet to be built. Complicating calculations of the profitability of the enterprise was the question of whether a seaway linking the St. Lawrence River and Labrador with the Great Lakes would be built. Such a seaway would dramatically lower transportation costs for the mined ore, but Humphrey decided he and his partners would make money even without it.

Building the St. Lawrence Seaway had been under consideration for several years, and Humphrey had been on record as an opponent of the idea, which he considered government overreach. On one occasion, he even called it a "socialist ditch."[34] But now he appeared before the Public Works Committee of the House of Representatives as a supporter. In typical fashion, he did not view his reversal as a source of embarrassment but merely an acknowledgment that the facts had changed. "It's perfectly simple, gentlemen," he told the committee. "You've got some material up there that you need down here."[35]

To make his argument as persuasive as possible before an audience of congressmen, he focused on the national security aspects of seaway construction. He testified that he felt "very definitively and positively" that the project was important to the nation's defense. Despite his obvious self-interest in the outcome, some congressmen said after his testimony that they understood for the first time what the seaway was all about. But the seaway decision would be wind up being deferred until after the election of 1952.

Humphrey assumed "that thrilling thing up in Canada" would be his last professional accomplishment before retirement. In 1950, he turned sixty years old and had no plans other than "to shoot some quail and raise some horses." But in 1952, Dwight Eisenhower became president, and his emissary, Lucius Clay, made him an offer he could not refuse.

4

Sizing Up the Newcomers

Their business credentials aside, Humphrey and Wilson brought differing personal qualities and administrative styles to their new roles. Humphrey had spent more time buying and selling companies than actually running them, while Wilson was absorbed in the innumerable details of managing a vast and complex enterprise. Humphrey had the typical executive's ability to make quick decisions based on limited data, while Wilson was accustomed to deliberating for hours, days, or even weeks before acting. "C.E. thinks like an engineer," said an associate. "He is a slow decider. He wants all the information he can get—he eats up big stacks of reports.... He never plays a hunch."[1]

Each man prided himself on his ability to recognize and hire good people. Wilson credited his experience growing up in a small town, where everyone knew everyone else, for his insights into human nature and behavior. "I think I got to be president [of G.M.] because I have the ability to know a good man on very short acquaintance," he later said.[2] Humphrey displayed equal self-regard. "I'm as good as any man in the U.S. at picking partners," he told a reporter.[3]

Humphrey and Wilson entered government at the end of their careers, with nothing to prove and no one they needed to impress, save the president. Neither man looked forward to being part of political Washington—in fact, their distaste for politics and politicians bore a striking resemblance to Eisenhower's. Neither considered his new responsibilities a stepping-stone to any other position. Wilson had an interest in cattle breeding and Humphrey in horses. Neither man had much interest in the life of the mind. Beyond occasional books on horses or cattle, neither man was a reader. Music, art and literature held little attraction. Wilson, in particular, enjoyed simple pleasures—among his best friends was the radio personality Arthur Godfrey[4]—and was not apt to find much in common with the Washington elite.

Humphrey did not hide his gloom about the immediate future. "I feel as though I had been shanghaied into the job," he wrote to a fellow C.E.O.[5]

He told a columnist, perhaps slightly in jest: "The whole thing is just terrible. I've had a happy, contented life, and now it's just shot out the window."⁶

Humphrey's Reception

No one had been surprised when the president-elect announced, in December 1952, that John Foster Dulles and Charles Wilson were joining the Cabinet. But the news of George Humphrey's appointment as treasury secretary was greeted mostly with blank looks.

Even in Cleveland, the headquarters of Humphrey's far-flung industrial empire, there was a scratching of heads and a certain amount of embarrassment at the inability of locals to recognize his name. Reporters knew that he was chairman of the board of M.A. Hanna, referred to humorously as an "ore house," involved in the mining and processing of iron and coal, but they scurried to their files in search of more revealing detail. All they turned up was a slim handful of clippings about a "quiet, canny Scot" with a passion for hunting and horses.⁷

Though he was one of America's most powerful corporate leaders, Humphrey had always been allergic to publicity. *Forbes* magazine reported that he had "never made a speech in his life, never appears on committees, [and] never issues pronouncements on national affairs."⁸ Humphrey spent most of his time and millions of dollars acquiring mismanaged or declining businesses and restoring them to health. None of this work required advertising, public relations, or speechmaking. "If you perform," he said about his corporate life, "you don't need to talk."⁹

The nation's business community did not expect the Humphrey appointment, but many of them slapped their foreheads in recognition of its wisdom. "I never once thought of George," recalled one of his competitors in Cleveland. "Then I sat back and said to myself, 'George Humphrey? Why, you poor fool, of course.'" Surprise gave way to enthusiasm. *Fortune* magazine reported a startling but unanimous belief among businessmen that Humphrey would "not only be a forceful and effective Secretary of the Treasury but a dominant personality in the new government."¹⁰

The *New York Times* also gave his background a positive spin, calling him "one of a new breed of master salesmen," a man who has the knack of "giving an inspirational, almost evangelical, lift to a homily on the virtues of free enterprise."¹¹ Humphrey freely admitted that he had a relatively narrow perspective. "I see everything through business eyes. It's only natural. All my experience, all my life has been in business." Individual voices in Congress added their approval. "If we had our choice of any man in the U.S. for Secretary of the Treasury," exclaimed Connecticut senator Prescott Bush, "we could not improve on George Humphrey."[12]

More liberally inclined observers were less enthusiastic about the corporate flavor of the new Cabinet. Ike was "not taking government out of business," worried Senator Wayne Morse, "he was giving government to business."[13] Historian Arthur Schlesinger, Jr., wrote that the Humphrey appointment was "putting the ideas of Mark Hanna in power," by which he meant a return to the William McKinley era of tight money and high tariffs.[14] Humphrey tried to reassure skeptics by acknowledging significant differences between government and the private sector and pledging to learn quickly on the job.

Personal Assets

As he made his initial rounds, Humphrey struck people as conspicuously lacking in self-doubt. He could cite many reasons why he was reluctant to accept a position in Eisenhower's Cabinet—lack of relevant experience, advanced age, anticipation of a quiet retirement, family obligations—but it never occurred to him that he could not handle the job. He had not only survived but prospered during the Great Depression, a crisis that had thwarted the ambitions of many other entrepreneurs and industrialists, and had gone on to serve his country in a delicate diplomatic task that brought him widespread acclaim.

His unbroken record of success inclined him toward optimism and bonhomie. Beyond his hearty personality and charm, what people noticed first about Humphrey was his reassuring presence. "This is a man you will want to look over carefully," one correspondent wrote: "It is not so much his outward appearance—conservatively dressed, a pleasant smile. It is instead the atmosphere he wears, one of soothing and cheerful confidence. You can imagine him going into a frantic board of directors meeting and calming it with a few practical and common-sense words."[15]

Praise rolled in from many quarters. Here was a rare combination of tough-mindedness and tact, exclaimed *Fortune*. He was a man who "managed by the mysterious alchemy of personality" and whose self-assurance reflected "neither complacency nor arrogance." He articulated "forceful" opinions with "sharp clarity" and a minimum of words, although one visitor said he felt like he had been on the receiving end of a pile driver.[16] Clifford Roberts, one of Eisenhower's closest friends, considered Humphrey "a sort of homespun, plain, easy to know type of person who had a way of changing complicated problems into very simple solutions."[17] Ike noticed that people began going to him soon for advice.

Reporters found his short, pithy sentences and lack of pomposity refreshing in a capital filled with people who loved the sound of their own voices. "You make up your mind you're going to do something, and you do the best you can," Humphrey told one journalist. "You don't blow hot and cold. You don't say first you will and then you won't. You do everything you can. When you can't do any more, you go home."[18]

So Humphrey was easy to like and he commanded respect, but what kind of policy perspective would he bring to his job? His life experiences had given him a conservative world view, though his occasional ruminations suggested a willingness to listen. Roberts said that, whatever the issue, Humphrey could always be found on the "basic side of the matter." He did not get bogged down in details or "wild-eyed philosophies."[19]

Those who knew him best said he was not a prisoner of preconceived notions. They called him "imaginatively orthodox"—a man who "starts with a tradition and strikes out from there on his own experience."[20] Herbert Brownell thought that he would be "on the progressive side," perhaps because of his past association with the Business Advisory Council.[21] Journalists Joseph and Stewart Alsop were among those who predicted that Humphrey's beliefs would take a back seat to the facts in recommending policy. They proclaimed him a "genuinely open-minded man."[22]

Some Doubts

Even with his many assets, it would be a huge step from Midwestern businessman to national economic policymaker. He was about to become the government's chief financial manager. He would help determine the budgets of all other Cabinet departments. And he would necessarily be at the center of Eisenhower's effort to prove that a Republican administration could competently oversee the economy.

Behind the warm welcome extended mostly by Republicans in the press and in Congress were several concerns. Humphrey's insulation from a decade and a half of hard times raised questions about the depth of his understanding of American society. The Depression and the war had barely registered as events affecting his personal life. (His son, however, had served in the military during World War II.) He had not known a moment of economic insecurity. He made his business decisions based on facts and numbers and could afford to ignore the human consequences. Policy advice from such a man might not have the greater good in mind.

Despite his appealing self-presentation as a facts-oriented technician whose goal was simply to put the nation's finances in order, it was clear to the attentive listener that he would be motivated at least in part by partisanship. One interviewer came away with a valuable clue regarding the new treasury secretary's predilections: "We've asked for this situation for a long time," Humphrey said in reference to Eisenhower's victory. "And now that we've got it, we obviously can't refuse to help."[23] These were the words of a man who intended to move the country in a conservative direction.

Wilson at Defense

Charlie Wilson had no experience in politics or public administration, but he had an intimate knowledge of defense production, some practice testifying before Congress, and a casual relationship with the new president. He was regarded as a "technical man," familiar with problems of research and development—a plus in an organization that produced some of the most complex weapons in human history.

As we have seen, Wilson thought deeply about management issues as well as labor relations. He had conceived of G.M. as a self-governing community and in doing so broke with conservative dogma in many ways. Management consultant Peter Drucker praised Wilson for his receptivity to ideas that many C.E.O.s of the time found heretical. Eisenhower was naturally drawn to a man with a reputation for fresh thinking. Most important, Wilson had proved that he could manage a large and complex organization. Wilson agreed that his strongest asset was his ability to "get people working well together."[24]

As he joined Eisenhower's team, Wilson had a much higher public profile than Humphrey. As leader of the nation's mightiest corporation during the 1940s and early 1950s, he made frequent speeches and granted interviews to the media. He was sufficiently well known in January 1949 to be selected for a *Time* magazine cover story. The writer of the story actually asked Wilson how running G.M. might differ from running the Defense Department. (He answered that G.M. was a much more decentralized operation.)[25] After Eisenhower's victory, *Newsweek* too placed Wilson on its cover.

Wilson had more publicly revealed his conservative views than his fellow C.E.O. at Hanna. He decried government interference in the economy and spoke on the evils of inflation. However, he was always ready to defend the relatively high wages G.M. paid its workers, displaying charts purporting to show that federal budget deficits, rather than higher wages, caused higher prices.

Wilson's first encounter with Eisenhower had been in 1949, when Ike was president of Columbia University. The G.M. president received an honorary degree that day and seems to have made a good impression on his host. As army chief of staff, Ike consulted with Wilson occasionally for help on weapons production and supply problems. The future president had a favorable view of Wilson in those days, regarding him as "anything but a yes-man."[26]

As the 1952 presidential election approached, Wilson often sent copies of his speeches to the leading Republican candidates, Eisenhower and Ohio senator Robert Taft, who he especially admired. In a talk titled "The Camel's Nose Is Under the Tent," he argued that the military must not be expanded beyond the minimum needed to defend the country and that the Korean war was being used to justify "more and more state planning."[27]

This message elicited a warm reaction from Eisenhower. "I applaud your purpose of demonstrating that we can and must produce national security without falling into national bankruptcy," Ike wrote. He went on to praise the "head-on fight you are making against the dangerous theory that bureaucratic control can solve our country's ... problems."[28]

Problems at the Pentagon

In assuming the relatively new post of defense secretary, Wilson was moving from the world's biggest company to the world's biggest government agency. The job did not have a happy recent history. It had been created as part of the National Security Act of 1947 in an effort to centralize defense policy and bring the uniformed services—army, navy and air force—together under a single management structure. Long-standing rivalries and competition for resources among the services had a serious impact on morale and efficiency and provided a vexing challenge. Wilson's predecessors had discovered that the new organization did not give them enough authority to rein in the service heads or enough funding to ensure adequate overall preparedness.

Not being able to do the job for which they were hired was a recipe for frustration. President Truman had four defense secretaries in five years, and they all found the position extremely stressful. Exhausted by his labors, Robert Lovett, Wilson's predecessor, declared the Defense Department a "monstrosity" and an "empire too great for any emperor."[29] For an older man with workaholic tendencies like Wilson, the assignment was not likely to provide much in the way of job satisfaction.

On some level, Ike may have recognized that the position was too big for one man, because he viewed his defense secretary-designate more as an administrator than a national security strategist. Wilson's role would be to explain, implement and defend policy but not make it—probably a wise decision in view of Wilson's "negligible" insight into foreign affairs and military strategy.[30] Ike wanted him to focus on organizational issues and take another crack at centralizing authority in the secretary of defense's office. If the three services were obliged to coordinate their operations, he anticipated considerable savings by eliminating duplication of effort.

Painstakingly Thorough

Though G.M.'s prominence made Wilson the better known of the two executives, his personality was not as compelling as Humphrey's. To be sure, he had an attractive warmth and sincerity, but his mentality and temperament were those of the engineer he was trained to be. Observers considered him a determined, rather than skilled, public speaker—a reference to his relative lack of polish and his shyness. In conversation or giving a talk, he often had difficulty summoning the exact words to communicate his thoughts. This failing would leave him vulnerable to being misunderstood in an environment like the nation's capital, where his every public sentence would be examined for its possible significance.[31]

Wilson's leisurely management style was highly unorthodox for a successful corporate C.E.O. He had rarely spoken or acted like a man concerned about profits. He never seemed to be in a hurry or did anything that suggested his time was valuable, whether it was getting somewhere, making a decision, or ending a meeting. He explored problems with what one journalist called an exhaustive and almost exasperating thoroughness. He talked to anyone who might be able to contribute a new fact or view on an issue. Often he would switch his position and play devil's advocate, in order to test the opposing arguments.

His executives called these lengthy deliberations "C.E.'s world tours." They dreaded a summons from him late in the day, because he had no sense of time. "Mr. Wilson doesn't seem to get hungry like other people," lamented one official. "Or tired or sleepy either," added a colleague. It drove crazy those subordinates of his who expected him to make crisp, firm decisions. "Why doesn't he cut the gab and tell us what to do?" exclaimed one vice president.[32]

His defenders countered that extended discussion and debate strengthened the final decision and secured all-important buy-in from junior managers. "It takes Wilson's kind of nerves, patience and mental capacity," said one, to make this approach work. There was no denying G.M.'s success with Wilson at the helm. "For solid results, for clear long-range policies, for getting a whole big organization pulling together in the right direction, I've never seen anybody up to Wilson," marveled a company vice president.[33] As a disciple of the legendary Alfred Sloan, Wilson believed in centralized authority and decentralized administration. He set broad goals but allowed subordinates great discretion on how those goals would be met.

He worked constantly. Four or five days a week, he spent the night in a specially designed suite at G.M. headquarters rather than make the twenty mile trip home. His concern for every aspect of production gave him a reputation for micromanagement, despite the semiautonomous status of the various G.M. divisions. He felt that if the people in the organization were working well together toward objectives they understood, profits would take care of themselves. Accordingly, he was more concerned with relationships than policies.

He also had a tendency to drift off into such intense concentration that he would apparently miss what was said to him and fail to respond. It was easy, but incorrect, to attribute this quirk to indifference or arrogance. Wilson's defenders insisted that he did hear but sometimes "filed away" the remarks of others and belatedly replied once he had thought them through. Colleagues counseled: "Give him time, and you will get your answer."[34]

Did Clay and Eisenhower know of Wilson's unorthodox leadership style? If they did, it must have raised some concerns. The organizational culture of the Defense Department bore little resemblance to that of G.M. Unlike the production of automobiles, the end product of the Pentagon's sprawling operations was not neatly quantifiable. The department was a vast, hierarchical bureaucracy, comprised primarily of men in uniform who were used to specific orders, not endless bull sessions. Decisions issuing from such undocumented discussions would be "likely to drift to a stop among cautious colonels in the middle echelons."[35] To be effective at the Pentagon, Wilson would likely need to adapt to its ways.

Like Humphrey, Wilson had other plans for the next few years that he was obliged to put on hold. He had been looking forward to spending more time with his family and caring for his prize-winning herd of cattle. He also had seen how other businessmen of the era—among them G.M.'s own William Knudsen, Donald Nelson, and the other Charles E. Wilson, the president of General Electric—had been "plowed under" trying to survive in the Washington pressure cooker.

The bubbling stew of problems at the Pentagon was dropped into Wilson's lap in January 1953. Unlike Humphrey, he occasionally spoke like a man uncertain of his ability to make the transition. "I will struggle through it and hope to make a worthwhile contribution," he said at the time of his appointment. "I hope the people don't expect too much of me." He promised that he would "give it the damndest whirl it's ever had."[36]

Wilson: Running the Congressional Gauntlet

Before he could do that, Wilson would have to get past his Senate confirmation hearings. Some congressmen questioned the wisdom of having so many corporate executives in Cabinet-level posts. Referring to the Wilson nomination, Senator Taft huffed that "it looks to me as if the government cars hereafter will be Chevrolets."[37] But with Republicans in the majority in both houses of Congress, the confirmation process promised to be quick and painless. Wilson upset this expectation by making a number of serious errors and ended up jeopardizing his chances of a successful tenure in office as well as embarrassing the man who appointed him.

The confirmation hearings of Wilson and Humphrey revealed a major difference in the surefootedness of the two men. Though Wilson was far more experienced in dealing with Congress, he carelessly told an associate before the hearings began: "I've got a feeling that I'm going to be pretty pleased and surprised at how easily these boys can be handled."[38]

"These boys" were the members of the Senate Armed Services Committee, and they took their confirmation responsibilities seriously. The main issue senators raised with both Wilson and Humphrey was how their extreme personal wealth might influence the conduct of their public duties. Wilson owned thousands of shares of stock in G.M., one of the Pentagon's primary defense contractors. His involvement in the awarding of such contracts struck the Armed Services committee as a clear conflict of interest, and it immediately became a sticking point.

Wilson informed his questioners that he would not sell his G.M. stock, because he was unwilling to pay the hefty capital gains tax required by the sale. The sacrifice is "too great," he told the committee, "and I do not know why you should ask me to do it."[39] He promised instead to work around the problem by delegating the defense contracting process to subordinates.

One of the senators asked if he could make a decision that benefited the country but negatively affected his stock portfolio. His answer became the most famous of Wilson's many memorable utterances. He could, he said, "because for years I thought that what was good for our country was good for General Motors, and vice versa."

The controversy set in motion by this comment could not have come as a bigger surprise to the nominee. Wilson had been saying the same thing in the same way before congressional committees and other audiences for years—it was one of his stock phrases. By it, he meant simply that G.M. did not place its interests ahead of those of the nation as a whole. Until now, no one had faulted him for it. But the committee focused on the "vice versa" at the end of his sentence. It sounded to them as though Wilson would have difficulty subordinating his loyalty to General Motors to his obligations as a public servant.[40]

Wilson's language and demeanor rankled the status-conscious senators. Foreshadowing his later tendency to use infelicitous words or phrases, he gave responses that were sometimes too blunt, sometimes too loquacious. He had a habit of addressing the committee as "you men," which he had also done on many previous occasions but now left the members feeling patronized. Wilson often betrayed a lack of patience with the sometimes politically motivated questions he was obliged to answer, displaying what amounted to a lack of proper deference in the eyes of many committeemen.

But the stock issue was paramount, and it was clear that he would not be confirmed unless he disposed of his holdings. Because he was being asked to leave a job that paid him $600,000 a year and to be happy with a government salary of $22,500, he found congressional demands for further financial concessions unreasonable. At an apparent impasse, the hearings adjourned, leaving the nomination in limbo.

Eisenhower finally had to order Wilson to liquidate his stock on the eve of his inauguration, but even then Wilson wanted to think it over. Two days later, he finally agreed to do so, but the reconvened Armed Services Committee questioned the terms under which Wilson would receive bonuses for past service to G.M. This was too much. After a long discussion of possible solutions to this problem, Wilson's anger got the better of him:

> WILSON: I really feel that you are giving me quite a pushing around. If I had come here to cheat, I wouldn't be here.
> SEN. RICHARD RUSSELL: I'm sorry you feel that way, Mr. Wilson, but I have my responsibilities too.
> WILSON: I understand that. But I am just human and I am making a great sacrifice to come down here.

Later, when asked questions he considered irrelevant to his confirmation, Wilson told another senator: "I am beginning to think that you would be doing me a great favor if you do not [confirm me]."[41]

A compromise solution was soon found for the bonus problem, which at long last allowed the committee to recommend Wilson's confirmation. The full Senate then approved it by a vote of 77–6. The focus shifted to Wilson's selections for his immediate subordinates and service secretaries, many of whom were also former businessmen. They received the same close scrutiny over their finances as Wilson had, and they, too, were ordered to sell their market assets.

Thus did Wilson's stewardship of the Pentagon begin on a note of distrust, as well as doubt about the relevance of the new team's credentials. Historian Arthur Schlesinger, Jr., wrote that the hearings provided more evidence of the "chronic incapacity" of the business community, which "has always botched the job when it tried to govern the country."[42] Political observer Richard Rovere also expressed deep skepticism about Wilson's suitability. No matter how many securities he is forced to unload, Rovere wrote, he has already displayed serious shortcomings as a public servant.[43]

If Eisenhower was hoping for an uncontroversial beginning to his "business" administration, he was disappointed. A perceptive judge of people, the president-elect noticed that Wilson was prone to lecture, rather than answer, when congressmen asked specific questions. Congress not only found this behavior annoying, Ike reflected, but it gave them "unlooked for opportunities to discover flaws in [his] reasoning and argument."[44] Chagrined by the Wilson hearings, Ike soon concluded that "able as he is, he is just a bungler" when it came to handling delicate situations.[45] Yet he also showed a certain sympathy for Wilson's plight when he confided to a friend that "it's not easy for a group of hard-headed businessmen, all important individuals in their own right, to kowtow to a group of legislators."[46]

Wilson never conceded the need to divest himself of his financial resources. He wrote to a friend that "the problem was mainly a political and public relations one, rather than a factual or legal one."[47]

Humphrey: Gliding Past the Senate

At his confirmation hearings, George Humphrey was faced with the same decision—whether to cash out large amounts of stock. However, he faced down his questioners on the Senate Finance Committee and argued that he knew of no legal reason why he could not continue to hold his various securities, as long as he excused himself from cases involving any of the relevant companies.

When this comment failed to satisfy the objections of some committee members, he pointed out that the Treasury Department was not the Defense Department. Even if he sold every share of stock he owned, the powers of his new office would allow him to influence the value of the proceeds once they were reinvested—even if they were merely sitting in a savings account. He urged them to use some common sense. "How would you account for what you received for it? Would you leave it in cash in the bank? Would you put it in government bonds? If you do not be practical about this thing," he concluded, "you just cannot have a Secretary of the Treasury unless he is a man who has nothing."[48]

The question moved from the abstract to the concrete when a committee member introduced the issue of the St. Lawrence Seaway. It was well known that M.A. Hanna's Labrador iron ore project would be a direct beneficiary of the proposed seaway, and Humphrey freely admitted to the committee that he had lately been attempting to persuade Congress to approve its construction. "You would be in a difficult position as a member of the President's Cabinet," said Senator Russell Long. "You are an enthusiast for the project ... and you would be subject to being accused of being interested as a stockholder of Hanna."[49]

Did Humphrey intend to use his position to encourage this legislation? "Well, Senator ... if I were trying to advance my own interests.... I don't believe I would be here at all. I am here for just one purpose and that is to try to do a job for our country." Did he feel that he could give the president his best judgment on the matter? Here, Humphrey dug in his heels. "I am so thoroughly convinced and so honestly believe that the seaway is very definitely in the national interest that I should be at liberty to say that in Cabinet meetings."[50]

The senators also took the opportunity to probe Humphrey's underlying beliefs and priorities as Treasury Secretary. He had no opportunity to coordinate his views with the president-elect, and he resisted the temptation to say too much. "It is a little difficult for me and I think probably not quite right for me to talk about where we are going and what we are going to propose," he told Senator Long. "I will say this, however, that I think our first job should be to attempt to balance the budget."

As he continued, it became clear that he interpreted the 1952 election as a mandate to return the country to more responsible financial practices, akin to those typical of American business. (On his first day in office, he hung on his wall a picture of Andrew Mellon, the last Republican treasury secretary.) His main target would be excessive federal spending—one of his favorite phrases was "The government cannot spend itself rich." He anticipated putting an end to "give-away" projects that wasted the country's resources, risked dangerous inflation, and led to high taxes and deficits. He went on to endorse a reduction of taxes "as soon as the expenses can be adjusted to permit it," and stated his intention "to retard and stop further depreciation of the dollar" by eliminating deficits.[51] These few words, spoken off the cuff even before taking office, turned out to be an accurate reflection of administration priorities over the next five years.

Humphrey's candor and sincerity won the day. One senator called his statements before the committee "quite refreshing." He also impressed the senators by knowing all of their names and what their main concerns were—a small thing, perhaps, but it went a long way in a status-conscious place like the Capitol. Unlike the Armed Services Committee, the Finance Committee decided not to question the motives of a man who had given up a huge salary and a satisfying life to do the people's business in Washington. With little further discussion, the committee voted unanimously to recommend Humphrey's confirmation. The hearings had lasted a single day.[52]

Both Humphrey and Wilson were about to leave environments in which they felt secure, confident and in control and assume difficult posts in which they would face a steep learning curve, encounter resistance, and endure fierce criticism from people they could not fire. They would face these challenges at a time in their lives when their physical energy was declining and the lure of a quiet and comfortable retirement life was almost too great to resist. They were within their rights to view it as a great sacrifice.

In every respect, Humphrey seemed better prepared than Wilson, an assessment that would be confirmed by time and events.

5

Eisenhower the President

Eisenhower needed Humphrey far more than he needed Wilson. He was hardly alone among presidents in his limited understanding of economic policy, but he was quite prepared to put his stamp on defense policy, with Wilson confined to administrative detail. Ike's collaborative work style—in particular, his faith in the efficacy of Cabinet government—gave additional running room to an assertive and persuasive treasury secretary.

Eisenhower's Cabinet

All presidents have preferred ways of receiving information. Eisenhower would rather engage in group discussion than read position papers. His reliance on the Cabinet and National Security Council for advice offered the more articulate members of his administration the opportunity to exercise outsized influence on policy.

As is well known, Eisenhower took his Cabinet more seriously than any other modern president. Under previous administrations, Cabinet meetings had been irregular and pro forma, but Ike's were held weekly and followed a detailed agenda. They allowed him to engage the members of his management team in regular discussions of policy issues. Cabinet members were expected to express their opinions, whether or not the matter under discussion related to their official duties. The ideal Cabinet official, from Ike's point of view, provided "broad-gauged" advice to the president, taking into account "the total national welfare, not merely the concerns and needs of one segment of society."[1]

Cabinet government was a good fit with Eisenhower's military background, as well as his need to get quickly up to speed on many unfamiliar issues. He had plenty of experience with group problem solving. He was a veteran of many frustrating and tempestuous meetings on strategy with some of the most egocentric military and political leaders in the world. After trad-

5. Eisenhower the President

ing verbal blows on matters of life and death with the likes of Charles de Gaulle, Field Marshall Bernard Montgomery, Winston Churchill, George Patton, and many hard-pressed generals, dealing with a room full of hand-picked Cabinet officials probably seemed relaxing by contrast.

Ike did not consider his Cabinet a decision-making body. The president never put issues up for a vote. He listened carefully and then made up his own mind. He was not hesitant to disagree in strong language with something said, although one gets the feeling in reading the transcripts that he often did so merely to get a reaction from the others or to play devil's advocate. At least one participant considered the Cabinet more of a "debating society" and believed Ike made the bulk of his decisions with small groups in the Oval Office, like most presidents.[2]

The reasons why most American presidents have paid little attention to their Cabinets are not hard to fathom. Cabinet officials in any administration are likely to cringe when issues within their purview come up for discussion, worried that a random or critical comment from another secretary might influence the president in an unpredictable way. They might hesitate to hazard a new idea in an arena where it might be attacked, preferring instead to raise it in a more controllable small-group or one-on-one conversation with the president. Cabinet members working at cross purposes, or simply trying to think of something useful to say, could easily undermine the value of the meeting to the president and to each other.

Despite careful planning of Eisenhower's Cabinet sessions, it was impossible entirely to eliminate ill-informed remarks and trivial subjects. Discussions could also wander and lose focus, resulting in a waste of senior officials' precious time. Given the uneven levels of expertise and preparation on the various agenda items among the participants, the quality of the exchanges was inevitably uneven as well. Herbert Stein, an aide to President Gerald Ford, noted that the force of personality could sometimes overrule the force of logic.[3] And not everyone was equally engaged. Labor Secretary James Mitchell told an interviewer that he would "talk about what we were doing over at Labor ... and it was clear that people like Dulles and Charlie Wilson could care less. But Ike insisted."[4]

A strong Cabinet was key to Eisenhower's intention to delegate responsibility for most aspects of domestic policy. He needed department secretaries who were not only bright and self-confident but independent enough to make decisions on their own. Judging by his effusive praise for his appointees, Ike felt that he had chosen well. "I believe in decentralizing," he told the first official Cabinet session. "That's why I took such care in picking this gang."[5] He wrote in his diary that "we have an extraordinarily good combination of personalities.

I know that I like them all; I like to be with them; I like to converse with them; and I like their attitude toward their duty and toward government service."[6]

Further, the president believed that regular group meetings with his top officials boosted morale, loyalty and support for his policies. He knew that Cabinet members would be subjected to many centrifugal forces—from their own departments, from Congress, from individual constituencies—all of them tending, in the words of one Eisenhower aide, "to grind special axes and sort of turn their heads away from the President who put them in office."[7] At Cabinet sessions, Eisenhower had a weekly opportunity to remind them of his concerns and priorities, as well as to reaffirm administration policy. The result was better buy-in from subordinates and less chance of mixed messages to Congress and the media.

Cabinet meetings also allowed the president to observe and evaluate his senior advisers, although not under the fairest of conditions. Those who operated well in a group setting naturally made the best impression. Ike liked big-picture thinking—cautious or parochial Cabinet members were at a disadvantage. It could be risky to hazard a comment on an unfamiliar issue, because Eisenhower tended to remember uninformed observations. Both Wilson and Humphrey made naïve comments about foreign policy, especially early in the administration. Such remarks were often met with instant rebuffs from the president and probably decreased the seriousness with which Ike regarded their future contributions on the subject.

Eisenhower's early reputation for passivity among scholars of the presidency was undermined when detailed accounts of Cabinet meetings became available. The president did not hesitate to break in if a participant went on too long. If someone had obviously not done his homework, according to an aide, "he'd just take his hide off."[8] The president did most of the talking anyway, so clearly he was not waiting to be told what to do.

It worked to Humphrey's advantage that Eisenhower used Cabinet meetings to remind the departments of his preoccupation with budgetary restraint. His response to a suggested new program might be to turn to his treasury secretary and ask for an impromptu cost estimate. Nearly every session, especially during the administration's first year, featured a comment from the president, Humphrey, or the chief of the budget office on the need for bringing federal expenditures into line with revenues.

In sum, the Cabinet environment rewarded assertiveness while punishing an unwise level of spontaneity. Humphrey, who had warmth, charm and a quick mind, immediately emerged as a Cabinet star. On the other hand, Wilson's propensity for thinking aloud and knack for the ill-considered remark sometimes set Ike's teeth on edge.

Along with his Cabinet, Eisenhower met regularly with his National Security Council to discuss foreign and security policy. N.S.C. meetings were highly structured affairs with many attendees and did not have the intimacy or spontaneity of Cabinet sessions, though they provided a similar forum for aggressive advocacy. Ike made an important change to the N.S.C. membership by including the treasury secretary and head of the Bureau of the Budget, in order to ensure that discussions of defense programs took into account their cost.

The early N.S.C. sessions were particularly spirited and contentious, as the new administration groped its way toward consensus on defense and foreign policy. Among the issues most hotly debated were the value of foreign assistance programs, the conditions under which nuclear weapons might be used, and the connection between the health of the nation's economy and its ability to sustain the necessary military expenditures.

The Modern Republican

By today's standards, Eisenhower was an inconceivably apolitical president. Most everything about politics and politicians bothered him—the name-calling, the job-seeking, the moral compromises, the short-term calculation of advantage. Even his presidential campaigns were elevated in tone. It would be up to Vice President Nixon and others to make the hard-hitting, rhetorically excessive speeches that drew fire from Democrats.

Ike instinctively sought middle ground. "All human experience" taught him that the most intelligent approach to any complex policy issue was located somewhere near the center of the ideological spectrum.[9] When confronted with difficult decisions, he tried to "apply common sense—to reach for an average solution."[10] He called his philosophy of government "the middle way." His allies called it "modern Republicanism." It seemed a political manifestation of Eisenhower's innate prudence and balance.[11]

His many years of service in the U.S. Army conditioned him to think in such terms. Ike had been taught since West Point to honor and obey civilian leadership regardless of party. He was used to productive dealings with Democrats and to sharing with them a view of the common good. He had worked throughout the war under Democratic president Franklin Roosevelt, a man who was no less a national hero than himself and who he greatly respected. When the war ended, he served President Truman as army chief of staff. Though Truman's intemperate criticism of Ike later destroyed their relationship, the two men worked closely and harmoniously throughout the late 1940s.

Eisenhower's "middle way" philosophy reflected his experience working with leading men in both political parties. It caused him to reject the idea that the first order of business in a Republican administration was to undo the liberal social programs of the Roosevelt and Truman years. This did not mean that he approved of the New Deal wholeheartedly. His letters to his conservative brother Edgar were full of worried references to the country's drift toward socialism. But he understood and accepted that the majority of Americans agreed with the New Deal's expanded view of government, including its obligation to manage the economy through troubled times and to provide for the elderly and sick.

To him, these were settled matters. Too many people in the Republican party, Eisenhower said, "want to eliminate everything the federal government has ever done that represents social advance. For example, all of the regulatory commissions are anathema to these people.... They believe that there should be no trade union laws and that government should do nothing even to encourage pension plans."[12] Plainly, Ike felt such views no longer served the public good. He hoped to slow or perhaps halt the growth of government but had no wish to reverse it. He had been part of the partnership between government and the private sector that won the war, and he was convinced that the state had an important role to play during peacetime in promoting social harmony and prosperity.

Instead of scrapping New Deal and Fair Deal programs, Ike meant to "apply gentle brakes" to them while taking care to "ensure that they were not damaged in the process."[13] His approach mirrored that of liberal Republicans such as Tom Dewey, who had encouraged him to become a candidate in the first place and who had staffed and helped fund his campaign. He risked the ire of conservatives, who had never been happy with Dewey's views and might be equally unhappy with an administration committed to the "middle way," even if headed by a member of their own party.

Eisenhower acknowledged that his outlook was more difficult to defend and sustain than a position on either political extreme. He believed that he risked being labeled a "kind of mugwump or wishy-washy compromiser," and that he could easily come under criticism from both the left and right.[14] That would certainly have been the case fifty years later. Today, many Americans would be amazed to hear that a Gallup poll taken in 1955 showed 60 percent of voters favoring a "man who usually follows a middle-of-the-road policy."[15]

Ike was determined to work in close partnership with the business community in promoting prosperity and national efficiency. But the views of leading businessmen would not always be in harmony with his middle-of-the-road philosophy. George Humphrey and others would attempt to pull him away from his non-partisan "fantasies" and in the direction of sound, business-friendly Republican principles. Economic aide Gabriel Hauge was clearly worried about the influence of conservatives like Humphrey when he called Eisenhower "just a little too naïve to be president."[16]

Eisenhower and Domestic Policy

Contemporary critics of the new president dismissed him as an exemplar of nineteenth-century modes of thought, reflecting the "hopelessly out-of-date attitudes of small-town America" and the "relatively simple life of turn-of-the century Kansas."[17] Even politicians who knew better viewed Ike's perceived deficiencies with concern, if not alarm. Republican presidential candidate Bob Taft, admittedly still bitter about his defeat at the Republican convention, worried that Eisenhower had little understanding of national issues. Even Tom Dewey, who had organized and led the Eisenhower campaign, called the candidate's ignorance of domestic policy "embarrassingly plain."[18]

Leading political journalists had similar misgivings. Columnist Richard Rovere pronounced Eisenhower untrained and untested and assessed his new team as the least professional and experienced group of government administrators in modern times.[19] Marquis Childs, an early critic of the administration, wrote that Ike was a "clean slate on which each citizen could write his own hopes and aspirations."[20] *Newsweek* ran a long story on Ike's domestic program, saying, "few think it's possible that he makes his own decisions."[21]

The full record, when made available, destroyed the vision of Ike as a hapless novice. His advisers quickly learned that he was an acute observer of contemporary America and a diligent student of policy. Though he had spent most of his adult life on army bases, the president knew that the country's problems bore little resemblance to those of pre–Depression small-town America.

Even so, the minutes of early Cabinet meetings suggested that the new president had not given much thought to a host of difficult domestic problems. He conceded his intention to delegate as much decision making as his domestic policy team could handle, in order to free his own time to think about the larger issues of war and peace. Chief of Staff Sherman Adams would have the job of resolving differences among Cabinet members before they could reach Ike's desk. Because his background in domestic affairs was weak, Ike's convictions and leadership risked being weak as well.

Washington newspapermen could easily be misinformed, but it was harder to dismiss the worries of insiders like Sherman Adams and Lucius

Clay. Adams confessed to being "impressed" by Ike's "lack of knowledge about details and [even] much of the generalities" of the domestic issues he would be facing. He felt that the president "was going to have to get really busy and school himself in what the country was thinking, what its internal problems were" and figure out how to solve them. Looking back later, Adams reflected that the president's great store of common sense allowed him to evaluate policy alternatives "fairly well" and to be "reasonably intelligent" about the forces at play in any given situation[22]—faint praise indeed. In an unguarded moment, even Ike's close friend Lucius Clay told a biographer that "the fact remains, this was a very simple man in a lot of ways."[23]

Ike and Economics

Eisenhower took office with a curious combination of limited economic experience and strong economic views. He had articulated only a few generalities about economic matters, but he did have some bedrock principles. He regarded fiscal discipline as a cardinal virtue. He told his economic aide, Gabriel Hauge, that he considered a country's currency a mirror of the qualities of a people and a symbol of integrity.[24] As he had written to Charles Wilson two years before, he saw a close connection between the health of the American economy and its ability to project military and political power abroad. In general, this was an unexceptional proposition, except he defined a healthy economy the way any conservative Republican of the era would— in terms of a balanced budget, minimum government interference, and avoidance of inflation. Ike wondered aloud whether "national bankruptcy or national destruction would get us first."

At the same time, the new president showed only a superficial grasp of both fiscal and monetary policy—these would become, over time, an "acquired taste."[25] Throughout his presidency, Ike would need instruction or reminders on basic economic concepts. White House staffers traded anxious notes about his frequent need for tutorials on economic topics. Typical was a 1953 memo from economic advisor Hauge to Humphrey that suggested Ike be given a detailed briefing on the Export-Import Bank, inasmuch as he "on a couple of occasions recently has shown an interest in and only a rather vague knowledge" of its loan policies.[26] Because economist Arthur Burns was given to abstruse "professorial expositions" during meetings, Hauge was often obliged to translate them for the president later.[27]

As late as 1957, Ike was still struggling with the complexities of monetary policy. He asked George Humphrey's successor as treasury secretary, Robert

Anderson, for a surprisingly basic outline of the subject.[28] Anderson's memo was entitled "The Money and Credit System of the US and How It Works."

The views of former administration figures on Eisenhower's understanding of economics ranged from polite to frank. Raymond Saulnier, who later worked for Ike, delicately described the president as "deeply interested" in business conditions and well informed about "many aspects" of the economy.[29] Less delicate was the view of Steven Benedict, an assistant to Gabriel Hauge, who characterized Eisenhower's grasp of domestic issues as "really rudimentary" and "skeletal on a great many of what were, to a politician, the burning issues of the day."[30] Deputy Secretary of State Douglas Dillon did not think that Ike "had any comprehension of or understood" Keynesian economics,[31] which had already revolutionized fiscal policy by sanctioning deficit spending as a weapon against recession.

But Eisenhower was a bright man, a fast learner, and a serious student of economic policy. He took advantage of his business contacts and the periodic tutorials from his staff. He always made sure that the administration's annual Economic Report, written by the head of the Council of Economic Advisers, reflected his views. His lack of specialized knowledge was certainly a weakness, but it did not translate into a lack of interest or necessarily hinder his ability to make informed choices. As Sherman Adams recalled years later, Ike was "more deeply concerned with economics than most people realized."

Moreover, the new president had considerable experience in one economic area: his army career had given him practical knowledge of the budget process. "Eisenhower was more budget-minded than any other executive I've ever known," remarked his third budget director, Percival Brundage. He saw it as "a mirror of the organization's operations, and no man ever served in government who understood it better."[32]

It would have been easy for a non-economist like Eisenhower to put undue emphasis on the importance of a national budget. Whether it is in balance or not is a simple mathematical matter, and he shared Humphrey's view that the consequences of a budget deficit were as serious as those for a family facing bankruptcy. The readily understood and easily communicated imperatives of equalizing revenues and expenditures may have been an important reason for the president's near obsession with the subject throughout his two terms in office.

Exorcising Hoover's Ghost

The country had at last allowed Republicans another chance to govern, but an economic crisis would dash any of their remaining pretensions to national leadership. Even a spike in unemployment would bring criticism and pressure to act. Eisenhower was as worried as anyone in his administration about being called another Hoover. He wrote to his brother Milton that "the maintenance of prosperity is one field of governmental concern that interests me mightily and one on which I have talked incessantly to associates, advisors, and assistants."

The lessons learned from the Great Depression had been embodied in landmark legislation—the Employment Act of 1946—which for the first time recognized the government's responsibility to employ "all its plans, functions and resources ... to promote maximum employment, production and purchasing power." It also created the Council of Economic Advisers to assist executive branch policymakers in carrying out this mandate.

Some understanding of the theories of economist John Maynard Keynes was essential to policymakers of the era. His advocacy of an active role for governments during economic downturns, even if their interventions led to deficits, influenced the Roosevelt administration's approach to combating the Great Depression. By the 1950s, Keynesianism was a widely accepted school of economic thought in academia though still controversial in political circles.

Eisenhower's mixed view of Keynesian economics foreshadowed his basic ambivalence about economic policy. Ike was explicit about his belief in strong federal action when necessary. To the charge of Democrats that his election would be followed by another economic collapse, he answered: "I pledge you this. If the finest brains, the finest hearts, that we can mobilize in Washington can foresee the signs of any recession ... the full power of private industry, of municipal, of state government, of the Federal government will be mobilized to see that this does not happen."[33] He reaffirmed this thinking in a letter to his brother Milton: "In these days, I am sure that government has to be the principal coordinator and, in many cases, the actual operator for the many things that the approach of depression would demand."[34]

This view alone separated him from the fiscally orthodox Taft wing of the Republican party and guaranteed conflict with his more conservative advisers. As a group, most of the party's business leaders argued that managing a complex economy was little different than running a company. A deficit was just as intolerable as a balance sheet in the red. Their view was conditioned in part by their dismay at the vast growth in federal spending during the Roosevelt and Truman years—from $4.5 billion in 1933 to $75 billion during Eisenhower's first year in office.[35]

If Eisenhower understood in principle the usefulness of deficit spending under certain conditions, he also believed that deficits led to inflation and should be avoided. He shared the conservative view that even a little inflation could be worse than a recession. The dangers of inflation would become one of his central preoccupations. Looking back in retirement, he wrote of an "inflationary psychology" that he believed prevailed throughout the 1950s—a psychology that was "necessary to defeat."[36]

The disruptions of the ongoing Korean War influenced Ike's economic views as his term of office began. The war's onset had brought a strong increase in consumer prices that was slowed only by a freeze in wages and prices in early 1951. President Truman chose to finance the war through steep tax hikes rather than by borrowing. By early 1953, high taxes and inflation topped the new administration's list of concerns.

As we will see, Eisenhower's dilemma was that he was torn between his intellectual acceptance of a strong federal role in maintaining prosperity and his instinctively conservative core beliefs. Despite his pragmatic bent, Ike's conservatism would, as a practical matter, act as a restraint on his actions. Arthur Larson, who understood Ike better than most, noted that the president would support "just enough government activity (and no more) to avoid extreme tendencies in the business cycle."[37] The central problem was to decide how much government activity was "just enough" to cure a recession without producing undesirable side effects. It would prove difficult in practice to find that balance.

Since Eisenhower, no president has taken seriously the importance of a balanced federal budget. All of his successors have paid lip service to the goal but have rarely achieved it. In fact, economic policymakers have moved away from strict rules of any kind concerning budget policy. As Herbert Stein has written: "[Economists] recognize ... that the decision about the size of the deficit, like any other decision about the budget, is a decision with its own costs and benefits and that it must be balanced with other decisions." By the 1990s, "the idea that there was some precise, knowable size of the deficit that was consistent with the stability of the economy had been dissipated."[38]

But to Eisenhower's way of thinking, avoiding deficits was just common sense. Criticized late in his presidency for making a "fetish" out of budget balancing, he replied: "I don't know why suddenly a balanced budget is getting to be a bad word. I think it is rather a good thing to be a bit frugal and say that we can live within our means."[39] For Ike, it was a moral issue. The nation should be just as prudent and disciplined as its best citizens.

A Reluctant President?

A more subjective ingredient in the climate of the Eisenhower White House was a certain lack of imagination, traceable to the president's limited view of government but also to his frequently unenthusiastic approach to his executive duties. Before he was prevailed upon to run, he expressed a reluctance to serve, and his behavior once in office sometimes suggested a man who wished to be somewhere else. "Anybody is a damn fool if he actually seeks to be president," he told friends in 1951 with apparent sincerity. "You give up four of the best years of your life. Lord knows it's a sacrifice."[40]

To be sure, he was not the disengaged figurehead many people thought him to be at the time. The closer one looks at his handling of the job, the more impressive seem his feel for the big picture, his mastery of public relations, and his understanding of the biases and weaknesses of his advisers. That being said, he did not act like a driven politician who had achieved his life-long dream. He was motivated by a sense of duty rather than burning ambition. Throughout his two terms, he complained bitterly and frequently about the constant demands of a job that he called the "unhappiest and loneliest on earth." At one point, he confided to his secretary, Ann Whitman, albeit humorously, that he "felt so sorry for himself that he could cry."[41] It is hard to imagine any other incumbent slipping into this kind of melancholy.

Because the White House staff was a fraction of the size it is today, much of his time was consumed with the trivial and ceremonial. Bernard Shanley, who managed his daily schedule, lamented the "absurd" number of routine activities, such as document signing, the swearing in of low level officials, and greeting of foreign dignitaries.[42] Many of these duties would in future administrations be delegated to subordinates. Ann Whitman wrote to Milton Eisenhower that his brother did too many things, such as giving unnecessary speeches or dabbling in defense minutiae, simply because of his generous nature.[43]

Ike often claimed that he needed a second, or "administrative," vice president to relieve him of many tedious chores. In the army, he once said, his policy was never to make a decision on which he was not fully informed. But in the White House he was finding that he must know or pretend to know about everything.[44] He floated the idea of having three vice presidents, two for domestic affairs. That's fine, counseled Sherman Adams, as long as all of them are under your control.

Available time for domestic policy was further reduced by the president's heavy concentration on foreign affairs. Shanley estimated that this subject consumed nearly 90 percent of his time by his second term, when every month seemed to present a new crisis. Secretary of State Dulles typically saw or called the president several times a day. Reacting to overseas developments increasingly crowded out the time available for thinking about other issues.

Also, Eisenhower spent a remarkable amount of time writing letters.

These were not simply routine greetings. They often consisted of lengthy musings on complex subjects, such as his personal and political philosophy, and conveyed his detailed views on current issues. He most often wrote to his brothers Milton and Edgar (whose sharp attacks on what he considered Ike's socialist leanings often elicited anger and sarcasm from the president) and a childhood friend, Swede Hazlett. One suspects that Ike found the letter-writing process both therapeutic and a way of figuring out his own mind. Either way, it was another drain on his time.

In response to a request from Milton Eisenhower, Ann Whitman identified additional activities that she felt required too much of the president's attention. Speech preparation was high on the list, as well as checking and editing outgoing messages, "since you know what a stickler he is for anything being right that does bear his signature." According to Whitman, he prepared so thoroughly for National Security Council meetings that he knew every word of the presentations before going. Still, he felt he had to sit through the meetings in order to maintain the interest of the participants. Her review of his schedule prompted her to conclude that "his generosity is part of the problem."[45]

Yet Eisenhower always found time for recreation. He spent nearly every free weekend in activities like hunting, bridge and golf. During the week, according to Adams, "he was always hopeful ... that if he could get his work cleared away early in the day, he might find time late in the afternoon to get out of doors on the golf course."[46] He raised his spirits during difficult afternoons by planning get-togethers with his "gang" of friends—sometimes for that very day.[47] During a thirteen-day stay at Humphrey's estate in Georgia in 1957, Cliff Roberts observed that he "seemed to have little demand made on him" by official business and that Humphrey "never seems to talk shop to Ike."[48] He was clearly in no danger of becoming a workaholic.

In a controversial book on presidential character, author James David Barber labeled Eisenhower a "passive-negative" president, because he gave the impression of being reluctantly and unwillingly involved in his work. Barber described him as in "continual retreat from the demands of the office" and serving only out of a sense of duty. He labeled Ike's general attitude as one of "irritated resignation."[49] One does not have to agree completely with this assessment in order to understand how the author arrived at it.

All of these limitations on his available time assumed that he was healthy. But after his heart attack in September 1955, followed a year later with a worrisome episode of confusion and an attack of ileitis, his closest aides made a concentrated effort to pare back his schedule in order to spare him unnecessary stress.

In sum, the quality of his work would always depend on the quality of the advice he received and his skill in selecting the proper course of action from those he was offered. His leadership style reinforced his reliance on such advice. According to a recent study, Ike was reluctant to issue unequivocal orders. His basic temperament was that of "a reconciler, an adjudicator, a compromiser ... a man willing, perhaps too willing, to split the difference."[50] These tendencies would surface in many contentious and inconclusive Cabinet discussions of policy options.

6

Eisenhower's Economists

As the new president began to confront the complexities of running a modern economy, he had a good deal of assistance. Along with his treasury secretary, at least three other executive branch officials had a voice in economic policy. Their expertise and standing with Ike made them Humphrey's most serious competitors. As members of the president's team, they all sought consensus, but with their overlapping responsibilities, occasional—and sometimes serious—disagreement was inevitable. Humphrey's skill in managing his relationships with the others would be of critical importance in getting his views accepted.

The secretary of the treasury had the advantage of being formally assigned the management of fiscal policy—that is, the federal government's revenue, expenditures, and debt. He was considered the administration's chief economic spokesman.

But Treasury shared policymaking involvement with four other officials:

- The most important of these was (and is) the chairman of the Council of Economic Advisers, which is charged with analyzing and forecasting economic trends and recommending policies to ensure national economic health.
- Sherman Adams persuaded Eisenhower to hire an assistant to the president for economic affairs, as a counterbalance to the advice he would receive from the Treasury Department and the C.E.A.
- The head of the Bureau of the Budget (now called the Office of Management and Budget) had the narrower task of preparing the federal budget and helping to set funding priorities.
- The chairman of the Federal Reserve Board was (and is) entrusted with the management of monetary policy. The Fed, then as now, was the country's central bank, charged with regulating money and credit. Its main tools for accomplishing this were the manipulation of interest rates and the purchase or sale of government securities—actions that increased or decreased the supply of money in the economy. By statute, the Fed was independent of the

executive branch, but it tried not to work at cross purposes with the administration in power.

Arthur Burns: Practical Academic

The existence of the Council of Economic Advisers was the result of Congress' acknowledgment in 1946 that the federal government had a responsibility to manage the economy in a way that maximized employment and maintained prosperity. Implicit in its charter was the progressive notion that business cycles in a market economy were not always self-correcting and that government intervention to manipulate demand was sometimes necessary. Before then, declines in production, accompanied by increases in unemployment, were not only accepted as inevitable but even considered useful in bringing supply into line with demand.

Because its usefulness to the president depended on its evenhandedness, the C.E.A. was staffed with economists rather than politicians. It got off on the wrong foot during the late 1940s under the leadership of staunch Truman Democrat Leon Keyserling for the cardinal sin of partisanship. When Eisenhower took office, the council's status had been tarnished and its future was in doubt. Ike might have been inclined to let it die, but his economic aide Gabriel Hauge argued that, given a "complete housecleaning," it could become a valuable advisory body and an essential tool for promoting economic stability.

The new president tentatively agreed. In March 1953, acting on Hauge's recommendation, he invited Arthur Burns, a prominent Ivy League economist and a recognized expert on the business cycle, to make recommendations on how the C.E.A. might be reinvigorated. Burns came up with such a compelling vision of a strengthened council that Eisenhower kept the C.E.A. and appointed him its new chairman.

Burns, then 48, had been born in Austria and immigrated to the United States as a boy with his family. After years spent in jobs as varied as washing dishes, painting houses, and selling shoes, he graduated Phi Beta Kappa from Columbia. Later, he taught economics at Rutgers. He joined the nonpartisan National Bureau of Economic Research after the war. His boss there, Wesley Mitchell, had been a pioneer in business cycle research. Under Mitchell's guidance, Burns became a practitioner of the new science of "operational economics"—the use of economic analysis and forecasting as a management tool.[1] The approach emphasized observable facts rather than theoretical models.

His appointment to the C.E.A. bothered many conservative Republicans because of his rumored liberal leanings and his Ivy League background.[2] Articles in the national media emphasized his belief in a strong government role in preventing another depression, but he was probably best described as on the center-right of a fairly liberal profession. During the 1952 campaign, he had been a prominent voice in the "Democrats for Eisenhower" organization. He turned out to be fiercely loyal to the president. Further, the appointment of a recognized expert on the business cycle served notice that Eisenhower was intent on avoiding the fate of his immediate Republican predecessor.

Rivalry with George Humphrey was guaranteed from the outset. Burns was a cautious analyst whose conclusions were backed up by careful thought and reams of data, whereas Humphrey made up his mind quickly, relying on instinct and business experience. Not only were the two men ideologically and stylistically apart, but they looked at the economy from separate institutional perspectives. The C.E.A. was concerned foremost with economic stabilization while the Treasury Department took a more money-focused position, like that of a banker.

Sherman Adams had a "sinking sensation" when he first laid eyes on Burns, the former professor, fearing a culture clash of major proportions between him and the president. Burns seemed a caricature of a New Deal egghead. He was cool and detached, with a "glassy stare through thick lenses, peering out from under a canopy of unruly hair parted in the middle, a large pipe with a curved stem: the very incarnation of all the externals that were such anathema to Republican businessmen and politicians."[3]

He turned out to be a pleasant surprise. Instead of being abstract and impractical, he was down to earth, hard headed, and realistic. He was determined to avoid being perceived as a partisan figure and was at pains during his confirmation hearings to emphasize the nonpolitical nature of his position. He promised to use professional and objective criteria and to be data-driven in recommending policy actions. As he told the media, his job was not to justify policy but to help frame it.[4] Burns admitted that he was a "perpetual worrier," concerned that no scrap of pertinent economic data or incipient trend escape his attention. Those who knew him best believed he would not allow politics to influence his view of economic policy.[5]

Some observers believed that Burns would be out of his depth in political Washington, but he proved to be a skilled operator with a sense of humor that captivated the president. Ike "listened to him with fascination"[6] and had such respect for his views that he was soon a fixture at Cabinet meetings where he delivered regular briefings on economic trends. He had an hour-long meeting with the president each week that frequently ran late. His relationship with Ike was not unlike that between a tutor and a bright, willing student.[7]

Burns' economic world view seemed a good fit with Eisenhower's, though it was perhaps a bit to the left of "modern Republicanism." He believed government had an obligation to act in reaction to worsening economic conditions, but he stressed the importance (and the difficulty) of timing interventions well. He believed corrective action needed to be taken early during a recession or it might wind up generating inflation later. He preferred steps that could be reversed quickly. The key was to strike a balance and to retain maximum flexibility.

Burns viewed the need for strong economic management in the context of America's many challenges, both foreign and domestic. He noted the growing menace of Communism, upheavals in trade, the advent of new technology, the legacy of economic breakdown in the 1930s. "Within this new kind of world environment," he concluded, "public responsibility for controlling depressions has become a necessity—and not only to safeguard our own people against hardship."[8]

But he also shared many assumptions of economic conservatives. He believed that the main danger of government economic intervention was the harming of business confidence. Like most Republicans, he preferred to rely on tweaks in monetary policy by the Federal Reserve rather than the more blunt instruments of changes in taxation and spending. Like the president, he thought even small budget deficits could bring on an unacceptable level of inflation.[9]

Gabriel Hauge: "Middle Way" Devotee

Sherman Adams believed that Ike needed a White House counterweight to Humphrey's likely business-friendly views—someone who would contribute a "breadth of view in keeping to the middle of the road."[10] If the administration was going to be graded on its skill in avoiding a repeat of the "Hoover Depression," Adams wanted to make sure the president could stand up to pressure from Republican party ideologues.

To this end, he lobbied hard to create the position of economic advisor to the president. For this job he had in mind Gabriel Hauge, the son of a Norwegian minister, a Minnesotan, and an economist of considerable intellect—he had taught economics at Harvard and Princeton and was a former editor of *Business Week*. In addition to his scholarly work, he was a close ally of New York's "modern Republican" leaders—he had done economic research for the Senate candidacy of John Foster Dulles in 1948 and had been an economic advisor to Governor Tom Dewey.

With Dewey's strong backing, Hauge had joined Eisenhower's speechwriting team aboard the candidate's train during the 1952 campaign. Bobby Cutler, later a close Ike aide who was also on the train, called Hauge "as sound, able and likeable fellow as I ever knew."[11] Hauge impressed both Cutler and Adams with his versatility, tact, and ability to explain complex issues in simple, accessible language—an essential skill for an economist advising a president. Adams considered him a "natural" for the White House economic post.[12] He went on to become one of the least known but most effective of Eisenhower's domestic advisors.

At first, Ike resisted the idea of having his own economist. His preference was to have well-rounded generalists at the White House, while relying on Treasury, the C.E.A., and the Bureau of the Budget for detailed policy guidance. Adams reminded the president that Hauge was much more than an economist—he could be useful in many areas, both political and economic, and he was a devotee of Eisenhower's philosophy. These arguments, plus the genuine affection Ike had developed for Hauge during the campaign, won Eisenhower over.

Working under Adams, Hauge took on a variety of ad hoc assignments for the president—evaluating economic legislation, assessing trade and investment trends, writing speeches, giving advice on appointments, and demystifying complex issues. His own description of his job was utility man, trouble-shooter and economic watchdog.[13] Adams, a tough taskmaster, declared that Hauge "threw a bright beam of light across the whole White House Staff."[14] Hauge's assistant, Steven Benedict, came to regard him as "an extraordinarily thorough and intelligent fellow, a very rare species…. He was incapable of doing anything superficially. He combined the activist and the reflective individual in a remarkable fusion."[15]

His job brought him into almost daily contact with Eisenhower, and he was in a position to exercise strong influence on both policy and personnel matters. Because Hauge was right down the hall, Ike frequently used him as a "reality check" on decisions he was about to make. According to Adams, the president admired his calm way of holding fast to his convictions under the stress of argument. Hauge's non-confrontational style and agreeable personality made him a useful arbiter among opposing views. His frequent tutorials of the president further consolidated his position as White House insider. Benedict noted that his gift for simplification made him a useful interpreter of Arthur Burns' occasional "tortured rhetoric" and "professorial expositions."[16]

Burns and Hauge were close friends and had a similar way of viewing public policy, though the latter distinguished between himself as an "operational economist" and Burns as head of an academic intelligence center.[17] Hauge accompanied Burns to his weekly meeting with the president. Above all, Hauge was an unabashed admirer of Eisenhower. In 1955, he took on the task of summarizing and codifying Ike's "modern Republican" philosophy, as he understood it, in a speech for the president as a birthday present—it was called "The Economics of Eisenhower Conservatism."[18] Milton

Top: Arthur Burns headed the Council of Economic Advisers under Eisenhower. Conservatives worried about his rumored liberal leanings and Ivy League background. Though at first glance he seemed a caricature of a New Deal egghead, Ike included him in Cabinet meetings and "listened to him with fascination" (Bettmann/Bettmann/Getty Images).

Right: Gabriel Hauge was Eisenhower's in-house economic adviser. A former speechwriter, he had the knack of expressing complex economic concepts in simple, accessible language. He was a staunch supporter of the president's "modern Republican" philosophy and was viewed as a counterweight to Humphrey's "conservative bromides" (Ralph Morse/The LIFE Picture Collection/Getty Images).

Eisenhower believed that Hauge's influence on Ike eclipsed even that of Humphrey.[19]

Bureau of the Budget: Economic Disciplinarian

Joe Dodge, the new head of the Bureau of the Budget, had been one of Eisenhower's easiest and earliest personnel choices. A prominent Detroit banker and former head of the American Banker's Association, Dodge had known Ike in Europe, where he had the complex job of managing the financial affairs of the American occupation under Lucius Clay. While thus engaged, he also developed a new banking system for West Germany, modeled to some extent on the Federal Reserve.

Clay considered Dodge one of his few intimates and described him as a "tower of strength."[20] When the U.S. occupation government in Japan under Douglas MacArthur ran into economic problems, Clay sent Dodge to Tokyo. With close ties to both Eisenhower and Clay, Dodge was a shoo-in for a responsible job in the administration.

The Bureau of the Budget had a long nonpartisan tradition. As with the C.E.A., economic expertise, rather than ideological leanings, had always been the required credential for a position at the B.O.B. However, Eisenhower was determined to cut federal spending, and he wanted the Bureau to play a major role in forcing the departments to hold down costs. Dodge and his several successors during the Eisenhower years were the president's nay-sayers. All were fiscal conservatives.

Dodge in particular was well suited for the role of White House curmudgeon. Steven Benedict called him a "crusty, conservative, not-very-personable fellow but very competent."[21] He had the requisite economic credentials, and he was also a hard-headed critic of deficits run by the Truman administration and a supporter of Eisenhower's budget-balancing goals. To magnify his voice in leadership councils, the president elevated Dodge to Cabinet status.

As a result, the B.O.B. under Dodge—and later Rowland Hughes and Percival Brundage—became an active member of the president's policy team rather than merely a group of apolitical technicians. Early on, Dodge got Ike to agree that "prior to the approval of any policy, the issue of the cost of implementing that policy should be raised and carefully considered."[22] Reputed to have one of the best minds in the Cabinet, Dodge employed it entirely to the one-dimensional task of limiting government expenditures.

William McChesney Martin: "The right kind of Democrat"

The head of the Federal Reserve throughout Eisenhower's eight years in office was William McChesney Martin. Though he had been appointed by President Truman and called himself a Democrat, he viewed the economy in similar terms as Eisenhower's people, who were happy to retain him.

Martin had made an astonishing rise in the financial world before coming to Washington. Only in his twenties, he had been put in charge of the Roosevelt administration's Lend-Lease program with the Soviet Union. By age 31, he was president of the New York Stock Exchange. The media called him "the boy wonder of Wall Street." Before his appointment to the Fed, he had been head of the Export-Import Bank.

Martin headed an independent agency that made decisions about monetary policy, a field that many people (including presidents) found difficult to understand. By controlling the cost and availability of money, the Fed could help end recessions or counter inflationary trends. Monetary policy had the advantage of being quick to implement and just as quick to reverse, while fiscal policy either required acts of Congress (as in tax reductions or hikes) or changes in total government spending.

The new administration was glad to learn that Martin was first and foremost a zealous inflation fighter who believed in the virtues of a balanced budget. Hauge called him "the right kind of Democrat." The president and other key officials immediately set out to build strong connections with the Fed, in order to assure its cooperation in setting a consistent economic policy. Martin was interested in close ties with the White House but not at the expense of the Fed's role as an independent agency. He could not afford to be seen as overly subservient to Eisenhower or Humphrey, but, with that caveat, prospects for harmony were good as 1953 began.

7

Humphrey Goes to Work

Humphrey had two main tasks before him—to demonstrate an ability to think and act as a national-level policymaker and successfully to cultivate Washington's political elite, which included congressmen, journalists, fellow Cabinet members, White House staffers, and, of course, the president himself. The policy challenges he faced during the first six months of the Eisenhower administration would have tested even the most experienced government executive. Humphrey had little in-depth knowledge of most of the issues on his plate, but there was no time to study background papers or embark upon lengthy training sessions. He just had to plunge in and rely on his instincts. And he had only two months to prepare himself.

The good news was that Eisenhower did not take office in a crisis atmosphere. In 1933, the incoming Roosevelt administration had the immediate task of rescuing the country from economic catastrophe. Twelve years later, Harry Truman assumed the presidency with weighty decisions to make about the use of atomic weapons and America's role in the reconstruction of Europe. In early 1953, by contrast, the United States was in an extended period of sustained growth. Thanks to technological advances, cheap energy, abundant credit, and pent-up demand, the basis for widespread prosperity was being laid. The main blemish in this otherwise rosy picture was the stalemated war in Korea.

The "Understanding"

Humphrey's first meeting with Eisenhower took place in New York a couple of weeks after the election. By all accounts, the two men immediately took a liking to each other. Upon seeing the mostly bald Humphrey for the first time, Ike made an oft-quoted remark—"George, I see you part your hair the same way I do." As they traded ideas, it became clear to Ike not only that their views on fiscal matters were compatible, but that Humphrey was the kind of "outgoing, cheerful, hunting and fishing person with whom [he felt] most at home," as one correspondent wrote.[1]

According to one account, Eisenhower admitted to Humphrey on the spot that "I guess you know as much about the job as I do." He noted that he might have some suggestions to make, but aside from those, Humphrey could do as he liked. Encouraged by the free hand he was being offered, Humphrey then made a bold request. He asked Eisenhower to promise to consult him before spending a single dollar of federal money.[2] Ike nodded in agreement, though he surely understood that his "promise" did not bind him in any way. Humphrey seemed to be sending a signal—one the president-elect appreciated—of his strong commitment to cutting federal spending and balancing the budget. The two men also agreed on a modest goal—that Humphrey would serve at least two years, long enough to prepare the 1955 and 1956 budgets.

Eisenhower had another pre-inaugural opportunity to get to know Humphrey and other Cabinet members while traveling on the *Helena* following his Korea trip. In the casual atmosphere aboard ship, Ike found Humphrey a man around whom he could relax. According to a *Time* correspondent, his "dry, quick sallies in the wardroom often broke the atmosphere of heavy deliberation, to Ike's relief."[3] On deck, Ike learned that Humphrey was every bit as good a skeet shooter as he was. The basis for a strong personal relationship had been laid.

When the group got down to business, Humphrey demonstrated a reassuring—and perhaps unexpected—familiarity with the issues of the day. One of the most pressing of these was the future of wage and price controls, which the Truman administration had imposed after the Korean War began. Some economists, citing the chaos that accompanied Truman's lifting of price controls at the end of World War II, worried that immediately ending the controls risked economic disruption. Aboard the *Helena*, however, Humphrey spoke for their elimination "with determination in colorful terms." He cited their deleterious effects on business and expressed optimism that lifting them would increase productivity and result in minimal inflation. This was a strong statement about national economic policy from a man who until recently had been preoccupied with the relatively parochial task of organizing a mining venture in Canada.

Settling in at Treasury

One of Humphrey's first tasks at Treasury was to select a deputy secretary. Somewhat surprisingly, he chose Marion Folsom, the president of Eastman Kodak and a liberal Republican who had been closely involved in the creation and passage of the New Deal's Social Security legislation in the mid-1930s. Folsom had became acquainted with Humphrey while serving with the Committee for Economic Development and the Business Advisory Council. His main job at Treasury would be to oversee preparation of a major administration initiative—a tax reform package.[4] A few years later, Eisenhower appointed him secretary of health, education and welfare, where he would anger his former boss by arguing for significant increases in the department's budget.

From the outset, it was clear that Humphrey planned to focus on only a few large issues. He told Folsom that he had reached an "understanding" with the president. "I'm going to be the boss as Treasury Secretary of everything having to do with money," he said. In order to free himself for this responsibility, he told Folsom that he intended to delegate day-to-day management of the Treasury Department to him. "I don't want to have to take my time administering these various agencies. They're old-line agencies, a lot of them can run themselves pretty well anyhow." It would be Folsom's job, not his, to oversee them. And he added: "Don't bother me with anything unless it's absolutely necessary."[5]

Folsom would go on to have a close personal relationship with his boss—one that transcended their occasional differences. He later spoke in glowing terms of Humphrey's strong character, forcefulness, powers of persuasion, and personality. He admitted that they had argued on many occasions, which he called "interesting times," but that, on the whole, Humphrey was a "wonderful man to work with."[6] After Folsom left for H.E.W., Humphrey replaced him with H. Chapman Rose, a Cleveland attorney and long-time friend. Like Folsom, Rose was the day-to-day administrator of the Treasury Department. He impressed Hauge as a "top-tier" lawyer and negotiator.

During the first few weeks, as Humphrey was briefed on Treasury's wide-ranging activities and responsibilities, his subordinates found him a quick study. An aide marveled as he worked his way down a list of highly complex issues and "handed down eight verdicts in less than forty-five minutes"—so quickly that the aide wondered if he had truly understood all the pros and cons.[7] An official who was responsible for preparing Humphrey for meetings of Eisenhower's National Security Council never spoke for more than ten minutes before being waved off. "He listens, then in a few words, cuts right to the meat of what you've been babbling about," noted one awed subordinate.[8]

Despite his quickness, Humphrey presented himself as the ultimate pragmatist, a professional problem solver, rather than someone who shot from the hip. "If you actually spend enough time so that you will get the facts—

all the facts," he would tell numerous audiences, "most of the time you will find that you haven't got a problem—that it answers itself." He did not seem bothered by the apparent inconsistency between his brisk decision-making style and his proclaimed passion for painstaking data collection.

Some of his new colleagues contrasted his natural friendliness with his icy analytic judgments. "He's a very warm person with a very cold, factual mind," marveled an assistant. "He knows finance—and people." A journalist praised his expansive personality but added: "His brain is as cold as the steel produced by M.A. Hanna."[9]

Budget Challenge

The new administration was preoccupied with money issues from the very beginning. Ike was still wrestling with the question of whether to remove wage and price controls. Despite Humphrey's strong advocacy, he was nervous about doing so too quickly. Others around him, notably counselors Henry Cabot Lodge and Harold Stassen and economic adviser Gabriel Hauge, were similarly hesitant. They reinforced the president's biases by warning that precipitous action might cause a sudden rise in prices and by advocating a more gradual approach.

But Ike was already "beginning to succumb to the radiant personality of the lawyer-businessman"[10] from Hanna, and he decided to take his advice, though he wanted stand-by controls in case inflation set in.[11] On February 6, back in Washington, he announced an end to wage and price controls. On his way out of the press room, he whispered: "I hope, George, that you know what you're doing."[12]

The next pressing issue was the budget. Ike shared with other Republicans the goals of fiscal discipline and tax reduction. Americans had borne a heavy tax burden during the world war, and taxes had remained high to fund the Korean conflict. Inflation, too, had accelerated as the Korean War intensified.

Joe Dodge, the new budget chief, had bad news for the president and his Cabinet. Until now, the specific consequences of increases in the defense budget caused by the Korean War had remained unclear. Dodge had been meeting periodically with his counterpart in the Truman administration and had just learned that the Eisenhower administration was going to inherit a fiscal year 1954 budget of about $78 billion, which meant a deficit of almost $10 billion.

The Dodge presentation "stunned" everyone present.[13] High inflation, high taxes and a growing deficit amounted to a perfect storm for the new

Republican Cabinet. Dodge tried to clarify the situation by using an analogy to the household budget that was popular among economic conservatives, likening the situation to "that of a family with an accumulated debt four times bigger than its annual income, with never more money in the bank than it needed to cover one month's living expenses."[14] Ike's campaign promise to cut the federal budget to about $60 billion within four years in order to eliminate the deficit and allow for substantial tax reduction now seemed a forlorn hope.

A little time still remained to make cuts in the inherited Truman budget for 1954. Humphrey and Dodge quickly agreed on the need for a crash program, resolving to take a hard look at the numbers. Ike wrote to a friend that he was "committed to an administration of economy, bordering on or approaching austerity."[15] Like many new Republican presidents, he assumed that the budgets of government agencies were bloated and wasteful, and that a Cabinet consisting largely of businessmen would quickly identify and eliminate the "fat."

With military spending consuming most of the so-called discretionary budget, it was obvious that the defense establishment would have to bear the brunt of any cuts. Ike knew the Defense Department well, and he believed that Truman's military planners had not made the hard choices necessary to bring spending down. He also understood from his Pentagon service that it was difficult, if not impossible, to terminate programs once they were funded.

It now became clear why Hauge called the job of treasury secretary "central to everything." As long as budget cuts were the order of the day, Humphrey had license to criticize the spending priorities of all other government departments, especially the Defense Department. On this occasion, after a cursory glance at the defense budget, he criticized the Pentagon's leaders for following several strategic plans simultaneously, an observation that went far beyond his job description.[16] At the very first meeting of the National Security Council, he took military planners to task for bloated programs. In reality, the ongoing Korean War was the main cause of the deficit. Humphrey conceded as much when he told the president: "You have to get Korea out of the way."[17]

Finding His Voice

Humphrey quickly proved himself adept at bureaucratic maneuvering. He could see that the State Department would be a potent rival, not least because it was headed by John Foster Dulles, the only Cabinet member with greater access to the president than he had. Even more unsettling, Dulles was a strong proponent of economic and military assistance to foreign countries, intended as a means of drawing them into the Western orbit. And Eisenhower strongly supported this program.

Humphrey viewed foreign assistance as just another drain on American financial resources. His goal was "very simple," recalled State Department official Douglas Dillon. "It was just to cut down on the amount of money that was spent abroad any place he could."[18] Instead of forcing the issue with Dulles, Humphrey sought out Undersecretary of State Herbert Hoover III, the son of the former president, and persuaded him to agree that any State Department document dealing with money had to be cleared by Treasury before it could be released. When Dillon held the post of deputy undersecretary of state for economics, he found himself frozen out of the decision-making process on foreign economic issues by Treasury officials, who often refused to meet with him. These moves by the Treasury Department, he charged, amounted to a "rear-guard action" directed at anything that might cost money.[19]

Humphrey had intended to keep a low profile for several months, but that turned out to be impossible. Immediately he was spearheading budget-cutting discussions in Cabinet sessions, consulting with policy experts, and speaking publicly about the danger of deficits and the importance of sound money. He was so busy attending meetings and receiving visitors that he complained to Ike: "When does anyone find the time to think around here?"[20]

Humphrey proved to be surprisingly skillful and sure-footed in handling veteran newspaper and television journalists. Because every issue facing the administration had spending implications, he felt free to express himself on a wide range of subjects. During the first half of 1953, he gave several addresses, wrote an article for *U.S. News and World Report*, and appeared on two television news programs.

If there had been any doubt that Humphrey held business-oriented, conservative views on economic issues, it was quickly dispelled. In an interview, he freely admitted to being a "hard shell, non-progressive"—a man who perhaps lacked the foresight of "more forward-looking fellows"[21]—but his air of certainty tended to discourage criticism. In political incorrectness typical of the era, he remarked that the things a woman knows in order to run a house are the same things necessary to keep government finances in order. Families and countries, he never tired of repeating, both need to live within their income.

The U.S. government, he was fond of saying, should keep a lid on the national budget except during a genuine emergency. While many economists and policymakers were concluding that an expanding economy naturally led to greater federal spending, Humphrey asserted that "just the opposite is true. The more we have, the better able more of us should be to do for ourselves and be less and less dependent on the government."[22]

As Sherman Adams later wrote, Humphrey came into office determined to balance the budget and was prepared to "swing his ax on anything that stood in his way."[23] In his view, the stakes could not be higher. Running deficits would "bankrupt the free world and force the U.S. itself to abandon its way of life."[24] He tried to impress upon his audiences the enormity of the inherited budget deficit of $9.9 billion by defining it in terms of purchasing power. He hammered home his belief in the evils of deficits, which he was certain would put the country "right back on the old merry-go-round of inflation." All Americans, including himself, wanted tax reduction, he noted, but with a deficit this big, any consideration of tax cuts had to wait until expenditures were brought under control.

Doing this meant making major cuts in the defense budget. He echoed one of Eisenhower's favorite themes—that excessive defense spending would one day destroy the American economy. The administration intended to provide more defense for less money. That goal put pressure squarely on Defense Secretary Wilson and set the stage for continuing conflict with Humphrey.

Despite having maintained a low profile throughout his business career, Humphrey expressed himself in public with passion and clarity. His comments were well received by the business community and drew praise from officials around the president. Ike's international affairs advisor, C.D. Jackson, wrote to say that friends of his were "quite lyric" on the subject of one of his speeches.[25] Following a May appearance on *Meet the Press*, Humphrey received a short note from Gabriel Hauge, who complimented Humphrey's "knowledge, confidence and realism" and the consequent "splendid result."[26]

Humphrey's early television performances were likewise surprisingly skillful. After his *Meet the Press* appearance, journalist Arthur Krock lauded his avoidance of economic jargon and his direct and well-thought-out answers. A *New York Times* correspondent likened Humphrey to a sly fox, concluding that "the hounds never once got the better of you." Humphrey and his wife Pamela also made a highly effective and sympathetic appearance from their living room on journalist Edward R. Murrow's iconic program *Person to Person*.[27]

Humphrey's early remarks made clear his rejection of New Deal policies—a common sentiment in the business community he represented. In his opinion, the Roosevelt administration had not demonstrated the value of deficit financing or of government intervention in the economy. World War II, rather than Roosevelt's programs, had broken the back of the Depression. This was an unremarkable view, still held by many today, but he took it a step further. "It was clear that the Government's policies during all the 1930s were wrong and worked badly," he told the American Banker's Association. "They were designed to solve unemployment, yet there were still nine million unemployed in 1939. Those unemployed only got back to work after war broke out in Europe." He added that he knew of "no one who thinks that war is the right way to cure unemployment."[28]

Humphrey soon gave an extended interview to brothers Stewart and Joe Alsop, two of Washington's most influential journalists. The Alsops came away convinced of the new secretary's flexibility and openness to new information. Like his new boss, Humphrey acknowledged that a serious economic downturn would be disastrous for the Republican party, and he pledged to provide firm leadership should things "get out of hand." But the American economy "is a delicate thing," he reminded them. "It's not something you can turn on and off like a faucet. You've got to move slowly, feeling your way, taking no precipitate action." If we can just get our confidence back in the value of the dollar, he said, "then our economy will operate the way it ought to, with a gentle ebb and flow."[29]

Humphrey in his office at the Treasury Building. He immediately impressed colleagues and journalists as a quick study. Subordinates sat open-mouthed as he absorbed complex economic issues and "handed down eight verdicts in less than forty-five minutes." He readily admitted to an interviewer that he was a "hard-shell non-progressive" (Western Reserve Historical Society, Cleveland, Ohio).

He concluded the interview with the Alsops by saying, "Those are some of my opinions today. Tomorrow I may change my mind." But Humphrey would never really stop seeing things "through business eyes." The world already knew enough about him to predict with considerable accuracy what his views and actions would be later.

Taxes and the Dan Reed Hearings

Even though the Korean War had not yet ended, congressional legislation provided that the tax increases funding it would be revoked later that year. Individual income taxes were scheduled to be reduced by 11 percent at the end of 1953, and a highly unpopular excess profits tax on business would be eliminated that summer.

Understandably impatient to pursue their agenda after twenty years of political irrelevance, some congressional Republicans got out ahead of the new administration. They did not want to wait even a few months for tax cuts. Representative Dan Reed of New York, the tall, austere, 78-year-old head of the powerful Ways and Means Committee and a long-time leader of the House tax reduction forces, declared that "tax relief must be the first order of business for this Congress." He introduced a bill at the opening of the new session to move both expiration dates forward by about six months—the income tax reduction to take place in July 1953, and the excess profit tax to be eliminated immediately.

Eisenhower and his Cabinet were sympathetic—after all, such action was consistent with Republican philosophy and administration goals. Also, many economists feared that an end to the Korean War and consequent reduction in defense spending would produce a sharp recession, which a tax cut might help avoid. But two realities intruded: the war was not yet over, and the administration was inheriting a budget deficit of as yet uncertain size. Allowing the excess profits tax alone to lapse would cut government receipts by a further $800 million.[30]

Humphrey thus considered Reed's bill ill-timed. The administration had not yet completed its review of the 1954 budget. With the outcome of the review uncertain, he felt it would be unwise to relinquish any sources of income. As soon as he had heard the Dodge budget projections, he advised the president that, in the absence of sweeping and immediate budget cuts, the tax relief scheduled for July had to be postponed. Coming from a man who considered tax cuts the highest administration priority, this view had high credibility.

Ike quickly agreed. He saw the decision as an early opportunity to demonstrate budgetary self-discipline. While some conservatives argued that tax cuts should precede deficit reduction, the new president insisted on attacking the deficit first. He reminded his Cabinet that he had never promised a tax cut until the budget was balanced. An earlier reduction, he believed, would stimulate inflation.[31] His budget message to Congress requested the postponement of both tax reductions "until we can determine the extent to which expenditures can be reduced."

The tax issue would test Humphrey's mettle and his skill in dealing with Congress within weeks of taking office. He would have to do battle not only with Democrats but with members of his own party, now holding a slim congressional majority. Representative Reed was obdurate. He vowed that his bill could only be stopped "over my dead body."[32]

The "Dan Reed problem" taught the Eisenhower White House an important early lesson. Reed had been a congressman for thirty years and a tenacious football coach before that. His persistence now in the face of opposition from the new administration appeared to be at least partly grounded in personal pique. He complained that the White House was paying no attention to him—despite his considerable experience in financial affairs, he had not been invited to brief or even meet the president. Someone at the White House "goofed up," recalled Marion Folsom later. It was proof that "you had to be awfully careful in dealing with these key people in Congress."[33]

By the time the administration realized its mistake, Reed had already introduced his bill and was committed to its passage. Too late, Eisenhower invited Reed to the White House for a chat, which turned into "quite an altercation," recalled Hauge.[34] Ike tried hard to change his mind. "I used every possible reason, argument and device," he later wrote.[35]

Compounding his problem was Reed's reputation for stubbornness. "As water flows over a rock without leaving a trace," said one White House budget officer, Dan Reed does not change his mind.[36] A "get-acquainted" luncheon initiated by Humphrey also did not move him. Reed would smile and listen, but Hauge sensed he would not move a millimeter. "If you people had any character," Reed said, "you would solve the problem I am creating, if indeed there is a problem, simply by cutting expenditures."[37] Even when Humphrey in May presented Reed with the results of the administration's 1954 budget review, which projected a $5.6 billion deficit, the congressman would not withdraw his opposition to an extension of the excess profits tax.

Aware that the business community would be the biggest supporters of Reed's early tax roll-back, Humphrey tried to explain the need for the continuation of a tax that he conceded was harmful to private sector growth. His careful and detailed presentations managed to convince many business leaders that keeping the tax in place for a few more months was a sign of fiscal integrity. He also pledged that the tax would be lifted in 1954.

Ike's economic adviser Gabriel Hauge aided the public relations effort by helping Humphrey select softer language for his explanation of the evils of the excess profits tax. On a nationally-televised news program, Humphrey had called it a "vicious" tax. From a public relations standpoint, Hauge advised, a better description would be a "poor way to tax corporate benefits," a formulation that would be harder for Democrats to attack.[38] Hauge was seeking to ensure that the entire administration took the same measured tone, a role that he would play many times in the future.

Reed's continued opposition evoked frustration from Eisenhower. He wrote to a friend in June, "We are in the midst of a bitter fight and many Republicans seem determined to pursue the old political objective of lowering taxes and increasing expenditures. Some of them will shout 'sound money' but they are unwilling to face the music in taking the steps that will keep the currency sound. This whole situation is exasperated by the legislative rules which make it possible for one individual in a strategic spot to keep necessary tax bills bottled up, and so prevent a vote. It is difficult indeed to call this characteristic of free government."[39]

Under pressure from other congressional Republicans, Reed consented to hold hearings on the excess profits part of the bill. Humphrey had the job of representing the administration at the hearings. Over three long days in June, he not only had to sell the administration's position on postponing tax cuts but soothe Reed's ego as well. By the time he went before Reed's committee in early June, he had a mere four months under his belt as treasury secretary.

His reputation as a fast learner proved well founded. In his testimony before Reed's committee, he employed many arguments for the tax extension, including its possible impact on national security. At the same time, he inspired the sympathy of many Republicans by expressing his profound distaste for an excess-profits tax, because of its negative impact on business. By voicing his personal disappointment that the administration had not made sufficient budget cuts to justify eliminating it, he subtly suggested that he shared the committee's concerns.

His bottom line was that the new leadership was resolved to tighten the ship. "I think if the administration has the courage to come in here and ask you gentlemen to extend this tax, it is the firmest good faith showing that we are determined to balance the budget and to accomplish sound economy."[40] Finally, he promised to resign his post if the administration requested another extension.

In parallel with his congressional testimony, Humphrey showed some political acumen. Going against Republican stereotype, he portrayed himself as the defender of the "little taxpayer," objecting to the reduction of business taxes six months before the ordinary American citizen would enjoy any relief. The statement was intended to show that the administration was not under the thumb of Wall Street.

Despite repeated rebuffs to his efforts at compromise over the spring and early summer, he also took a conciliatory and respectful approach to Reed and consistently avoided personalizing the issue. "I have the very highest regard for Chairman Dan Reed," he told a television panel show in June. "He is a hard fighter. He is a man who has trained football teams and taken the guff that goes with it. He believes very firmly in his position. We ... believe very firmly in ours."[41] The only fair way to resolve the issue, he concluded, is to put it up to a vote.

In the end, the committee found Humphrey's arguments and candor persuasive. Representative Wilbur Mills called him "as good a witness as we have had before our committee," adding that "you disarm us and leave us perfectly helpless to resist anything you propose."[42] (This flattery was too much for Reed, who disassociated himself from Mills' final comment.)

Reed's main problem was that the Republican leadership of the House did not wish to embarrass the new administration, and they had the power to circumvent Reed's committee while bottling up his bill. Some of those leaders now reminded him that no individual Republican was greater than his party. Without their support, his bill quietly died. Reed's obstinacy had made his defeat all the more painful, but in the end he felt he had been fairly treated. He soon declared that he held no grudge against the president.[43]

The Dan Reed affair was a baptism of fire for Humphrey. The opportunity to work closely with Eisenhower on a major domestic policy goal and the positive outcome that followed helped to cement their growing bond. A Cleveland historian later called the Reed hearings "the most spectacular political victory of [Humphrey's] entire service." This was certainly an exaggeration, but the hearings did help to establish his credibility with Congress, underlined his status as Eisenhower's primary economic spokesman, and strengthened his voice in administration councils.

St. Lawrence Seaway

The one issue of immediate importance to the new administration with which Humphrey was thoroughly familiar was the thirty-year debate over federal financing of a seaway connecting the Atlantic Ocean with the Great Lakes. Plans for the project called for a joint effort between Canada and the United States. President Truman had favored the seaway, but when he failed to persuade Congress to finance it, Canada vowed to move ahead unilaterally.

The strongest proponent of the waterway in the Cabinet was, of course, George Humphrey. The M.A. Hanna company stood to benefit from its com-

7. Humphrey Goes to Work

pletion, and he had served notice at his confirmation hearing that he would feel free to lobby for it.

Humphrey's supportive view of the project had strengthened since he told *Business Week* in 1950 that a St. Lawrence Seaway was not necessary for his Labrador mining venture to be profitable, "but it would help." A year later, in four hours of testimony before the House Public Works Committee, he argued for the seaway, emphasizing the national defense argument that shipping iron ore to Great Lakes mills could be essential in wartime. He considered the project so important that he said he would be willing to take over construction of the seaway as a private venture. In appreciation for his analysis, one congressman told him: "You've helped me more than all the rest of the witnesses who have appeared here."[44]

Curiously, Eisenhower was dubious. Though the seaway seemed to guarantee a faster and cheaper means of transporting goods between the Atlantic coast and the interior, it was opposed by several special interests, notably the railroads. He also knew that several leading congressional Republicans opposed the project and did not want to antagonize them on an issue he considered of lesser importance. In early Cabinet meetings, he expressed concerns about whether the seaway was worth the cost. On April 3 he startled Humphrey by declaring the project more complicated than he had thought and postponing a decision.

With many Cabinet members, including Attorney General Brownell, Sherman Adams, and Humphrey favoring American participation, Ike realized that he was hearing mostly the pro side of the argument. He decided to invite representatives of several Midwestern railroads to the White House. For three hours, he listened carefully to their views, including their cost estimates, which were much higher than those of the project's proponents. He concluded that it was premature to take a public position on the issue.

At the next Cabinet meeting, on April 10, Humphrey went on the offensive, ostensibly to "provide the pertinent facts and figures" for debate but in reality to press for Eisenhower's consent. Having recently met with railroad officials, Ike played devil's advocate by restating their arguments. Humphrey countered with strong reasons for approval, which included the need for Labrador ore in the Midwest and the value of an inland waterway as a security measure. He also warned that if Canada pursued the project on its own, it might establish exclusive control over seaway traffic. The strangeness of the treasury secretary taking a leading role in the issue was highlighted when Ike turned to the secretary of the interior, under whose jurisdiction the seaway would fall, with a follow-up assignment.

Humphrey's arguments brought the president around. Once persuaded that the costs could be reduced through user fees and shared with state and private entities, he endorsed the project, mostly on national security grounds. But congressional approval was still far from certain. Humphrey was required to play a major role in marshaling support from companies who would benefit from the seaway and in lobbying key senators to vote for passage. It was not until February 1954, after exhausting negotiations and extensive logrolling, that the House and Senate approved the St. Lawrence Seaway.

Ike was present in 1959 when the completed waterway was dedicated. Its construction was probably inevitable in the long run—the president admitted as much during a Cabinet meeting. But after watching the weekly give and take, Attorney General Brownell concluded that Humphrey "almost single-handedly pushed through the program."[45]

First Among Equals?

Even when they vigorously disagreed with him, Eisenhower administration officials found Humphrey a most congenial colleague. His relaxed good humor put people at ease. Even Gabriel Hauge, who often disagreed with Humphrey on economic policy, remarked on his "remarkably winning personality." Hauge "seldom saw him when his ruddy face was not possessed by a magnificent smile."[46] At least at first, his "outsider" status and lack of political ambition increased the appeal and perceived honesty of his arguments. Nearly every leading figure in the administration came to believe that Humphrey was the most articulate, polished, and persuasive member of the Cabinet.

Eisenhower encouraged his Cabinet members to form personal friendships, and Humphrey took him seriously. Early on, he cultivated close relationships with Attorney General Herbert Brownell and Secretary of Commerce Sinclair Weeks. Their attachment may have stemmed from their close involvement in Republican politics; both Weeks and Humphrey had raised a lot of money for the party. The three men and their families vacationed together annually at the Weeks home in New Hampshire and at Humphrey's Georgia estate, where they engaged in many of the same recreational activities as Eisenhower's "gang."[47]

A perceptive observer of Cabinet dynamics during the early days was Emmet Hughes, one of the president's speech writers. Watching Humphrey in a group setting, Hughes was struck by his "unusually warm and expansive" manner." When his ability to reason did not carry the day, his conviction and determination often overcame the doubts of others. Hughes marveled how he plunged into debates "vigorously and bluntly, enliven[ing] almost every Cabinet session with little polemics" on deficits and the dangers of inflation.[48]

Others in the Cabinet and N.S.C. felt similarly. Agriculture Secretary Ezra Benson was especially impressed that Humphrey asked for tutorials on farm policy, about which he knew little, and ended up knowing agricultural issues better than any other Cabinet member.[49] Humphrey even delivered a speech before the National Grange Convention in 1955 that Benson proclaimed "remarkably effective." Dillon Anderson, Ike's national security adviser, called Humphrey a strong voice at N.S.C. meetings "just by sheer force of his intellect and the strength of his personality."[50] Another frequent N.S.C. attendee recalled that, aside from the president, Humphrey "was the strongest personality and had the strongest influence."[51]

Robert Cutler, who managed the National Security Council during much of Ike's first term, also succumbed to Humphrey's charm. Cutler regarded him as his "particular friend." In his memoir, he described a birthday party he gave for Humphrey, at which the table centerpiece included a miniature bronze statue of Humphrey's favorite horse. Cutler would spend many "happy, informal times" with the Humphreys at their home in Washington.[52]

Even more effusive praise came from administration insider and Eisenhower intimate Arthur Larson. He called Humphrey one of the most effective public officials he had ever encountered. Observing his performance at a Cabinet session, he said, was "worth a year at Harvard Business School." The secretary was always completely prepared, remembered Larson, with appropriate facts and figures, and his demeanor was that of a man "suffused with inner contentment because of his comfortable (and well justified) assurance of his own ability." Larson continued: "With unerring instinct, he would wait until everyone else had had his say and until the meeting was on the verge of dissolving in confusion and then he would say, 'Why don't we try this?' Quietly he would unfold a well-worked-out line of action, and the exhausted participants would gratefully seize upon the course Humphrey knew all along would prevail."[53]

Cultivating Congress

Beginning with the Reed hearings, congressional committees welcomed Humphrey's appearances. He left the impression that he would be willing to testify until every matter of interest to every congressman was thoroughly covered and explained. Senator George Malone of Nevada compared Humphrey favorably with William McChesney Martin, the head of the Federal Reserve. "I would not know Mr. Martin if he walked through the door.... I know you, I knew you the second day you were here," Malone said years later. "You are easier to get acquainted with, and you have not elevated yourself above ordinary mortals."[54]

In another example, Humphrey testified before the House Ways and Means Committee on the issue of raising the public debt limit. One of his questioners took the time to commend the "straightforward answers that you have always given in appearances before this committee." Taking note of a recent wave of resignations in the administration, the congressman expressed the hope that Humphrey would not be among them.[55] When an early tax bill barely passed the House, Humphrey entertained ninety-three of the ninety-six senators at lunch and briefed them on the details of a bill they probably had no time to read. It then sailed through.[56]

Humphrey numbered several important congressmen among his new Washington contacts. As a long-time supporter of Robert Taft, he would have been a valuable administration conduit to the senator had Taft not died suddenly in mid-1953. He was also a friend of the influential Virginia senator Harry Byrd, soon to become chairman of the Senate Finance Committee, whom he had met when a Hanna subsidiary built a plant in Byrd's state. Byrd and Humphrey saw each other socially and held similar views on budgets and taxes.

Cultivating the President

An important reason for Humphrey's appeal to the president was his "self-presentation as a vigorous, practical businessman whose mind was uncluttered with either complexities or doubts and who knew the simple truths in a very complex world."[57] Ike dashed off notes of thanks after many of their meetings. "I cannot tell you how much I enjoyed our talk," he wrote to Humphrey on typical occasions—on one of these, he even asked for a written recapitulation of their conversation so that he would not forget anything.[58]

Humphrey's ability to operate comfortably and effectively in large groups, such as the Cabinet and National Security Council, guaranteed his influence with the president. As a man who preferred to hear issues thrashed out in debate rather than to study long memoranda at his desk, the president admired Humphrey's lucidity and surefootedness in these forums. In May 1953 he confided to his diary: "He is a sound business type, possessed of a splendid personality.... He is almost a direct opposite of the caricatured businessman that so often appears in the columns of the 'liberal' press. He is persuasive in his presentations and usually has his facts well in hand."[59]

7. Humphrey Goes to Work

Humphrey's charm and style in expressing what were often conventional and even simplistic economic ideas came across to Ike as "imaginative orthodoxy." In a note to his brother Edgar at the end of the first full month of the administration, the president called Humphrey "one of the soundest and, I think, wisest men I have had the pleasure of meeting."[60]

Eisenhower's affection for Humphrey made him more receptive to the secretary's advice. It proved difficult for Ike to resist Humphrey's constant lectures on the need for cost cutting, even when he sensed that opposing views had more merit. Advisors chalked up his occasional indecision to the treasury secretary's persuasiveness, saying: "Well, you know how the boss is when someone talks economy—especially when that 'someone' is George."[61]

In perhaps his greatest admission of Humphrey's influence over him, he once said: "In Cabinet meetings, I always wait for George Humphrey to speak. I sit back and listen to the others talk while he doesn't say anything. But I know that when he speaks, he will say just what I am thinking."[62] Other Cabinet members were well aware of this. They were often timid in countering Humphrey's exhortations, because they suspected he was speaking for the president.

Looking back later, Eisenhower spared no accolade in expressing his appreciation of Humphrey's service. "We got along famously from the beginning," he wrote. "My admiration, respect and liking for him ... never ceased to grow."[63] A couple of years into his first administration, Eisenhower was moved to concur with the judgment of a White House visitor that Humphrey had been his most enlightened Cabinet selection. "I agree," Ike admitted, "Humphrey was my best."[64]

The feelings of affection and respect flowed both ways, as Humphrey took every opportunity to make clear. In an apt metaphor, he once said of Ike that "his political battleship drew more water than all the other politicians put together."[65] Early in the administration, he told the *New York Times*: "I have never worked with a man in my life who was superior to General Eisenhower in his grasp of things, his ability to understand them. He will listen to both sides of the question. He will listen to reason. He will reverse himself if he sees he is wrong. He is just the greatest boss you can imagine."[66] A skeptical reader might notice that Humphrey seemed more impressed with the president's ability to receive advice than with the quality of his thinking. But he also praised him for his knack of getting things done without seeking credit for it.

As Humphrey settled into his job and solidified his relationship with the president, the scope of his activities expanded well beyond the Treasury Department. He often served as an informal channel between the White House and individual congressmen. He also tapped his widespread network of business and political contacts to gain support for administration initiatives and to explain its policies. Far more of a party loyalist than Ike, Humphrey threw himself into fund-raising activities during election years and campaigned for Republican congressmen.[67] After the 1954 election, he concluded that the American public's image of the party had to change. "The Republicans needed to be more positive—future-oriented—by building up, not tearing down," he later wrote.[68]

Ike respected all the officials in his administration, but he invited only Humphrey to join the group of friends with whom he played and vacationed. He and his "gang" of bridge players, golfers and hunters convened whenever the president had a free weekend and engaged in non-stop recreation and banter. In the evenings, while the men played bridge, the wives joined Mamie Eisenhower for rounds of Bolivia—a variation of Canasta, a popular 1950s card game.[69]

Ike's acceptance of Humphrey into the fellowship was probably contingent upon the implied consent of the other gang members. But because Humphrey was one of them in background and outlook, he was never in danger of being black-balled. "What a grand person and able Cabinet member he is," remarked businessman Ellis Slater, "and how fortunate it is that the president can count on this kind of man to handle the financial affairs of the country."[70] The door was wide open as well for his wife Pam, whom Slater proclaimed a fine person and a good Canasta companion for Mamie.

Remarkably, Humphrey was terrible at both bridge and golf. According to Eisenhower intimate Cliff Roberts: "He was a very poor bridge player, if you could call him a bridge player at all, but Ike was so fond of him that he would often invite him over to the White House to play bridge, and would undertake to try to teach him and point out his errors and mistakes. George would listen very patiently but he was not a man who had card sense, and you could never have made a good bridge player out of him, no matter how hard you tried. But Ike never gave up on him." Humphrey was equally unskilled with a golf club. Hoping to spark some enthusiasm for the game, Roberts bought him a complete set of golf clothes and scheduled lessons for him with a professional, "but our efforts to make a golfer out of him were a complete flop."[71] Yet so great was the affection Eisenhower and his buddies had for the man that they were willing to endure his lack of competence at the very pursuits about which they were most passionate.

Humphrey's ace-in-the-hole was ownership of his magnificent 13,000-acre estate at Thomasville, in southern Georgia. He made available this residence, with its horse and cattle breeding facilities, ample guest quarters, large staff of servants, and fine food, for several gang get-togethers over the course of the administration. Thomasville's mild winter climate made it a good choice for outdoor activities when Washington was bleak and cold. Ike

7. Humphrey Goes to Work

and Mamie were frequent visitors, most notably while the president was recovering from his September 1955 heart attack.

All the president's friends were captivated by Humphrey and his property. As the busy executives repaired to the warm south for their soon familiar routine, Slater observed that "the relationship between the Humphreys and Eisenhowers is very close.... I would guess Humphrey is closer personally to the president than any other member of the Cabinet" and "George is the president's greatest help among his top men."[72]

Over time, Eisenhower's admiration of Humphrey's policy acumen began to lessen, even as the two men remained personally close. Soon enough, the president would discover that Humphrey was not as flexible or open to new information as he was thought to be and that he had few original prescriptions to offer. He began to hear complaints from his other economic aides that Humphrey was overconfident of the correctness of his views and difficult to reason with.

By any measure, however, Humphrey's first few months in Washington were wildly successful. Wherever he performed—on Capitol Hill, before the media, or in meetings with his Cabinet colleagues—he made a strong impression. To top it off, he was a member of Ike's social circle. Altogether, it was a giddy experience, though Humphrey appeared to take it in stride.

With his key relationships thus secured, Humphrey plunged into the debates about spending that would dominate Eisenhower's presidency. By May 1953, when he gave his first major budget presentation to the Cabinet, he was ready to take the offensive. His main target was the secretary of defense, to whose travails we now turn.

George Humphrey boards a plane en route to a conference. Humphrey bruised egos in his aggressive campaign against federal spending, but few could resist his charm and powers of persuasion. A colleague "seldom saw him when his ruddy face was not possessed by a magnificent smile" (Western Reserve Historical Society, Cleveland, Ohio).

8

Wilson in the Maelstrom

With his confirmation hearings at last behind him, Wilson, like his friend at the Treasury Department, hoped events would allow for a smooth transition to his new job. While neither man had that luxury, Wilson soon seemed in over his head.

His first year as defense secretary was an ordeal. He knew running the Pentagon would be a big job, but he soon found that it was even bigger than it looked. Despite being a proven manager, he had little understanding of the political world he was entering and little in common with America's senior military officers. In a move guaranteed to increase their discomfort, he brought in a team of fellow businessmen to occupy senior administrative positions. His deputy, Roger Kyes, had been one of his vice presidents at G.M.

Beyond those drawbacks, a "perfect storm" of circumstances conspired to present Wilson with an unenviable challenge. No previous administration had made much progress in bringing authority over the military's varied budgets and resources into the secretary's office. Ike wanted Wilson to begin this process, which was certain to earn the enmity of the individual services. A competition for resources among them would threaten the relative parity among the army, navy and air force and thus exacerbate their rivalry.

The deepening Cold War with the Soviet Union raised the questions of how to configure U.S. forces to meet a nuclear threat to the country's survival. Many politicians in both parties regarded the international environment as more dangerous than ever and believed that Eisenhower's plans to cut the defense budget were unwise. An explosion of defense-related technology during the 1950s constantly called into question the relative priority of the service missions and caused endless recalculations of military expenses.

Pressure and criticism from many quarters, including the president and Congress, would often leave Wilson frustrated. Though he put up a bluff, hearty front and, as always, worked extremely long hours, he was not happy during much of 1953. His wife, Jessie, told a journalist that for several months he was uncharacteristically withdrawn and unwilling to talk about his work.

Issues of Judgment

While Humphrey adapted quickly to Washington's unique rituals, procedures, and ways of measuring effectiveness, it was apparent from the beginning that Wilson had spent his entire working life in a different universe.

The new defense secretary was an unpretentious man who enjoyed a modest lifestyle unusual in status-conscious Washington. He turned down many of the normal perks of senior government service, driving himself to work and waiting in line at the ticket counter at airports. His wife Jessie would sometimes bring him a fresh suit after he worked what he called the "night shift" at the Pentagon and did not have time to come home.[1]

An episode at the outset showed him strangely lacking a sense of proportion. Before taking office, the president-elect circulated a draft of his State of the Union speech to Cabinet members for any comments they might have. Wilson took this assignment very seriously. He suggested four trivial wording changes in the foreign policy section of the speech, which was not his area of responsibility. When a second draft revealed that Ike's speechwriters had not made the requested changes, Wilson called to insist that they do so. He continued to insist after they informed him that Eisenhower had gone over the speech carefully and was happy with it.[2]

Wilson's admirers suggested that such tenacity accounted for his success at G.M., but it also raised a question about his judgment. Fortunately, he was not as tenacious in defending his choice of radio personality Arthur Godfrey as the Defense Department representative to the Psychological Strategy Board. He backed down under White House pressure.

Like most civilian defense secretaries, Wilson had a lot to learn about the armed services. He proceeded in his typical fashion, spending the first several months in lengthy meetings, considering problems from every possible angle, and conducting what one historian called his "scatter-gun education."[3] His lack of hesitation in displaying ignorance of the most elementary military facts left the impression that he was a provincial man and a slow learner.[4]

Wilson had immediate difficulty winning over the career military. For example, General James Gavin called Wilson "the most uninformed man, and the most determined to remain so, that has ever been Secretary." Gavin charged that Wilson "tended to deal with his Chiefs of Staff as though they were recalcitrant union bosses."[5] Wilson professed to understand the feelings of Gavin and others. "Of course, they would like to run their own particular service and not ever have anybody check up on it," he conceded. "That is just human nature."[6] *Time* magazine reported that Wilson's refusal to change his mind once he had made a decision "sometimes emerged as arrogance and bullheadedness."[7]

Relations with the President

On the same day that he set down his preliminary impressions of George Humphrey in his diary, Eisenhower wrote a few words about Charles Wilson: "In his field, he is really a competent man. He is careful and positive, and I have no slightest doubt that ... he will produce the maximum of security for this country at minimum or near minimum cost. If he fails, it will be because of his inability to sell himself or his programs to Congress.... On the other hand, Mr. Wilson is prone to lecture, rather than answer, when asked a specific question."[8] Ike's comments about Wilson's relations with Congress and his tendency to deliver long monologues reflected his troubles during the recent confirmation hearings, but they also hinted at future problems with Wilson's style and approach.

Wilson's biggest handicap was working for a president who happened to be the country's leading military authority. Ike well understood the Defense Department's competitive budgeting process, in which the fierce rivalry among the services often led to padded resource requirements—indeed, he had once been part of that process. He was predisposed to be skeptical of all Pentagon budget numbers, and he was already frustrated by the department's strong resistance to change.

Eisenhower affirmed that he had no intention of micromanaging the Pentagon, yet somehow he expected Wilson to enter this alien environment, bring order and transparency to the department's finances, and to set in motion a specific series of reforms. Needing Ike's guidance but discouraged from asking for it, Wilson would find himself in an impossible position much of the time.

Wilson irritated the president by requesting an hour a week to discuss routine problems—departmental issues that Ike felt had not been sufficiently "shaken down."[9] In addition to this regular meeting, Wilson sometimes dropped in unannounced and, according to Sherman Adams, "discombobulated" Ike with his "rambling, exploratory discourses" on defense problems.[10] "He comes in here and sits here and asks me questions about details of his own job," the president fumed. "If he wasn't able to do them he shouldn't have the job."[11] Ike famously reprimanded Wilson when he brought one too many minor decisions to his desk for resolution: "Charlie, you run defense. We both can't do it, and I won't do it."[12]

8. Wilson in the Maelstrom

Despite his difficulties at the Pentagon, decades of success in the corporate world had given him an air of imperturbable self-confidence. According to Sherman Adams, Wilson was usually the first member to speak up at Cabinet meetings and was "preposterously opinionated," with views on "most anything that anybody said around the Cabinet table."[13] Press Secretary James Hagerty found his default style argumentative.[14] A 1953 newspaper article alleged that the White House staff was distressed by his "bull-in-the-china-shop behavior."[15] After a series of "dogmatic irrelevancies" at a Cabinet meeting, Ike aide Wilton Persons joked: "From now on, I'm buying nothing but Plymouths."[16]

Even so, his comments included the occasional bull's-eye. Once in a while, he would ask a penetrating question that "would sort of blow a proposition out of the water."[17] For example, during a discussion of the option of launching an attack on China during the Korean War, Wilson listened for a long time and then said: "Mr. President, I understand from what's been said that we could lick China. What I don't understand is what we would do with China after we got them licked."[18] According to insider William Ewald, Ike admired his "bluff courage," as revealed in his willingness to confront Russian behavior when necessary.[19] Adams conceded that Wilson was a "smart cookie," particularly on the subject of labor relations. Wilson, he recalled, suggested James Mitchell for Secretary of Labor as a replacement for Eisenhower's least successful Cabinet appointee, Martin Durkin.[20]

But Eisenhower found Wilson more often annoying than helpful. At the very beginning of the term, Wilson tried the president's patience by seeking help from the entire Cabinet on a relatively minor decision concerning the Pentagon's purchase of generators and transformers. A British firm had submitted the lowest bid, but an American supplier whose bid was second lowest was said to make more reliable products. When Wilson raised the issue in early March, a lively discussion ensued, after which Ike suggested that Wilson seek the views of the appropriate congressional committees. But the decision remained unmade for several weeks and continued to be debated at subsequent Cabinet sessions, consuming more of the time and attention of such highly paid officials than it was surely worth.[21]

Speechwriter Emmet Hughes noted that Wilson's frankness, directness and infelicity of phrase sometimes made the president "grind his teeth, tighten his mouth, [and] roll his eyes." Wilson himself listened only grudgingly, "as though the words of another were imposing rude delay upon his next remarks."[22] Though the president as a matter of policy welcomed the participation of all Cabinet members in any issue being considered, Wilson sometimes monopolized the discussion, even on matters unrelated to defense. Of course, this was a primary disadvantage of Cabinet meetings.

Eisenhower learned early that Wilson lacked a sophisticated grasp of foreign affairs. At the very first Cabinet meeting, as Ike was extolling the virtues of trade in breaking down barriers with the Communist world, Wilson shook his head. "I'm a little old-fashioned. I don't like to sell firearms to the Indians." The president reacted sharply, delivering a little lecture in support of his view. "If you trade with them, Charlie," he concluded, "you've got something pulling their interest your way." Unconvinced, Wilson replied: "I'm going to be on the tough side of this one." Ike had the last word: "Charlie, I'm talking common sense."[23] Later, he growled: "Damn it, how did a man as shallow as Charlie Wilson ever get to be head of General Motors?"[24]

Despite Eisenhower's growing concerns about Wilson, he did not seriously consider replacing him. Wilson would remain a key player in one of the central bureaucratic dramas of the Eisenhower administration—the attempt to trim and shape the American military into a force the nation could afford to sustain over the uncertain length of the Cold War. Congressional opposition to these plans, often on both sides of the aisle, as well as resistance from the military services themselves, left the president so frustrated and angry that he would end his second term with a famous broadside against the unchecked growth of an entity he labeled the "military-industrial complex."

Early Accomplishments

The easiest and most successful part of Wilson's first year involved purely managerial tasks, relating to organization and personnel. These were bound to be his strong suits, having been core responsibilities during his G.M. tenure. "No organization will protect you against the stupid fellow," he once said with typical humor, "but good organization should prevent a concentration of stupidity."[25]

His intent was to centralize the department while saving money by eliminating inefficiency and waste. In the first several months, he made progress in restructuring the Pentagon chain of command. He relied on the recommendations of a high-level commission, which included prominent Americans such as Nelson Rockefeller of New York, former defense secretary Robert Lovett, and Ike's brother Milton. The commission tiptoed around the controversial concept of unifying the services under firm civilian control, an idea for which Eisenhower had long been fighting.

But it managed to come up with a plan that added significantly to the powers of the joint chiefs of staff and the Office of the Secretary—a solid step in the direction of greater centralization. Wilson was also granted authority to create six additional assistant secretaries of defense, corresponding to General Motors vice presidents. Media critics feared that the new structure left the army with too much power, labeling the plan a "Hydra-headed monster"[26] that would lead to "military absolutism,"[27] but Eisenhower endorsed the approach and sent it to the Hill. Congress gave its blessing in June.

Early personnel decisions also proved uncontroversial and provided some forward momentum. Wilson and Eisenhower appointed a group of experienced and able joint chiefs whose backgrounds and views satisfied key Republicans in Congress. Senator Robert Taft, whose support of defense policy would be important in the months to come, was shown the list of appointees and proclaimed it "entirely satisfactory."[28]

The new chairman of the joint chiefs would be hawkish Admiral Arthur Radford, a supporter of the aggressive use of air power. Radford was a formidable figure with strong views who was highly regarded by the president.

Wilson, Humphrey and the Military Budget

Foreign challenges had forced the Truman administration to triple the defense budget between 1950 and 1951. In this new age, it seemed necessary to be ready for war at any time, rather than try to mobilize when it might be too late.

The basis for U.S. thinking on defense at the time of Eisenhower's election was a policy paper called NSC-68. It assessed the Soviet Union as an irredeemably hostile nation that was building a dangerous arsenal of weapons. This assumption, plus the outbreak of the Korean War in 1950, stimulated the military spending that led to the FY-1954 federal budget deficit. Between 1951 and 1953, the defense budget almost quadrupled—from around $12 billion to $46 billion. Truman accepted the need for greatly increased spending and did not worry too much about the strain on the economy. The Office of Defense Mobilization assured the administration that the country had the resources to support whatever level of defense spending might be required.[29]

Eisenhower did not share this sanguine view. He wanted military budgets to be sustainable, year after year, during what he was certain would be a long-term struggle with the Soviet Union. His goal was a defense that was adequate to the task but not so expensive as to bankrupt the country or to interfere with other administration goals, such as tax cuts and balanced budgets.

The president had insisted he would not "run" Defense, but from the outset of his administration he sought to shape the strategic and budgetary aspects of a policy that he called "security with solvency." Behind the slogan was an approach to defense spending that downplayed the urgency of the Soviet threat and thus provided a rationale for the desired cuts.

George Humphrey was only too happy to assist. Before the administration was a day old, he and Dodge were driving a government-wide hunt for budget fat, with the primary goal of reducing the defense budget as soon as possible. Despite the ongoing war in Korea, the administration intended to submit an interim budget for 1954 that would begin to close the inherited gap between expenditures and revenue. Forcing cuts at domestic agencies, such as the Interior and Agriculture departments, was part of their program, but the amounts involved were not nearly enough to turn a deficit into a surplus.

Humphrey became focused on military spending because that was where the money was. He argued that such spending shifted "productive resources" into weaponry that might never be used. He reasoned that the country would be better off lowering taxes to spur innovation than pouring money into inherently wasteful Pentagon programs.

President Eisenhower (left) with George Humphrey. The two men "got along famously from the beginning." Humphrey was the only Cabinet official to become a close friend of the president. "When he speaks," Ike once said, "he will say just what I am thinking" (Ed Clark/The LIFE Picture Collection/Getty Images).

From the outset Humphrey set himself up as a sharp critic of how the Defense Department operated. He reserved special contempt for army generals who wanted larger budgets for conventional warfare. They were "just Army-minded morning, noon and night. If you gave a nickel to anybody, the Army had to have a lot more."[30] After studying the Truman administration's defense posture, he decided it lacked focus and financed too many redundant capabilities. He described the ideal military budget much as Ike would: a "middle way between extremes which—on the one side would stupidly cheat our defenses to save money, and—on the other side—would amass weapons and strength with an abandon that would wreck our economy."[31]

Wilson supported the cuts, but he had a much tougher task than Humphrey. He had to translate lower budget numbers into a leaner military program that would still adequately defend the country, all the while learning on the job, reevaluating the evolving threat of a nuclear-armed Soviet Union, keeping his service chiefs from rebelling, and overseeing the continuing war in Korea. Wilson would have preferred a decent interval to build relations of trust with military brass and cushion the blow that was coming. But Humphrey's demand for cuts was immediate and unrelenting. Wilson had to get used to the idea that his Cabinet colleague was going to make his life very difficult.

Always a conscientious manager, he made a genuine attempt to understand the relationship between the budget and military strategy, and in time his extra hours of time and effort made his defense views more informed than Humphrey's. But Eisenhower never quite believed that Wilson could free himself from the influence of the service chiefs. It was the treasury secretary who had the president's ear, and Wilson knew that Eisenhower was unlikely to push back against him. He recalled a strong note Ike had sent him a year before his election. It strongly criticized those who did not believe that the country's security and economic health were interdependent. Such people, Ike said, "should not be entrusted with any kind of responsibility in our country."[32] Wilson did not want to be one of those people.

In their zeal for Pentagon reductions, Humphrey and Budget Director Dodge focused relentlessly on the bottom line rather than the content of defense programs. Humphrey firmly denied the obvious—that he had a bias toward economy—asserting that "our defense must be measured not by its cost, but by its wisdom," and he always insisted in public that a strong defense was more important than a balanced budget.[33] However, his real priorities were clear.

In fact, the administration's budget goals seemed to suggest an arbitrary limit on defense expenditures, even if those expenditures might not be suffi-

Charles Wilson at his desk at the Pentagon. Genial and hard-working, Wilson attacked problems with an almost exasperating thoroughness and favored lengthy, unstructured discussions with subordinates. Army officers in particular chafed under his leadership and publicly criticized his "woeful lack of comprehension of the role of the foot soldier" (courtesy Anderson University & Church of God Archives).

cient to protect the country. Only a president who was also a military hero could hope to gain acceptance for reducing the size of the defense establishment as foreign dangers seemed to multiply.

Thrashing Out Security Policy

The clash over military spending and its connection with the economic health of the nation played out with particular force at early policy meetings. Week after week, the National Security Council engaged in vigorous debate about the overall goals and priorities of American security policy—a debate that set the stage for several years of pitched battles over defense resource allocation. As an N.S.C. member, Humphrey was prepared to use a platform for fiscal arguments that no previous treasury secretary had enjoyed. At the first meeting, in February 1953. he greeted his new colleagues by stating ("very emphatically," according to the notes kept) that all major security recommendations must henceforth be accompanied by an estimate of how much they would cost and how the cost would be covered. He also declared that defense programs could not be discussed piecemeal—they must be viewed in relation to the country's total foreign policy posture. Joe Dodge of the budget bureau immediately concurred.

Several administration officials were immediately alarmed by the attack on defense spending. Speaking at a March Cabinet meeting, Secretary Dulles reminded his colleagues and the president that America faced many foreign policy challenges, including Communist aggression in Europe and the Third World, which made drastic national security cuts inadvisable. Bobby Cutler, the Cabinet secretary, added his view that the country could afford both "guns and butter."

Eisenhower adviser Gabriel Hauge agreed. The budget hawks, he believed, underestimated U.S. ability to cover growing defense costs. He made that case to Humphrey privately in a March memo. "I think the President should be reassured that the economy can support whatever he thinks he needs as he undertakes to turn around some of these situations in the world where we are on the defensive against Communism," he wrote.[34] Harold Stassen, a former governor hired by Ike as an outside-the-box thinker on foreign policy, made the same point at several N.S.C. meetings. Humphrey dismissed such heresy. He also took note of the fact that influential opponents were operating close to the president.

Ike soon realized that costing out a national security policy was not possible without a fresh assessment of defense needs. He asked Wilson to consult with the joint chiefs and make a preliminary estimate of what a streamlined military might look like. The job was far too complicated to be finished in a couple of months. Wilson reported back to the N.S.C. that, without the necessary reconsideration of the basic objectives of American security policy, little could be squeezed out of Truman's projected 1954 defense budget.

But where Wilson saw decisions without adequate information, Humphrey saw unreasonable delay. His stridency and forceful calls for cuts made the joint chiefs nervous. He and Dodge came to the N.S.C. in early March 1953 with a plan that called for military reductions steep enough to enable a balanced budget by 1955. Humphrey threw in exhortations drawn from his former world. "It's just like reorganizing a whole business," he told his skeptical audience.[35]

Eisenhower recognized that his top officials were still learning to know and trust each other. He didn't want either side of an important argument to be stampeded, so he intervened to even the scales—a debate management technique he would employ throughout his presidency. As Humphrey became more insistent, Ike came down on the military's side, sensing that the ground had not been prepared for the "meat-axe" cuts Humphrey was pushing. But when the session ended inconclusively, the president saw no harm in pressuring his defense secretary a bit more. He told Wilson that he was still bothered by waste, overhead and duplication of effort. He asked him to burrow into the defense budget and look for "avoidable costs."[36]

Beyond debate management, Eisenhower's immediate reaction to the clash between the two schools of thought on military spending revealed his sense of realism. He shared Humphrey's concern for economy, but he knew at heart that the quality of America's defense had to be taken into equal account. Even before the intramural arguing began in earnest, he decided he would be content with making a good start in the revised 1954 budget toward a leaner government and military and worry about deeper cuts later.

Initial Defense Cuts

Meanwhile, Dodge was sending a blizzard of memos to the various agencies, directing them to scrutinize costs and revise budgets downward, In response, Wilson immediately ordered a freeze on civilian employment. But Humphrey expressed disappointment with the initial projections of money saved. "If we end up lifting [wage and price] controls and don't cut government expenditures," he told the Cabinet in early March, "then boys, we're in trouble."[37] He told his colleagues that the cuts made in the next month or so would lay the foundation for the success or failure of the administration's budget and tax policies all the way through the election year 1956. Dodge warned the departments to expect further orders from the president.

Although the prospective personnel cuts at the Defense Department were relatively modest, they drew fire from both inside and outside the Pentagon. Democrats in Congress charged that the administration was giving short shrift to national defense at a time of rising danger. A navy officer fed the sentiment by telling the press that Wilson was "fiddling with our national security." Influential journalists and even other Republicans joined in the criticism. A *Time* magazine columnist called the idea of reductions, coming as they would during wartime, "dangerous and irresponsible beyond belief,"[38] even though sizeable military budget cuts at this stage were still little more than rumors.

But most Republicans had no problem with Eisenhower's initial moves toward fiscal retrenchment. In fact, Senator Taft faulted Wilson for not going far enough. The defense secretary, he said, was too willing to accommodate the military's unreasonable demands for resources.[39] Conflicting pressures of this kind would plague Wilson throughout his tenure, as he was whipsawed among the military professionals in the Pentagon, their allies and opponents on Capitol Hill, and his masters at the White House.

In late March, Wilson brought a compromise budget plan for FY-1954 to the N.S.C., one that probably accorded with the president's sense of the possible. The plan determined that $5 billion could be cut, mostly through improved procedures, consolidation of functions, and the elimination of 40,000 civilian jobs. Eisenhower approved it immediately. The defense budget he submitted to Congress totaled around $43 billion.

The reductions were fleshed out and made public in April. The overall plan slightly favored the army, whose funding would increase slightly to accommodate the ongoing war in Korea. The navy and air force, as well as the Pentagon's research and development budget, stood to be assessed cuts. Wilson also proposed a new way of selecting defense contractors, which ran into predictable opposition from congressmen whose districts had companies that did contract work for the military. The upshot of these still relatively minor tweaks to the defense budget was to rile both the military services and their key allies in Congress.

The R&D cuts sparked much opposition, given the importance of remaining on the cutting edge in weapons development. But neither Wilson nor Humphrey professed to see much benefit in military R&D. "It is very easy to waste money in what you call research, that is, people hide behind the name and go ahead with a lot of boondoggling," Wilson said in his infelicitous way. "Just because somebody calls it research, don't think it's wonderful."[40]

Dealing with Congressional Dissent

Despite the grumbling, Eisenhower felt that he had taken an important first step in a long-term effort to bring down the cost of government. It came as a shock, then, to learn that the Republican leadership in Congress was far from satisfied. As the new president briefed key legislators on the fiscal picture for 1954 in late April, Senator Taft reacted with explosive anger when informed that the overall budget would still be in deficit. His intemperate remarks, which included a threat to go public with his opposition, left the president trembling with rage.

Following a brief "stunned silence," Humphrey, supported by Dodge and Dulles, parried Taft's criticism at some length, allowing Eisenhower to calm down and come up with a well-reasoned response. The moment passed, and the two men went on to have a productive relationship until Taft died of cancer a few months later. Humphrey's intervention in this emotional confrontation helped to cement his friendship with Ike.

Despite strong objections to the administration's budget from members of the president's own party, Eisenhower's relations with Capitol Hill were fairly harmonious during the first half of his term. Democrats of the period were in the minority in both houses of Congress, as well as divided into several camps. Working in Ike's favor was the strength of a conservative Democratic faction, composed mostly of southerners, who tended to agree with the policy of fiscal economy. A liberal faction, committed to larger budgets to meet what they felt were obvious national needs, including defense, would emerge as the most vocal critic of Eisenhower's war on spending.

Some liberal Democrats took the opportunity throughout the spring of 1953 to score political points. After the president's briefing of congressional leaders on the 1954 military budget, Senator Stuart Symington, a former air force secretary, charged the administration with sacrificing security for the sake of a balanced budget and following a "perilous course."[41] Former president Truman weighed in by challenging Eisenhower's rationale for the cuts. "There can be no doctrine more dangerous than the notion that we cannot afford to defend ourselves," he warned.[42]

In the first of many dissents from within the Pentagon itself, the outgoing air force chief of staff criticized Wilson and the president in congressional testimony for not matching Soviet force levels and for leaving the joint chiefs out of the decision-making process. Like all the administration's critics, he alleged that arbitrary budget targets were endangering American defenses. Disloyalty of this sort especially rankled Ike, who declared himself "damn tired of Air Force sales programs."[43] Wilson also castigated opponents of cuts for having a "desire to build up such forces as could defend the whole world."[44]

Wilson tried and failed to reassure Congress in testimony a few days later. *Time* magazine's Capitol Hill correspondent considered his appearance a disaster—the secretary seemed stumped by the most predictable inquiries.[45] As he fumbled for words, Senator Margaret Chase Smith finally presented him with a list of thirty-two questions and asked him to find someone "capable of answering them."[46] The harsh criticism so early in his tenure may have been a legacy of his disastrous confirmation hearings. The dust-up with Congress and the rebellion of the career military were troubling. Eisenhower, a former army officer himself, had been in office only four months, and he and Wilson were already being berated for defense cuts that had not even begun in earnest yet.

In June, Eisenhower and Wilson managed to bring the Congress around—in particular, by gaining the support of Republicans whose party loyalty was stronger than their opposition to military cuts. It helped that some of the quieter party members were just as economy-minded as the president. Wilson, in a much improved performance on Capitol Hill, made a persuasive case that the dissenting air force officers were challenging the principle of civilian control of the military. A radio address by the president also helped swing popular opinion over to the side of the administration. According to a Gallup Poll taken in July, 55 percent of the public did not believe that the defense cuts endangered national security.[47]

The revised 1954 budget passed on July 29 was actually about $1 billion less than Eisenhower had asked for and about $4 billion less than the Truman administration had projected. With congressional approval and a truce in the Korean War, which was signed in June, Wilson reached a breathing space.

It proved to be fleeting, because hardly anyone was satisfied. Congressional Democrats sensed the political potency of the debate over military sufficiency and resolved to continue attacking the reductions. At the Pentagon, military leaders, realizing that the years of easy money were over, were circling the wagons and girding for battle with the new president. On the opposite side, George Humphrey was preparing to force further defense reductions. Wilson had been defense secretary for four months. His troubles were just beginning.

Humphrey's Persistence

Humphrey ignored congressional criticism of the administration's frugality and, as budget planning for FY-1955 began, continued to push for deep cuts. He had been hoping for a FY-1954 defense budget closer to $38 billion instead of the $43 billion to which the president had finally agreed. At a Cabinet meeting on May 22, he suggested that the administration aim for an overall FY-1955 budget of $60 billion, a sum which he agreed seemed "almost impossible" but might allow a "Republican tax reduction" in 1954.

Possibly annoyed by Humphrey's unwelcome injection of politics into the discussion, the president seemed to consider the budget goal unrealistic. The "psychology of the country" might not allow major budget reductions just now, he cautioned. Americans had become accustomed to "heavy subsidies," such as veterans and farm programs, and defense cuts had inspired opposition from both parties. Ike showed some sympathy for the plight of

The incoming chairman of the joint chiefs of staff, Admiral Arthur Radford (left), at a Pentagon luncheon for President Eisenhower (second from left) in May 1953, along with Defense Secretary Wilson and outgoing JCS chairman General Omar Bradley (right). Over the next four years, Wilson would be caught between Eisenhower's demands for military budget cuts and the fierce resistance of the service chiefs (U.S. Army photograph/courtesy Anderson University & Church of God Archives).

Wilson, who was "already in the position of having to defend what he isn't spending rather than what he is." He concluded by repeating a refrain from his critics—that national security must not be endangered "merely" for the sake of balanced budgets.[48]

A Cabinet meeting on June 26 marked the early appearance of another contentious spending issue—one that would find Humphrey and the president on opposite sides. Because tight credit was having a negative impact on the government's ability to finance its operations, the secretary noted, it would be an especially bad time to consider any new foreign aid measures aimed at "financing the world."[49] The sarcasm was lost on no one. Ike immediately countered that more foreign spending might actually allow reduced military expenditures at home. Over the next five years, Eisenhower would seek, with limited success, to convince Humphrey that U.S. foreign assistance was money well spent.

Along with the Cabinet, the N.S.C. was becoming another key arena for Humphrey's anti-spending campaign. At a July 14 session, he gave a surprisingly aggressive lecture on the need for a "thorough reexamination of our entire foreign policy," a much tougher attitude toward foreign aid, elimination of "all duplication and overlapping" among the military services, and an investigation of the "possibilities of nuclear warfare," all with the aim of saving money. And this must be done quickly, he concluded. "If we just sit here for another three months without making these vital decisions ... the result would be unqualified disaster," and the administration might as well "abandon all hope of being retained in office."[50] Finally, he turned to Wilson with a demand for an additional $10 billion in military reductions. "We've got to revise whole programs," he argued, "and this means surgery."

Humphrey's passionate arguments aroused immediate, almost reflexive, opposition around the table. The military services felt that they were under siege. Wilson immediately insisted that he was finished making defense cuts for the time being. Secretary of State Dulles, focused on fighting the Cold War with the Soviet Union, did not consider balancing the budget a priority. But many conservatives, in Congress and elsewhere, were convinced of the need to recover from the perceived profligacy of the Roosevelt-Truman years, and they cheered Humphrey on.

Only the president could resolve the conflict. Though he understood the risks involved in scrimping on defense, the treasury secretary's arguments squared with his intuitive sense of what the national situation demanded. And the more he heard them, the more persuasive they became.

9

Humphrey and the 1953–54 Recession

Economic Trouble Brewing

Eisenhower's promise to use the power of the federal government at any sign of recession was put to the test during his first full year. At the beginning of his term, the president told Humphrey pointedly that inaction in the face of economic difficulties was not an option. "We must not allow businessmen to be charged with indifference to the country," he said.[1] The brief recession of 1953–54 provided the first economic challenge to a Republican administration since the Depression. It yielded important lessons for the president and his economic team that governed their conduct for the next seven years.

The economy seemed strong when Eisenhower took office in January 1953. Though business was doing well and unemployment was low, Gabriel Hauge was already preparing the president for more volatile times ahead. Six months from now, he warned, "visibility isn't so good. This boom isn't going to last forever.... America hasn't found the secret of perpetual economic motion."[2] He wrote to Humphrey that an economic slow-down seemed to him the main danger. "We are going to have to shift our mental gears on this preoccupation with inflation sometime before long," he concluded.[3]

The nervousness of Hauge and others did not change Humphrey's "mental gears." Representative Reed had also predicted an economic downturn during his hearings, and he had warned Eisenhower and Humphrey that the administration's opposition to immediate tax cuts would make matters worse. But Humphrey was preoccupied with inflation and budget cuts, which impaired his ability to see the warning signs of the recession that began toward the middle of 1953. In fairness to Humphrey, the Federal Reserve had also been more concerned about inflation than recession and had used its monetary toolbox to rein in the economy shortly before Eisenhower took office.

9. Humphrey and the 1953–54 Recession

The Treasury Department took an early action that left the economy even more vulnerable to a recession—an action that Chief of Staff Sherman Adams later described as a regrettable "rookie mistake." It was an outgrowth of Humphrey's promise to the president that the end of wage and price controls would not cause any inflation. He decided to back up his promise by having his department issue a high-paying thirty-year bond, designed to attract funds from long-term investors and take a lot of money out of circulation.

The reasoning behind this decision was complex but, as future C.E.A. chairman Raymond Saulnier later pointed out, it was "in accord with the financial orthodoxy of the time."[4] The problem with the Treasury bond issue was that it was immediately over-subscribed and drew too many funds that might have otherwise been invested, thereby slowing several sectors of the economy. The action would have been more prudent if the economy showed no signs of flagging, but such signs were even then becoming visible.

The Federal Reserve, headed by William McChesney Martin, "rescued" Humphrey by lowering interest rates and reserve requirements in June, but the bond issue drew considerable criticism from the economist community.[5] Congressional Democrats also blasted Humphrey for failing to realize that inflationary pressures had abated. Saulnier later wrote: "It is clear that the Treasury's move took more chances with the economy's stability than it was prudent to take." In his memoirs, Eisenhower conceded that the Treasury action "may have" helped cause a recession, though he seems to have approved of it at the time.[6]

The Recession Arrives

In any case, Hauge's prediction was correct—an economic downturn came into view as summer turned to fall. C.E.A. data showed that unemployment and the cost of living were inching up, durable goods orders and residential construction were dipping, and the incidence of business failures was increasing.

The immediate causes of the slowdown were clear. The end of the Korean War in June had sharply reduced defense spending, and the administration's recently enacted budget cuts had further slowed economic activity. "We are glad to know the brakes work," *Business Week* wrote, "but we don't want to go through the windshield."[7] The *New York Times* sensed that the new administration's first economic challenge was imminent. Ike's team "might be heading into the first test of the adequacy of a hands-off approach to the national economy," it reported in September.[8]

Humphrey was not concerned, because he balanced this bad news against other developments that he believed would move the economy in a more positive direction. The postponed tax cuts, now scheduled for early 1954, would stimulate spending. The administration was preparing a tax reform package that would contain various business incentives. The Federal Reserve had begun to take expansionary measures. There seemed no reason to panic or to reverse the government's cost-cutting initiatives.

In September, however, C.E.A. Chairman Arthur Burns brought the Cabinet a different message. His data suggested that a downturn, which he euphemistically called a "rolling economic adjustment," was in progress. In response, the Eisenhower team began to debate the need for government action. Ike again reminded his aides that he did not intend to stand by and do nothing if a crisis was brewing. Then he turned to Burns and said: "Arthur, you are my chief of staff in handling the recession. You are to report every week … on where we are going and what we ought to be doing."[9]

Over the next nine months, Ike listened to the conflicting counsel of his primary advisors and tried to decide what to do. In the intramural debate, Humphrey held the advantage—he was first and foremost a policy advocate, while Burns felt it was his primary duty to gather data and interpret it as objectively as possible. As the two men competed for the president's attention, the stakes mounted. Considering Republican vulnerability on the issue of economic management, the wrong policy outcome could easily make Eisenhower a one-term president.

The Burns-Humphrey Rivalry

While the storm clouds gathered, Humphrey continued to bask in media praise. In November the journalist Drew Pearson called him the "Cabinet member Ike listens to most."[10] A *New York Times* political reporter wrote that the "smashingly forceful" Humphrey had "in a year amassed a reputation in the capital which approaches in size the debt he is called upon to manage."[11]

But Arthur Burns' star was also rising. His sudden prominence was a reflection not only of the growing influence of the reinvigorated Council of Economic Advisers but of Eisenhower's obvious respect for the tweedy academic. Burns had been anticipating a low-key role—he had hoped to simply render non-partisan judgments on economic conditions week by week and remain in the background. Now he would find himself involved in anti-recession planning that often had political implications. The presence of

Burns at Cabinet meetings and Ike's attentiveness to his presentations attested to the president's appreciation for the C.E.A.'s data-driven point of view. Burns was an immediate hit with the rest of the Cabinet as well, speaking knowledgeably in language the members could understand.

He even became a minor celebrity—similar, in some ways, to the media's fascination with Henry Kissinger fifteen years later. Articles in national journals noted his pivotal role in economic policymaking. They were often illustrated with photos of the smiling, rumpled, pipe-smoking professor working hard at his desk. A *Business Week* piece in July 1953—called "He's Watching for Trouble"—identified him the administration's primary inflation fighter.[12] An article in *The Nation* a few months later, titled "Meet Arthur Burns: He'll Influence Your Future," praised his diligent gathering and weighing of facts and figures. Burns, it said, shared the president's belief in strong government action when and if necessary.[13]

Harmony among the president's key economic players had prevailed throughout most of 1953. They emphasized publicly their close consultations despite their "frequent disagreements."[14] The appearance of a real economic slowdown was bound to intensify those disagreements.

Humphrey eyed the Burns phenomenon warily. For a man who considered himself the final word on anything having to do with money, the attention being paid to Burns was irritating. Continued talk about the possibility of government intervention when he felt that the economy was in no discernable trouble made him nervous. He saw his main tasks for the next several months as reducing the president's level of concern and staving off any interference in the workings of the free market.

Watchful Waiting

The negative economic trends sparked the creation of several task forces to study possible government responses. At the president's direction, Burns took charge of the contingency planning. He devised a three-part program that would rely, first, on monetary policy (notably, the lowering of interest rates), then on tax reduction, and, if those did not work, increased federal expenditures, including public works. When fully implemented, these measures were intended to give substance to Ike's pledge to do everything possible to avoid a Republican recession.

As a blueprint for government action, the program made sense, except that just one of the three steps—more public works spending—could be accomplished by the executive branch alone. Only the Federal Reserve could lower interest rates, and only Congress could lower taxes, though the administration could propose a tax cut.

So Burns focused on devising a modest public works program. He would always have at the ready a list of projects that could quickly be set into motion in the event of an economic slump. This was so even though he admitted that launching public works programs would take far too long to have any impact on a rapidly deepening recession. He also emphasized that they should be employed only as a last resort. Yet Cabinet debates often assumed that such programs could make a big difference. Humphrey resisted them because they would cost money and, in his view, spook the business community.

The main problem with any plan that included additional spending, even on public works, was that the administration was engaged in a strenuous effort to do the opposite. Well aware of these conflicting goals, Burns appeared to be giving contradictory advice when he told the president in October 1953 he should "scrutinize the demands of the Joint Chiefs [for additional resources] with the greatest of care" while not losing sight of the possibility that "some military demands ... may deserve the very highest priority in any expansion of government spending ... to relieve unemployment."[15] Such muddled counsel reflected the dilemma a recession could pose for those who wished to reduce the role of government in the economy.

The administration was fortunate that Federal Reserve Chairman Martin was willing to coordinate its actions with the White House, as long as the Fed's independence was not compromised. Republicans greatly preferred the use of monetary policy as an anti-recession tool. As John Kenneth Galbraith observed: "No businessman, or indeed no citizen, was told what to do. Instead, they were guided by forces of which they themselves were not wholly aware."[16] In normal times, Martin's primary concern was inflation, but he recognized that the times called for abandoning, at least temporarily, the anti-inflation playbook.

Skillful cultivation of Martin and occasional pressure from Eisenhower through Humphrey paid dividends. The Fed lowered interest rates and reserve requirements steadily from mid-1953 to mid-1954, pursuing a policy of "active ease" and thereby stimulating the economy. Burns later described his relations with the Fed as harmonious, but behind the scenes he sometimes commented that Martin did not act fast enough to suit him.

Despite Fed actions, concern about an American recession was growing in Europe, whose continued recovery from the war depended partly on America's ability to buy European products. In November, a respected British economist rattled many Republicans by predicting a painful depression in the United States. At a fall Cabinet meeting, Eisenhower advisor Harold Stassen, back from a meeting on the continent, relayed the strong sense of concern that he found there. Burns then cited figures showing a rise in unemployment. Pressure on the president to recommend some kind of action mounted.

Humphrey downplayed the unemployment data presented by Burns. He countered that jobless numbers could continue to rise for several more months before the situation would become critical. Perhaps a "few readjustments" might be necessary, he conceded, but nothing more. Humphrey also ridiculed the "sensational headlines" in the press that had accompanied the recent slight increase in the cost of living.[17]

But the C.E.A. increasingly feared a recession and sought ways to boost business confidence in the economy. One such action was to make a public promise that the tax cuts Congress had agreed to postpone until early 1954 would be enacted on schedule. Burns believed that "there was considerable uncertainty in the business community whether [they] would actually take place." He encouraged the treasury secretary to "come out with solid reassurance," which he regarded as a "necessary psychological move."[18]

With a balanced budget looking less and less likely, Humphrey resisted making that commitment. The staffs of Burns and Humphrey met and argued throughout October but remained at loggerheads. Finally, and reluctantly, the two sides had to go to the president for a decision. Ike listened to the competing arguments and decided to support Burns. He tasked the unhappy Humphrey with making a public commitment to lower taxes in early 1954.[19] Though it was a relatively minor decision, it showed that the president valued economic stability over a balanced budget, at least in the short term. It was also a tentative step in the direction of accepting deficit spending—at least in principle—as a recession-fighting tool.

Despite recession concerns, the executive branch remained under orders to reduce spending. Wilson's defense cutbacks were well under way, and the president was taking every opportunity to remind the other departments to economize. Here, too, the different missions assigned to Burns and Humphrey led to muted but clearly discernable infighting. Burns counseled the president to think twice about continued defense cuts[20] and ramped up contingency planning for public works projects. Such projects, he told Eisenhower, "involved certain sacrifices of other values," by which he meant budget balancing.[21] Budget chief Joe Dodge joined Humphrey in opposing Burns, but they were thrown increasingly on the defensive by the C.E.A. director's pessimistic weekly reports.

Publicly, Humphrey had already conceded that a balanced budget was not a short-term goal. "I don't think we ought to wait to get our budget completely in balance before we anticipate the release of some of the money that we are expecting to save for the people themselves," he said in mid-1953. "I think we have to take a gamble that we can make some of the savings we think we can."[22] Humphrey fought hard for his views in private but never forgot who he worked for.

Humphrey Holds Out

The root of Humphrey's concern about the direction of government policy was his knowledge, derived from his corporate experience, that economies and markets are ultimately based on public confidence. He worried that the business community would interpret any significant government action to address negative trends as a sign the economy was in trouble, which in turn would undermine confidence. If that action should result in a deficit, he believed that private investment would be reduced far more than government spending would rise—a theory that a historian of the period pointed out was "almost unanimously rejected by the economic profession."[23] Whenever he was asked about the role of government in fighting recessions, he insisted that it should simply get out of the way. Prosperity is "almost completely dependent upon the efforts of 160 million people.... If you don't interfere with them ... that's what makes this country go."[24]

The blunt expression of this view unnerved the mainstream economic community as well as the C.E.A. chairman. Burns did not fear deficits when necessary, but he was loathe to propose additional spending in the conservative environment of the Eisenhower administration until he saw no reasonable alternative.

By and large, the president went along with Humphrey on the importance of maintaining confidence. He was determined to project an aura of calm. His consistent message to the public, expressed at many news conferences in late 1953, was: There is no need to worry. We have a strategy, and we will employ it if circumstances warrant.

The question always was: What would follow if circumstances *did* warrant? Burns wanted to reassure the business community by announcing the administration's contingency plans, such as they were. At a Cabinet meeting in January 1954, he said that his draft of the President's Economic Report to Congress, a public document, would reveal the "arsenal of weapons" the government could use in addressing a downturn.[25]

Humphrey opposed calling attention to this "arsenal." He criticized Burns for being too specific about possible government actions and for implying that the government by itself could "make or break prosperity." He told his Cabinet colleagues that government needed instead to remove restrictions on business and give them room to act. But Eisenhower took Burns' advice and went public with the list of measures being held in readiness. He even appropriated from Burns the strong word "arsenal," which *Time* magazine quoted in a February article.

This decision was influenced by the growing number of people, especially in Congress and labor, who were clamoring for some kind of action. On Capitol Hill, senators Wayne Morse and Paul Douglas worried that signs of a depression were already visible. Republicans in Congress feared that continued economic weakness would turn public opinion against the president by the November elections and lead to the loss of a Republican majority in the Senate. Labor union leaders, concerned about possible job losses, joined the chorus, demanding tax cuts, public works spending, and increased unemployment benefits. U.A.W. leader Walter Reuther said that three million unemployed people proved more was going on than a mere "corrective process," the term used in the administration's 1954 Economic Report.[26]

The charge from Reuther that really stung the president was that of "political indifference." During this and nearly all Cabinet economic debates, Eisenhower worried aloud about the negative consequences of doing nothing. "Now look," he said sharply to Humphrey in early 1954. "Let's not quote too much Mr. Hoover. I remember 1929 and prosperity around the corner, and basically sound economy." The administration must be prepared to "act positively," he said.

Humphrey worried that the Burns report would sow panic by sending the message that the administration was preparing for a depression. Ike shook his head. "You just don't hear this the same way I do," he said. Humphrey said that the report underplayed the small steps that were already being taken. Defense Secretary Wilson did not help Humphrey's cause by expressing concerns that Burns' list of possible government actions looked like a prelude to a "planned economy."[27]

In January, Humphrey was a guest on the television interview show *Meet the Press*. Determined to project a business-as-usual air, he dismissed any cause for concern about the recent negative economic data, seeing "absolutely no evidence of a substantial recession at this time." He conceded that there had been a "little downturn," but he thought the economy was already on the rebound. Would public works spending be necessary? he was asked. Only if a lot of bad things happen that have not yet happened, he replied. Is the government prepared to meet a recession "head-on"? "Well, that's a good deal like asking have you stopped beating your wife," he answered.[28]

By February, Eisenhower was telling his Cabinet that recession fighting had to take precedence over other domestic policy goals. "We've got to have good economics," he told the Cabinet, declaring that it would be best to err on the side of doing too much. Again, Humphrey sought to calm the waters and pled for patience. He offered faint praise for the idea of public works, conceding that they might be desirable if other efforts fail, but added that those efforts "might well succeed." The president again declined to take action. He did order the various departments to provide a small economic stimulus by spending their authorized budgets earlier rather than later.[29]

At the Bureau of the Budget, Rowland Hughes had replaced Joe Dodge. He fully shared Dodge's enthusiasm for cost-cutting and was alarmed by Ike's flirtation with the idea of public works spending. He wrote to Humphrey in February that such a decision risked "encouraging the proponents of big government and big spending to go into action." The treasury secretary acknowledged that "we have a continuing fight on our hands to control expenditures." But he added carefully that the administration had to have some plans ready, "perhaps even radical" ones, in the event conditions warranted. He reassured Hughes that "we will simply have to control the bad effects of such thinking as best we can." He concluded by expressing confidence that no significant action would be necessary.[30]

On occasion, Burns offered an anti-recession step that Humphrey blocked through his access to and influence with the president. For example, the C.E.A. chairman pushed for a liberalization of the terms of government-guaranteed mortgages in early 1954. Humphrey's determination to minimize government intervention apparently ended this initiative, even though some Cabinet members supported it.

Eisenhower continued to try to talk himself into doing something. Every week, as Burns presented more negative data, the odds seemed to improve that he would succeed. Humphrey continued to speak out against all forms of economic intervention, hoping that the situation would resolve itself. He explicitly rejected the "lesson" most economists had learned from the Great Depression—that federal stimulus programs provided a route to economic recovery. "If we go into some type of New Deal project, we'll lose the confidence of the country overnight," he said. "It was tried for years and never did succeed in making any real jobs until war broke out."[31]

Economic indicators continued to worsen. The internal battle was joined again on March 12. Secretary of State Dulles brought word of "near panic" among his contacts in New York.[32] Eisenhower acknowledged that he had Burns' counter-cyclical plan in his pocket and was poised to put it into effect, but he seemed to be waiting for a recommendation from someone.

Humphrey was "calm as a cucumber, as usual," according to Robert

Donovan's inside account. He shook his head. "Drastic action" would not be necessary until the unemployment rate went higher, he counseled. A bit sarcastically, the president responded that action taken now might forestall the need for "drastic" action later. "Radical moves can't be turned on and off easily—and can cause trouble," Humphrey cautioned. He recommended that the president wait until April or May for the situation to "clarify." Ike, according to Donovan, "meekly agreed." His decision, once again, was to not decide.[33]

The Tax Package of 1954

One of the reasons for Humphrey's fierce resistance to spending aimed at short-circuiting a recession was that the Treasury Department was simultaneously engaged in a laborious negotiation with Congress over the administration's most important piece of legislation—a tax reform package. The main purpose of the bill was to stimulate investment by reducing the tax burden of business. Specifically, it would remove what then amounted to double taxation of dividend income and accelerate business depreciation allowances. Announced by the president in January 1954, the draft bill called for a total tax reduction of $6.4 billion.

Because he anticipated its passage, Humphrey regarded additional recession-fighting measures—undertaken hastily, he believed, in an environment of panic—as upsetting the delicate balance he was trying to achieve over the long term between expenditures and revenue. In May, he told a conference of labor officials that the tax reform bill would improve the jobs picture more than the public works program being considered in administration councils.[34] He viewed it as key not only to prosperity in the Eisenhower years but to Republican success in the off-year elections of 1954.

Once the Treasury Department drafted the legislation, it went to Congress, where there was no shortage of views on how tax reform should be carried out. When briefed on the administration's plan, key Republicans thought it did not go far enough to reduce excise and corporation taxes, but they agreed not to oppose it.

Others faulted the plan for containing few measures that would directly assist lower-income Americans. It seemed to be an early example of the "trickle-down" theory, in which business expansion would create jobs that eventually benefited ordinary workers. In fact, Democratic senator Hubert Humphrey referred to the treasury secretary as "trickle-down George."[35] Senate Democrats pointed out that middle and upper income groups would realize six to seven times more money in benefits than those near the bottom.

As Senator Paul Douglas remarked at a session of the Joint Committee on the 1954 Economic Report, "before the poor can have a bite, the rich must have a banquet."[36]

Humphrey defended the administration's emphasis on reducing business taxes. "The goose that lays the golden egg is production," he pointed out. "If you haven't got a payroll, you haven't got consumers."[37] He also tried to convince congressmen that dividend rebates benefited ordinary workers as much as corporate managers, but statistics seemed to show otherwise. Some Democrats pointed out that Humphrey would personally reap great financial rewards from the dividend provision.

Needing an alternative to the administration's program, the Democrats decided to make a case for an increase in personal exemptions for individual taxpayers. The measure, sponsored by Senator Walter George, would raise the exemption from $600 to $1000 by 1955, thus eliminating any tax liability for many earners.

Humphrey considered this idea a dire threat to his plan for a balanced budget, because the missing revenue would "throw us back into substantial deficit financing." In opposing the exemption increase, he had strong support from Arthur Burns. "You have to be careful not to erode away the income tax base," the C.E.A. chairman warned Congress. On the whole, Burns felt that the tax reform package "might not be a bad idea for counter-cyclical reasons"—in other words, as helpful in fighting a recession.[38]

The rest of March saw an exhausting round of procedural maneuvers, negotiations in smoke-filled rooms, lobbying by Humphrey and his associates, and a nationally televised appeal by the president. Humphrey's bottom line was to be flexible about anything except the personal exemption, and he and Burns were prepared to agree to a slight lessening of excise taxes in order to secure enough votes for passage of the administration bill.

After a bitter debate, the Internal Revenue Act of 1954 was finally enacted. The administration had managed to accomplish most of its original goals, even though the protracted negotiations liberalized the final product enough to achieve sufficient Democratic buy-in. However much the act fell short of his hopes, Humphrey proclaimed it a monumental achievement.

Over time, it proved to be a boon to American business. The dividend exclusion, rapid depreciation allowances, liberalization of the capital gains exemption, and more generous treatment of business losses—coupled with the expiration of the excess profits tax—provided a total tax cut of $5 billion per year. In the early 1960s, congressional Democrats charged that the law had allowed over $100 billion in revenue to escape taxation, with a loss to the government of over $40 billion.[39]

The Internal Revenue Act was not specifically designed to fight the recession—the drafting of the bill had begun long before then. But once it had passed, Humphrey used its expected effects to support his belief that no further federal action was needed to stimulate the economy.

Adrift into Spring

At the Cabinet session of March 19, Burns gave a balanced report on both positive and negative economic trends, judging that unemployment seemed to be peaking. He played into Humphrey's hands by recommending continued vigilance but no immediate action. Harold Stassen ventured the view that business confidence remained high because business leaders believed the administration's promise to act if necessary. Humphrey gave it a different spin. Confidence was high, he responded, because business knew the administration had the sense not to act prematurely.

With Burns leaning toward inaction, the danger of "pump priming" seemed to ebb. Humphrey thought he could relax a bit, but now several Cabinet members argued for concrete steps to address the situation. Vice President Nixon's concern was political—he judged that positive measures were needed to preempt increasingly shrill demands from Democrats and thus to avoid Republican losses in the upcoming November election.

Burns and the C.E.A. came up with another accounting device, called "budget flexibility," that had some potential as an anti-recession measure. Under this approach, the rate of spending for already-approved projects—particularly involving the military—would be accelerated, or front-loaded, to get the money into circulation more quickly. One economic historian called it Burns' most innovative contribution to recession fighting.[40]

Nixon liked the idea. "If anything sound can be done today," he advised, "do so now rather than three months later."[41] Even better, it was a concept Humphrey and the Budget Bureau could get behind, because it involved no new obligations. At a Cabinet meeting, Humphrey conceded that "projects which the administration would undertake eventually" could begin now. Ike hesitated at first but the idea easily gained acceptance around the table, and it was widely implemented.[42] Eisenhower met the press on March 24 but did not mention the economic debate that had been roiling his Cabinet for months.

Two days later, Burns briefed the Cabinet on a series of "purely administrative actions" that might be taken to stimulate the economy. However, he provided no further guidance on when, other than to warn that government could not "wait for indices to reach any magic point." Once again, Ike expressed his view that it was time for "liberal action," but asked Burns yet again to study the situation further. Humphrey did not even bother to oppose Burns' mostly marginal recommendations, though he cautioned the members not to expect them to accomplish much.

At the first Cabinet meeting in April, Burns, as instructed, brought to the table a list of possible action items. Aside from the suggestion that the Fed make available cheaper credit, the items were again low profile and undramatic. Ike now seemed worried about the possible negative public reaction to any government remedies, saying, "if you tell a soldier you're doing something to help his morale, he'll start running."[43]

Ike's retreat, preceded by so many months of sparring with Humphrey and debating when to act and what to do, had made Burns increasingly frustrated. Though he had made a point of not advocating one policy over another, he ended his action list with a pointed warning that turned Humphrey's view of confidence on its head—confidence could be weakened "by any indication that the administration was timid or impotent in dealing with this subject." Ike heard this loud and clear. In a diary entry on April 8, he wrote that "the dangers of doing nothing are far greater than those of doing too much."[44]

The Burns economic report was again the main attraction at the April 9 Cabinet meeting. It was cautious and equivocal, noting the continued worsening of unemployment along with a surprisingly strong financial sector. These trends, he believed, would soon be reconciled in one direction or another. As usual, Humphrey denied any sense of urgency and underlined the importance of business confidence. He suggested that a late spring surge of consumer spending might make a difference in the economic climate.

At the same time, he assured the public that there was no need for special programs designed to counter a recession. In a speech to the American Society of Newspaper Editors, he admitted that "some people, fearing downward trends, ask when the Government is going to get 'in' and do something about it. The fact is that the government is always 'in,'" he reminded them. He then summarized ongoing programs, such as small business loans and increased old age insurance, that would at least peripherally help an ailing economy.[45]

The president remained torn. He and Humphrey had met the day before with David McDonald, the head of the United Steel Workers, who cited widespread joblessness in the steel industry and called for vastly increased federal spending. Ike rejected McDonald's more radical suggestions, calling them "contrary to our policy," but his vacillation continued. In his written account of the meeting, he mused that the "point of no return" had been reached—

it was time to resolve any uncertainties in favor of doing something rather than doing nothing. But at the same time, in a telling entry, he confessed that "only the future will determine whether or not this is a fairly accurate estimate or merely the expression of ignorance."[46]

For Humphrey, doing "something" did not include unauthorized spending increases. On April 7 he wrote to budget director Hughes recommending that he instruct every agency that any expenses incurred during the next three months in excess of one-twelfth of their yearly appropriation per month would be regarded as a charge against next year's budget. In this way, he pointed out, the savings achieved so far this year would not be nullified.[47]

During April, worsening unemployment prompted Burns and the president to turn to the Federal Reserve for help. They concluded that the Fed was not expanding credit as much as the economic situation warranted. The central bank had lowered interest rates the previous fall and again in February, but the administration thought it could be doing more. Eisenhower noted in his diary on April 8 that he had asked Humphrey to "develop real pressure" on Fed chairman Martin to act. According to Ike, Burns believed that bankers "have always acted 'too late and with too little' in the face of approaching recession."[48]

This criticism of Martin was unfair. The chairman often faced strong internal opposition to his preferred policies, especially from Allan Sproul, the chairman of the prestigious New York Federal Reserve Bank, who was a vigorous and persuasive debater during internal Fed meetings.[49] As a manager, Martin was a consensus builder and was frequently obliged to postpone action until he could build sufficient support for it.

The perception that the Fed moved too slowly to reverse tight money policies in the face of an economic slowdown sometimes made it seem more conservative than the administration. Now that Ike had passed the buck to the Fed, Burns wrote to the president in April in evident frustration. "We are moving at a *timid pace* in the monetary field, and some precious time may be lost," he summarized (emphasis in original).[50]

At such times, Ike reflected that his pressure on the Fed to loosen the reins might seem to the country like he was abandoning his anti-inflation principles. But during the spring, the Fed found itself on the same page as the administration, agreeing to roll out all of its recession-fighting tools. Between April and July, it lowered reserve requirements of member banks, again reduced the discount rate (to 1.5 percent), and added to its holdings of government securities.

On April 9, Defense Secretary Wilson offered oral support for Humphrey's non-interventionist philosophy. He pointed out that the automobile industry was experiencing an upturn, possibly a harbinger of better times. But Ike cut off his argument with an account of recent conversations with the president of C.B.S. and Wilson's former colleague at General Motors, Roger Kyes, who both expressed pessimism about the immediate economic future. Again, the Cabinet meeting ended without any plan of action.

Another month went by—a month of more inconclusive economic reports and desultory Cabinet discussions. Outside pressure on the administration continued to build. With nearly three million workers now jobless, C.I.O. head Walter Reuther took Eisenhower to task on May 11 for "doing nothing" to fight unemployment and suggested a national conference on the subject.[51] Two days later, former president Truman weighed in, warning of "creeping McKinleyism" and pressing for more federal spending. The A.F.L. charged that Ike had not kept his promise to act at the first signs of recession. In response to all the criticism, the president said that he would do what was necessary but would not be stampeded into a "slam-bang emergency program."[52]

A Crisis Averted

By mid-May, Burns had happier news. His data suggested that the economic situation was finally improving. A sense of relief settled over the Cabinet during the next few weeks, and any urgency among the members about recession fighting began to fade.

But lingering uncertainty among the experts kept alive Ike's concern. On June 4, Labor Secretary Mitchell cited evidence of a manufacturing decline that refuted the more encouraging Burns figures. The president once again declared that the government must act, "even though it jarred the sense of logic of Cabinet members."[53] He emphasized the importance of visible results and again directed Burns for what seemed like the hundredth time to report back with a list of possible additional steps, including a more detailed public works program, with the goal of putting them into effect by July if events warranted. Humphrey now realized that the danger of unnecessary action still existed.

On June 11, Burns returned to the Cabinet with a mostly upbeat account of economic improvement and another list of action items. As before, these items were at best minor tweaks: they included more rapid processing of Veterans Administration loan guarantees, informal Treasury advice to banks on interest rates, expeditious contract letting by the Forest Service, and prompt IRS repayment to over-assessed taxpayers. Again, congressional action and public announcements were deemed unnecessary. As Cabinet members discussed the list, Ike repeatedly urged them to do quickly whatever the government could legitimately do to strengthen the economy.

Things continued to improve. By July the signs were so unmistakable that Ike was finally able to lay his fears to rest. He announced the end of the year-long recession—or, as he termed it, the "economic decline." The administration never had to deploy more than a fraction of its contingency plan, let alone come up with more serious measures. For example, the C.E.A. had decided that its trigger point for requesting public works funding was an unemployment figure of six million. It never even reached four million.

The administration's year-long obsession with what turned out to be a mild and short recession reflected its terror at the prospect of another economic debacle presided over by Republicans and the political fallout that was certain to follow. The urgent and frequent appeals for action from American industrial leaders showed that memories of the Great Depression were still fresh. But output had declined by only 3 or 4 percent and unemployment had risen only 2.5 percent. Previously scheduled tax cuts that took effect at the beginning of 1954 and timely action by the Federal Reserve had kept the downturn from becoming more serious and long lasting.

It is difficult to give the president's performance during the recession of 1953–54 a definitive grade. On the one hand, he insisted many times that the government should take vigorous action. On the other hand, he shrank from actually pursuing most of the options offered him, expecting the Federal Reserve to leap into the breach. The main step taken by the administration was to speed up already approved budget expenditures. The president also signed with some reluctance a bill sponsored by congressional Republicans to cut the excise tax.

Thanks mainly to Humphrey, the inconclusive and tentative Cabinet discussions of 1953–54 never built a consensus behind an activist counter-cyclical program. The outcome suggests that Humphrey was often "the highest, and sometimes the unassailable, hurdle standing between the various options and their implementation."[54] Because the recession ended before much harm could be done, one cannot criticize his inaction too harshly. Indeed, on the whole, Humphrey's caution had been borne out.

Where did Ike's economist, Gabriel Hauge, stand on this issue? Some of Ike's intimates feared Hauge's liberal influence on the president, but he claimed later not only that he sided with Humphrey but that all three advisers were more or less in agreement on the policy of watchful waiting. In his memoirs, Hauge wrote: "It seemed to him [Eisenhower] and to the rest of us in his administration that there was no reason why the downturn would not work itself out by the spring."⁵⁵ The passage of time may have obscured Hauge's memory of the long and inconclusive Cabinet debates, but the burden of his argument is that the main impetus for action came from outside the administration rather than from within. Hauge even professed to oppose the 1954 tax cut package, on the grounds that the budget deficit had not yet been brought under control.

Burns had been helpful to Eisenhower in analyzing economic events and framing his choices, but the data he was analyzing nearly always pointed in conflicting directions. While industrial production languished, for example, the financial sector, construction and retail remained strong. These opposing trends reinforced Burns' innate caution. Yet Eisenhower lavished public praise on Burns. "Arthur," he exclaimed at the June 11 Cabinet meeting, "you'd have made a fine Chief of Staff during the war."⁵⁶ By now, he had learned that his administration's "theorist" had a more nuanced and even-handed view of the economy than his dogmatic treasury secretary.

Also, the key fiscal issue during the crisis was whether or not to allow scheduled tax cuts to take effect in early 1954, and Burns had been on the winning side of that argument. His aide Neal Jacoby considered Ike's decision to cast his lot with Burns on taxes a pivotal event, because the president thereby became willing to accept a deficit of more than $4 billion in FY-1955 in order to combat the recession—which was, consciously or not, to go against a generation of Republican dogma.

More generally, Burns deserved credit for injecting the ideas of modern economics into a debate that might have been dominated by knee-jerk business-centered arguments. The options he put forward were important in reconciling traditional Republican conservatism with the modern conviction that every administration had counter-cyclical responsibilities. "The president needed him," said one observer of Burns. "He was the one egghead among a crew of millionaire businessmen; [and] he had an effective bedside manner."⁵⁷ No wonder Eisenhower was grateful.

A Failure of Imagination?

What would Eisenhower have done if the situation had continued to worsen?

Assuming that Eisenhower's comments during Cabinet meetings genuinely reflected his thinking at the moment, the most striking aspect of the nine-month economic debate was his almost crippling indecisiveness. Burns' arguments did not convince him to act, even when he thought it was time to do so. Ike understood that Humphrey viewed the situation through a rigid ideological lens but was still loath to go against his non-interventionist counsel. Had both the recession and Humphrey's resistance continued, would he have ultimately gone along with Burns?

And would Humphrey have rejected government action no matter how serious the recession became? Apparently, yes. In a telling note to budget chief Hughes in October 1954, he wrote: "A time might come which would justify the deliberate running of a budget deficit, but it will be done by a different treasury secretary."[58]

He was not afraid to say the same thing publicly. Asked in early 1957 if he approved of increased government spending during an economic downturn, he made one of his most quoted statements. "I don't think you can spend yourself rich. I think we all went through that for a good many years [the 1930s and 1940s], and we kept spending and spending and spending, and we still didn't help our employment or help our total position."[59] On that occasion, as we will see in Chapter Eight, the president decided it was necessary to "correct" his treasury secretary's remarks.

An argument can be made—and several economists have made it—that doing nothing while allowing the Federal Reserve to tinker with interest rates and open market purchases was precisely the right call. Unemployment rose but not to alarming levels. A tax cut had gone into effect in January. A major tax bill, incorporating important business incentives, was about to be enacted. Under these conditions, it made sense to Humphrey to plug away at cutting government expenditures—even though doing so was the opposite of conventional wisdom on how to deal with a recession—and to trust that the downturn would be brief and mild.[60] This turned out to be the case.

But the reality was that the president and his Cabinet had no available policy for combating a more serious downturn. Burns made lists of possible actions, but they were either too small to make a difference or would have required too much time to implement.[61] No plans were on the table to involve Congress in an emergency spending plan or tax cuts. No plans were being made to reverse the government-wide spending reductions and embark upon new programs that might stimulate the economy. The fear of undermining business confidence eliminated every option that might be effective. The administration seemed to be reduced to crossing its fingers and hoping the crisis would pass.

In reviewing the internal administration debates, Raymond Saulnier later praised Eisenhower's constant readiness to push for strong recession-fighting measures.[62] But the readiness never translated into action. As the threat receded, Burns pointedly reminded everyone of the government's responsibilities. "Our system of free and competitive enterprise is on trial," he said in October 1954. "The government cannot stand aloof from the private economy, but must be ready to take vigorous steps to help maintain a stable prosperity."[63]

Toward the end of Ike's first term, journalist Robert Donovan published an assessment of the administration's performance to date, based on insider interviews and leaked Cabinet minutes. The book caught the attention of Raymond Moley, a Roosevelt aide in the 1930s turned conservative columnist in the 1950s, who wrote that Humphrey emerged from the Donovan account as the "hero" of the economic scare of 1953–54. Despite Democratic panic, Humphrey "kept his head" as news worsened and showed "wisdom and balance" in opposing an emergency spending program.[64]

The positive outcome certainly strengthened the hand of the administration's non-interventionists. They had stared down a recession and refused to be stampeded. Events demonstrated that the economy could repair itself with relatively minor tinkering. In fact, the budget deficit actually narrowed a bit during the downturn. The president's Gallup Poll numbers had stayed high throughout the year. Even liberal economists agreed that "watchful waiting" had worked.

But the end of the recession had not removed the albatross of Hoover and the Depression from around the Republican neck. A Republican administration had still not proved that it could handle an economic crisis. Eisenhower could easily conclude that recessions were best dealt with through automatic stabilizers and timely changes in monetary policy alone. The heady experience of a happy ending in this one instance could not help but affect perceptions of the next recession.

Even as the downturn ended, polls showed that Americans still believed that the economy would fare better with Democrats in charge. The nine months of uncertainty seem to have brought back the voting public's skepticism about the economic leadership of both the administration and its Republican supporters in Congress. Vice President Nixon's fears were borne out when the Democrats again became the majority party in the elections of November 1954. Those fears would return with greater force four years later, when his own political future was on the line. In 1957 and 1958, an even sharper downturn would give rise to a similar debate about Republican economic policy and carry a higher price for misjudgment.

10

Humphrey and His Critics

As the threat of a major recession slipped away, Humphrey had every reason to be pleased with his first year in office. In mid-1954, he wrote an article for *Collier's* magazine comparing government with the business environment he left behind. It made a positive impression on official Washington, because he seemed engaged in the useful process of sorting out how much of his business experience could be applied to his public responsibilities.

The *Collier's* piece expressed Humphrey's unhappiness with the slow pace of government and the sheer difficulty of getting anything done. The interests of lobbying groups, congressmen, other federal agencies, and public opinion had to be taken into account and reconciled. In private industry, "you get a final decision and that's it.... There is an automatic check on every businessman through the quarterly and annual reports.... In government, there is no check that I know of ... except what people believe." He also found fault with federal employees, who lacked the "snap and vigor" and "responsive discipline" common in the business world.

He went on to lament the tendency of Americans, after twenty years of liberal administration, to turn to Washington for money and support. But he believed that was about to change. "Nearly everybody knew that, sooner or later, extravagant government had to come to an end," he wrote, "and the expansion of government functions had to be stopped." It would take some time to alter people's thinking from fiscal carelessness to watchfulness over every dollar, "but we are determined to bring about the change."[1]

In an interview with *Newsweek*, he confessed that he still had a lot to learn. Though he thought he was "reasonably well informed on government operations" before coming to Washington, he had discovered that "there was an awful lot I didn't know anything about at all." Of course, the sheer size of the federal apparatus bothered him. "You've got to do something," he concluded, "to bring this octopus that the Government has become back under control."[2]

Mixed Reviews

In 1954 and 1955, most press analyses of Humphrey's performance continued to be reverential. Columnists and editorial writers referred to him as the "star of Ike's team" and the "most powerful man in the capital"—indicative of his impact on the administration and official Washington. A cover story in *Newsweek* praised his skill in convincing Congress that a proposed tax cut was unwise and cited a poll showing him to be the most popular Cabinet member with the media.[3] The *St. Louis Post-Dispatch* described him as the most powerful treasury secretary in years and one of the Republican party's best fund-raisers. "There has been no break in the rise of Humphrey's stock," the article concluded.[4]

Amid the glowing public tributes, some administration insiders were increasingly troubled by Humphrey's attitude and style. Sherman Adams, for one, looked upon the developing rapport between Ike and Humphrey with some wariness. He regarded their close personal relationship as inevitable, given their good chemistry, but not necessarily desirable. He understood that Humphrey's success in private finance had led Eisenhower to believe he would make a good treasury secretary, though he remained unsure why Ike had come to that conclusion.[5]

As he later expressed in his memoir, Adams believed that Humphrey was "sometimes too quick to think of government economic problems in terms of private industry and occasionally too impatient for fast action." The extent of Humphrey's conservatism, once revealed, seemed to startle him a bit, but he was confident that the interaction between him and the administration's more liberal economic voices, like Hauge and Burns, would result in the kind of "middle way" policies Eisenhower naturally favored.[6]

Gabriel Hauge was another figure who questioned Eisenhower's confidence in businessmen. He further doubted that either Humphrey or Wilson thought their skills were directly transferable into their new environment. In Hauge's judgment, Humphrey's crusade against deficit spending was "a task he ultimately found more difficult than he ever dreamed."[7]

Humphrey may have sensed Adams' grudging acceptance, for he seems to have regarded him as little more than an obstacle to be gotten around. He was determined not to allow the chief of staff to decide when he saw the president, so he usually sneaked in a back way to Ike's office. He told historian Herbert Parmet that Adams was "building his own little empire in the White House for his political future," a charge that had little justification.[8] (Humphrey was hardly the only administration official who objected to Adams' peremptory style and tight control of Eisenhower's calendar.)

After a strong beginning, Humphrey's relations with Capitol Hill were also fraying. An observer of a Humphrey performance before the House Ways and Means Committee noted his "somewhat elevated, school teacher, doctrinaire attitude toward members of Congress, coupled with a propensity to belittle the ideas of others as 'silly,' 'foolish,' and 'irresponsible.'"[9] Others noted that he tended to dismiss any congressional criticism of the administration's economic policy.[10] Democrats offered more partisan criticism. Senator Paul Douglas charged that, despite his undeniable ability, Humphrey "judges the prosperity of the nation by the condition of the wealthy."

Even his strongest supporters acknowledged that Humphrey could display a single-mindedness and "take-no-prisoners" style that made him difficult to deal with. The same columnist who called Humphrey the "strong man" of the Cabinet described him as "haughty, quick-tempered and quick tongued" with an anti-intellectual bent and an impatience with those who disagreed with him. Humphrey, he wrote, can deflate an opponent with "one stroke of his steely sarcasm."[11] Republican supporters of aid to anti–Communist Asian nations called his approach to foreign policy "dangerously unimaginative."[12]

As the depth of Humphrey's commitment to business principles became evident, media pundits and academics alike questioned anew the wisdom of his appointment. "There is no one more doctrinaire and impractical in public affairs than some successful men of private affairs," wrote economist James Tobin.[13] Former New Deal economist Rexford Tugwell blamed the 1953–54 recession on Humphrey's "obsolete thinking." The president had received better advice from the C.E.A., said Tugwell, but he had been slow to accept it.[14] When news of Humphrey's threat to resign in the event of a budget deficit leaked out, Harvard economist Seymour Harris called him "a really dangerous man."[15]

Using Business Eyes

Many economists noted that Humphrey's business-centered views seemed to lack an intellectual foundation. One wrote that his orthodox Republicanism seemed unleavened by exposure to current thinking on how a modern economy functioned. His insistence on budget cutting regardless of the circumstances bothered people with formal training in economics and left him vulnerable to their well-informed criticism. Within a few months of his taking office, many of them were dismissing his views as "conservative bromides."[16] He was a man who "believed his own rhetoric and expressed himself in clichés widely heard and revered in corporate board rooms."[17] A Federal Reserve official asserted flatly that "he just didn't really understand how the big forces in the economy work together."[18]

Humphrey's obvious intelligence muted early concerns about his views. Eisenhower and others showed an amused tolerance of his occasionally dogmatic statements, which they attributed to inexperience. Emmet Hughes wrestled with his ambivalence about Humphrey. Like many others, he was impressed with the man's "effortless grace," natural warmth, vigor and conviction, but he also called him a man whose "intellectual baggage [was] uncluttered with complexities" and who "served as an uncompromising spokesman for a world view peculiarly grudging and parochial."[19]

The main question Hughes and others pondered was his capacity for growth. With additional exposure to national economic issues, "it seemed unlikely that much time could pass without his acquiring a wider vision."[20] When no such vision appeared, Hughes attributed it to the political environment rather than his inherent limitations. But Eisenhower seemed pleased with Humphrey's flexibility. "All of us have learned a lot since we came into office," said the president. "I guess no one has changed more than Humphrey, which shows how big a man he is."[21]

Humphrey also revealed himself as an extreme political partisan, which Eisenhower had to overlook if they were to remain close. Two more years of the Truman administration, Humphrey had said, would have caused the "utter collapse" of the nation.[22] Once in office, he worried constantly about the negative electoral consequences of the administration's failure to follow his guidance. Even his economic views sometimes tested the president's patience. In response to one of his frequent lectures comparing government budgeting to that of a household that cannot spend more than its income, Ike said: "Yes, but what if the kids get polio?"[23]

The Burns-Humphrey Rivalry

Disagreements are inevitable in any administration. What matters is how they are handled. For the most part, Ike's economic advisers avoided airing their dirty linen in public. They were motivated to rise above interpersonal tensions by their strong loyalty to and affection for the president. Insider Steven Benedict confirmed that cooperation was more common than competition. "I don't recall any very notable or serous personal frictions," he later said. "It wasn't a staff that was rent with rivalries and conflicting ambitions, people knifing one another in the back."[24] It helped that conflict was thrashed out in deliberative bodies like the Cabinet and N.S.C. rather than being allowed to fester, and that Arthur Burns was determined not to be a partisan figure.

That being said, after the recession of 1953–54, it was no longer possible to believe that the Eisenhower team spoke with one voice on economic policy. The members of that team "differ, and differ hard," the *Christian Science Monitor* observed.[25]

Staff relations might have been relatively harmonious, but the men at the top had a fraught relationship. Arthur Burns later admitted to "serious clashes" with Humphrey over policy options during the recession and found his stubbornness and dogmatism "appalling." "We fought hard at times," he acknowledged, "and each lost some battles to the other." In his exasperation, he exclaimed that Humphrey did not understand counter-cyclical theory, on which Burns was an expert.[26]

C.E.A. officials found the uneven and unreflective quality of Humphrey's counsel ever more worrisome. Some of these men did not bother to sugar-coat their views. Burns' deputy, Neal Jacoby, was a former dean of the U.C.L.A. School of Business and an experienced government consultant who shared Humphrey's faith in the free market. But he expressed great frustration at dealing with a man whose influence, he felt, derived more from his relationship with the president than from the correctness of his views. Jacoby asserted that Humphrey "had not learned anything from the Keynesian revolution.... [He] either didn't understand this, or if he did, he didn't believe in it."

Yet Jacoby found Humphrey difficult to oppose. His status gave him "a great amount of power and self-assurance, which he carried, in my view, to the point of arrogance."[27] Jacoby suspected that many top Treasury officials often disagreed with Humphrey but were afraid to say so.[28] He also believed that Humphrey purged Treasury officials sympathetic to the C.E.A.'s viewpoint.

In discussions of recession-fighting options with Burns and Jacoby, Humphrey made it clear that he regarded academic economists as dreamers and theorists unacquainted with the "real world." Prior to Humphrey's arrival at Treasury, the department had built a close relationship with economists at major universities around the country and had assembled an advisory group to interact with top policymakers. After ignoring this group for several months, Humphrey abolished it.[29]

Jacoby recalled many meetings at the Treasury Department where he, Humphrey and Burns would talk long into the afternoon. Humphrey would constantly remind them that he had been chosen to pursue a "sound" fiscal policy, "come hell or high water." Jacoby continued: "He would pound the table and raise his voice." He said he "had run a big business and he wasn't going to have professors tell him how to run the Treasury of the United States."[30] Since Jacoby was a professor who had also run a large organization, he was offended by Humphrey's anti-intellectual stereotyping. On the record, he called Humphrey "an economic illiterate. Not only illiterate but uneducable." Contrary to early assessments of Humphrey, Jacoby did not find him the least bit open-minded.

Relations between Humphrey and Burns continued to worsen after the recession. In an example often cited by historians, Humphrey was strongly critical of the administration's Economic Report for 1955, which Burns had drafted. The report reflected Burns' view of government's responsibility to stimulate demand during a recession, even at the price of deficit financing. Incensed, Humphrey called Burns and insisted that it be rewritten. He was "so brutal in condemning the report," Burns wrote later. "He didn't make one specific criticism, besides calling it 'socialistic.' I really doubt that he had even read it."[31]

According to White House staff member William Ewald, Burns told Humphrey that he was "not changing one comma. If you don't like it, you tell the president." After Gabriel Hauge got wind of their conversation, he called Burns and volunteered to support him against Humphrey on the issue. Burns refused the assistance. He told Hauge that he "wanted to take on Humphrey and his big tycoons" and "had confidence in the end in the President—in his making the fair and right decision."[32]

On the day the Cabinet was scheduled to discuss the report, Burns lightened the atmosphere by bringing two pipes to the meeting, instead of his usual one. "Well, Mr. President," he announced, "I am well prepared today."[33] After his presentation (according to Ewald), several members burst into spontaneous applause. Eisenhower called it a "brilliant effort" and later wrote Burns a note of thanks. It is a "magnificent document," Ike assured him, "even if some of our radical liberals will unquestionably call it a reactionary treatise, while the real reactionaries will call it a 'blueprint for socialism.' All of which probably proves that you are just about right."[34] Despite his victory, Burns remained angry about his confrontation with the treasury secretary. "After this episode was over," he said later, "I made no effort to conceal my feelings toward Humphrey."

Raymond Saulnier, who succeeded Burns as chairman of the Council of Economic Advisors, agreed with his predecessor about Humphrey's limitations as an economic thinker. "He had his positions pretty well formulated and could or would give you his judgment on a question pretty fast," Saulnier recalled. He added that he did not mean to imply that Humphrey's opinions on economic questions were not well thought out, but his breeziness "tend[ed] to be a little disconcerting to the academic and reflective mind." Typically, Saulnier added, there would be "no 'on-the-one-hand, on-the-other-hand' discussion, just a quick response." He softened this criticism by adding that he had the "greatest admiration for his intellectual ability, his absolute honesty, integrity and forthrightness."[35]

Though Eisenhower and Humphrey thought alike on many issues, it did not take the president long to figure out that the Ohio executive would not be a natural proponent of "modern Republicanism." Periodically he braced Humphrey with reminders of his more liberal leanings. In response to a written argument from the treasury secretary that economic theory often ignored practical workability, Ike wrote back that "we cannot completely ignore" such theory. He added: "Somewhere we have to find that middle of the road again."[36]

In late 1954, Ike called Humphrey and began thinking aloud about world events. "I hope I am not one of your spendthrift people," he said, confessing that he had been bothered by recent defense cuts. He recommended that they both "look facts more broadly in the face." Humphrey came back with the suggestion that the administration limit its objectives and then "go to town on them."[37]

But the two men, being friends, could disagree without damaging their relationship. They were even able to joke about their differences. For example, in the summer of 1955 Ike phoned Humphrey in a bantering mood to remind him that he had not come over recently "to threaten me with the dangers of inflation." The secretary replied that he had not wanted to add to his worries, but that he would be glad to resume such visits.[38]

Hauge as a Counterweight

The competition between the C.E.A. and Humphrey increased the value to Eisenhower of Gabriel Hauge. One of Hauge's jobs was to summarize the positions of key administration players in short memos designed to help Ike sort through his options. At times, he also provided specific advice. For example, in mid–1953 he sent the president his analysis of a military salary measure making its way through Congress, concluding strongly that "it would be a mistake to be saddled with this bill."[39] We can assume that he used his many opportunities to engage, tutor, and, when necessary, correct his boss.

Hauge's easygoing personality and sense of humor defused some of the acrimony between Humphrey and Burns and made Eisenhower's life much easier. His close ties with Burns worked to the latter's advantage. He liked to poke affectionate fun at Burns and his "Old Testament prophet manner." The two men arrived at a logical division of labor, with Burns overseeing economic research and in-depth analysis and Hauge handling ad hoc issues that required a presidential decision. He modestly called these "housekeeping duties," but they gave him almost daily contact with Ike.[40] Also, he and Burns had a private half-hour meeting with the president each week to discuss current economic developments.

As we have seen, Hauge's views were much closer to the economic mainstream than Humphrey's. His March 1953 note to Humphrey criticizing his "preoccupation with inflation" was one early sign. Later that year, in a memo to Ike that was unmistakably critical of Humphrey's two main goals, he argued

Arthur Burns (right), chairman of the Council of Economic Advisers, with his eventual replacement, Raymond Saulnier, and Assistant to the President Sherman Adams (left). Burns' academic background guaranteed clashes with Humphrey, who said he would not let professors tell him how to run the U.S. Treasury. Saulnier agreed with Humphrey's conservative views but called his blunt statements "disconcerting to the ... reflective mind" (National Park Service/Eisenhower Presidential Library and Museum).

for a more activist economic program. Americans, he wrote, are "not going to be content with budget balancing and sound money. They are a building people, a doing people, and for better or worse they see government as having a significant role in this matter."[41]

Hauge also set down his thoughts in a memo to Humphrey that showed he did not share many of the new treasury secretary's assumptions and priorities. Yes, taxes are high, he said, but they have not interfered with investment or prosperity. Yes, the budget should be balanced, but there is no great urgency about it. Hauge sided more often with Burns than Humphrey on matters of substance. He confessed to an aide in early 1954 that Humphrey was too doctrinaire and was "one of our larger problems,"[42] but he noted that the president was usually on "our side though."[43]

Ever the diplomat, he managed to flatter and befriend the treasury secretary while harboring serious doubts about his economic views. He sent many warm notes praising Humphrey's work in several areas. In one of these, written in mid-1955, he was "moved to say that you seem to have the knack, despite changes in your original team, to keep the average [performance] up to A-1."[44] On another occasion, he wrote Humphrey to compliment the "fine, straightforward job you did this afternoon" before a committee of the House of Representatives.[45] Frequent praise was consistent with Hauge's deferential style and strong interest in maintaining the unity of the president's economic team.

Humphrey could be equally diplomatic. When a journalist asked if he disagreed with Hauge's preference for flexibility in handling the economy, he replied somewhat evasively: "I don't think that necessarily there's any disagreement anywhere. Flexible policies can be used, but, as I say, the various things that you would and might do should be used at various times…. It's very difficult to pick out the timing of when one method would be appropriate or another would be appropriate."[46]

Despite his strong affinity for Eisenhower's "modern Republicanism," Hauge's views on military spending ran contrary to administration policy at times. In the interests of a strong defense, he was willing to postpone a balanced budget for as long as necessary. At the height of the debate on defense cuts, he tried to convince Humphrey that America's expanding economy could cover increased costs. This was the central contention of many liberal economists of the period, and it undercut the economic rationale for the defense reductions of the 1950s. Hauge undoubtedly sensed that he would not get far pressing this view on the president.

But he and Ike sometimes exchanged humorous notes at Humphrey's expense. "I don't know whether you have heard this description of George

Humphrey," wrote Hauge to Ike in 1955. "The greatest extractor in the U.S.A.—and he uses no Novocain."[47] A year later Hauge sent an article to Ike citing a growing belief among corporate executives that some inflation was essential to full employment. Ike wrote back: "Send this to [Humphrey] when he returns from London. (Send a doctor along.)"[48]

Hauge understood the limits of his role and was always careful not to exceed his authority. He often downplayed his own policy preferences in order to serve Eisenhower better. Even so, some conservatives were dissatisfied with his appointment, worried about the "radicalism" and Ivy League backgrounds of key people around the president.[49] Several of Ike's "gang" of friends also thought Hauge "leaned too far to the left" and told him so, but the president did not agree.[50] Hauge's counsel certainly broadened his outlook and gave him a basis for pushing back against that of his treasury secretary.

11

"A banker's mentality": Humphrey and Foreign Aid

One of the most contentious issues between Humphrey and Eisenhower was foreign economic assistance. Humphrey viewed foreign aid purely from a budgetary perspective, while Ike considered it an important tool in America's Cold War competition with the Soviet Union. It deserves brief mention here because Humphrey's refusal to countenance what he considered ill-advised hand-outs to other nations made the subject a persistent irritant in his relations with the president.

Humphrey's attitude alarmed the nations of West Europe, which were still recovering from the devastation of World War II and increasingly worried about potential Soviet aggression. But the problem was larger than that. In the mid-1950s the U.S.S.R. mounted an ambitious program of assistance to developing nations aimed at securing their allegiance—in part by proving the superiority of the socialist economic model. In response, the Eisenhower administration launched its own grant and loan programs. Soon, a full-blown contest between the two superpowers for influence in the Third World was in progress. Ike believed foreign aid was money well spent. He had spoken often of the importance of spreading American economic resources and know-how in less developed regions as a means of fostering stability, helping poor nations resist Communist influence, and "pulling their loyalty our way."

Unfortunately for the president and his like-minded advisers, foreign assistance was a hard sell with Congress, the American public, and his own administration's budget hawks. Foreign aid was more vulnerable to congressional cuts than other expenditures, because it had no natural constituency among the electorate. Many conservatives objected on principle to assisting autocratic governments or financing "socialistic" projects abroad. Ike tried to explain that socialist countries did not necessarily present a threat to American interests. In frustration, he declared that cutting foreign aid was "very penny wise and pound foolish."[1]

Humphrey's Opposition

Within the administration, Humphrey led the fight against this use of public funds. He considered foreign assistance just one more category of expenditure that needed to be reduced if the country were to live within its means. He regularly warned of the dire consequences of foreign "giveaway" programs and fought with the president about the wisdom of specific aid projects.

Even if he thought that the United States could easily afford foreign aid, Humphrey argued that it would not accomplish its intended goals and would foster dependency. "You can't spend all that money wisely and well," he told a friend. "Some countries are too ignorant to be helped." The danger, he felt, was that "every time a country catches cold it [will come] running to us for cough syrup and a quarter."[2] He told a business trade group that "large grant programs not only burden the American taxpayer but do not always produce either stronger or more friendly allies."[3]

Humphrey did not oppose all kinds of aid. He was willing to promote trade liberalization policies and encourage American businesses to invest overseas. This preference was shared by much of the nation's business press, corporate elite, and the U.S. Chamber of Commerce, and was captured in the slogan, "trade, not aid." These groups believed that carefully negotiated bilateral investment agreements would demonstrate to the host governments the superiority of free enterprise in promoting growth. But many Third World governments considered private investment another form of colonialism, of which most were even then ridding themselves. They preferred low-interest, long-term, "soft" loans from recognized international lending institutions, like the Export-Import Bank and World Bank.

Humphrey sought to condition all foreign assistance on a set of strict requirements that revealed a banker's mentality. He insisted that host countries guarantee American investment against expropriation and confiscation, as well as promote monetary and fiscal policies that assured a stable environment for investors. These were no doubt reasonable protections for American investors, but Eisenhower, Dulles and other advisers believed that more was at stake in many foreign countries than the amount of the loan. Achieving political goals, they felt, sometimes required taking economic risks.

Humphrey flatly opposed political loans. His rivals in the administration viewed his insistence on imposing strict rules as a reflection of his poor understanding of the different histories and political cultures in the Third World, as well as American interests abroad. To their frequent dismay, his forceful opposition made him a major stumbling block to administration grant and loan programs.

Though Humphrey argued that aid programs were ineffective, his fundamental goal was unrelated to program outcomes. He wanted to avoid additional financial commitments that would make the attainment of a balanced budget and tax reductions at home more difficult to achieve.[4] Success in these pursuits, he believed, would be the measure of his performance as treasury secretary.

Conflict with Administration Heavyweights

The administration's evolution on foreign aid, through many twists and turns over the four years of Humphrey's tenure, played out as an organizational struggle—mostly between the Treasury and State Departments—for control of the various aid programs. It also pitted Humphrey and his allies in the Bureau of the Budget against the administration's leading proponents of a vigorous foreign aid policy—notably, Nelson Rockefeller, Harold Stassen, Secretary Dulles, and the president's brother, Milton Eisenhower. Humphrey's combativeness on the subject and Ike's disinclination to overrule him angered and frustrated all of these men.

Milton Eisenhower was a distinguished scholar who favored aid to Latin America as a way of countering a growing resentment of U.S. policies there. Humphrey opposed this aid at every turn, leading Milton to call Humphrey's appointment to the Cabinet "tragic."[5] He later blamed Humphrey indirectly for the continued growth of anti–Americanism in the region throughout the 1950s, culminating with Fidel Castro's take-over of Cuba. To the detriment of U.S. interests, he believed, the treasury secretary had shown himself to be arbitrary, stubborn and convinced of his infallibility.[6] "I liked George personally," Milton said, "[but] I disagreed with him profoundly on many problems."[7]

At the time, Milton tried to be fair to Humphrey. "Let me say that I consider [him] one of the most intelligent men I have ever met, in his field," he wrote to his brother. "He is pretty narrow, but is growing. He is awfully sure of himself ... [but] if he keeps on growing he will come out all right." Still, he could not get past Humphrey's provincialism. "Basically, George is an isolationist who is gradually learning that isolationist policies won't work," he concluded.[8]

The president seemed surprised by Milton's comments. "I have not encountered [such an attitude] in the same form as you have," he wrote back. "Possibly he has merely been less objective with me."[9] In another letter, Ike agreed that Humphrey was "instinctively isolationist" but speculated that it may be "difficult for George to free himself completely of old convictions to the effect that the U.S. really needs nothing from the outside world. But I think that ... he has a clear enough understanding of present-day circumstances to overcome his instinctive reaction."[10] He expressed confidence that his treasury secretary would be a "good team player."

Humphrey's parochial views clearly limited his value as a foreign policy advisor. When he began to express his disapproval of foreign aid in Cabinet and N.S.C. sessions, Eisenhower believed he was not seeing the big picture. In typical fashion, rather than simply overruling Humphrey, the president worked hard to convince him of the benefits of foreign assistance.

But open disagreement persisted. On one occasion, Ike criticized the treasury secretary indirectly by pointing out that America's business leaders failed to understand the importance of the administration's aid program.[11] In late 1954, Humphrey made a comment at a Cabinet meeting about "lavish" American spending in Asia. Ike reacted strongly against the word "lavish" and emphasized that the United States had interests to protect there.[12]

The president especially objected to the argument that American loans and grants promoted socialism in the beneficiary countries. In a 1955 Cabinet meeting, Humphrey hazarded the remark that "the Russians had not done 10% as much socializing in the world as the United States." Showing some frustration, Eisenhower quickly pointed out that socialist governments did not prevent such countries as Denmark, Norway and Sweden from being American friends.

Humphrey also had "rousing" battles with Secretary of State Dulles over financial commitments overseas.[13] According to Douglas Dillon, Treasury was always fighting a "rear guard action against anything that might cost anything" at the State Department. It was an argument that went on "all the time."[14] As Humphrey told a historian years later, Dulles "used money, or was inclined to use money, as a tool of his trade. I just didn't like it at all."[15]

The two men sparred over the issue at early N.S.C. meetings. In October 1953, after Humphrey and Dodge spoke for curtailing economic grant aid and loans, Eisenhower mounted a vigorous defense of such programs, saying he was weary of hearing them maligned. Dulles quickly agreed. Economic assistance to some countries would not only add to American security interests, he noted, but would later produce actual savings by, for example, allowing the return of U.S. servicemen stationed in these countries.

Humphrey admitted that he and Dulles came at the issue of foreign aid from different perspectives. The secretary of state "was more interested in keeping in good standing abroad, and I was more interested in jobs here at home."[16] Because Dulles shared Eisenhower's opinion of foreign aid as an important foreign policy tool, his views usually carried more weight. However, Dulles did not consider foreign assistance one of his top priorities, and his disagreement with Humphrey did not poison their relationship. In fact, the two men got along well, respected each other, and amicably attended NATO summit meetings together.

Other men in the administration opposed Humphrey's stance on foreign assistance. Eisenhower had enlisted two leading liberal Republicans and former governors, Nelson Rockefeller of New York and Harold Stassen of Minnesota, to advise him on security and aid policy. Humphrey's conflicts with these men caused occasional fireworks. Though Stassen was often a loose cannon, Eisenhower defended his role as an "ideas person" who would challenge the status quo. He and Eisenhower agreed on one goal—generous assistance for developing Asian countries—which Humphrey went to great lengths to undermine. Ultimately, Stassen's headstrong nature and fraught relationship with the turf-conscious Dulles made him an easy target and limited his ability to influence the president.

Aiding India and Egypt

By far the most contentious of the administration's foreign aid candidates were India and Egypt. Both were strategically important underdeveloped nations teetering between West and East. Both had a colonial past and ambitious plans to modernize their economies, for which they needed lots of help. Though both had an active private sector, they also flirted with socialist forms of state planning.

Humphrey always grumbled about proposals to assist countries like India. He spoke up at one N.S.C. session in opposition to an aid program to the government of Jawaharlal Nehru, once again on the basis that the United States should not be offering financial support to a socialist country. Eisenhower brought the proceedings to a halt and delivered a tutorial to Humphrey on the economic and social differences between India and the United States. "So it's quite a mistaken idea," he concluded, "that we should judge the Indian situation or the Indian needs or the Indian policies by criteria which may be relevant for us."[17] The two men had another "sharp exchange" when Humphrey worried aloud that he could see no terminal point in the U.S. effort to prevent the emergence of Communist regimes everywhere in the world.[18]

The India aid issue led to conflict between Humphrey and Nelson Rockefeller. As a special assistant to the president for foreign affairs, specifically for Cold War strategy, Rockefeller was an advocate of an activist foreign policy, which included high-profile political loans to India and other Third World countries. Humphrey regarded Rockefeller as a "left-wing spendthrift."[19] He was particularly incensed when Rockefeller had the temerity to go around him and appeal to the president on the issue. He accused the New Yorker of "running around here like a dog yipping at everybody's heels."[20] In the end, the president did not allow Humphrey's opposition and foot-dragging to interfere with his larger policy of engaging with India.

A similar argument took place when the administration was trying to decide whether to help the British finance Egyptian president Gamal Nasser's Aswan Dam project. Humphrey saw danger in seeming to reward an ideological foe. The United States, he said, would simply be "building up a socialized economy in Egypt for all the world to look at."[21] Eisenhower viewed the project as a way to solidify relations with England and France and to impede Soviet influence in an increasingly important region of the world. The arrangement unraveled in the face of Nasser's assertive policies and belligerence toward Israel. In the long run, however, Eisenhower was fully committed to economic competition with the Soviet Union, which included additional spending for mutual security and technical assistance in Third World nations.

Humphrey continued to object. At Cabinet sessions, he kept trying to derail or reduce aid programs in order to keep federal expenditures down and allow for tax cuts. He used the worsening balance of payments situation, which greatly worried Eisenhower, as another weapon to demand more selectivity in foreign assistance. "We've got to revise our thinking and stop these trends," he warned. "Someone has to say 'We just can't afford it.'"[22]

The President and Humphrey's Dissent

As we have seen, Eisenhower disagreed openly with Humphrey on the subject of foreign assistance. He dressed the secretary down at Cabinet meetings when he could no longer stomach his warnings about the dangers of aiding socialist countries. Beyond that, he often forced him to work out compromises with other administration officials, especially Dulles. This expedient had the effect of shifting policy away from the merits of the issue and toward what two strong-minded Cabinet officers might be able to agree on. It was a manifestation of the president's well-known preference for delegating, but it may also have revealed a reluctance to come down strongly on one side or

11. "A banker's mentality": Humphrey and Foreign Aid

the other. In a 1954 example of splitting the difference between advisers, Eisenhower scaled back an ambitious Asian aid program advocated by Harold Stassen while accepting only part of Humphrey's suggestion that Stassen's Foreign Operations Administration be abolished.[23]

When it came to the general usefulness of foreign assistance, Ike continued trying to "talk sense" into Humphrey, rather than overrule or work around him. He even asked like-minded allies to help him in this task. On one occasion, he and Paul Hoffman braced the treasury secretary on the issue, but to no avail. As his various gambits failed, Ike lost patience. He wrote Hoffman that Humphrey relied too much on his business experience and failed to understand that Third World countries cared more about a reliable food supply than liberal ideals.[24] But he also knew that Humphrey's views were mirrored in Congress.

The disagreement took a toll on Humphrey's relationship with Eisenhower, though Humphrey tried to make peace with as much of the new policy as he could and to limit its impact on the domestic budget. Toward the end of his term of office, Humphrey decided to test the limits of his authority. In discussions about the establishment of a Third World development fund, Humphrey came close to defying his boss. "The maintenance of fiscal responsibility is my job," he insisted at one point, "and whatever is ultimately done must meet these requirements."[25] He promised that if Dulles and the president agreed with his conditions, he would give the program his full support. On this occasion, his stubbornness worked. He met with Dulles and the president a few days later and got them to agree to a scaled down initial appropriation and, more important, congressional review and approval. In return, he testified enthusiastically in favor of the loan fund before the Senate.

In March 1957, three months before Humphrey resigned, the president was still taking valuable time to write long memos to him, laying out his now familiar arguments on behalf of foreign economic assistance and perhaps reassuring himself of the correctness of his position.[26]

12

Wilson, Humphrey and the "New Look"

The first year of the Eisenhower administration was a time of intense debate over defense spending. On one side were those convinced that budget cuts would seriously erode the nation's military strength and readiness during a time of high international tension. On the other side were the advocates of a smaller, more affordable defense structure that would be economically sustainable over an extended period of confrontation with the Soviet bloc. As we have seen, Eisenhower and Humphrey belonged to the latter group. The dispute led to unprecedented levels of acrimony, not only among administration officials but in Congress and the uniformed military services.

Wilson's reduction in active duty military personnel in early 1953 was just a prelude to a major rethinking of the country's defense posture. In midsummer, the administration was developing its first full-year budget, for fiscal year 1955. A recently-signed Korean War armistice would allow the deep defense cuts Ike and Humphrey wanted. But Wilson proposed a budget of $42 billion, which represented little change from Korean War levels. In Humphrey's mind, this was a shockingly high figure that would mean a $9 billion deficit in fiscal year 1955, the postponement of further tax cuts, increased inflationary pressures, and a decline in Republican electoral fortunes.

In October, the N.S.C. launched an in-depth review of American security policy. The discussions were broad and at times bordered on the academic—Robert Cutler, who set the agenda, worried aloud that the group would become a "debating society." But the outcome seemed likely to have real-world consequences for administration priorities and budgets, so the participants expressed their views with vigor. The give and take among these heavyweights would enable Humphrey to smoke out opposition to his plans and to see which arguments carried most weight with the president.

The N.S.C. meeting of October 7 was both contentious and revealing.[1]

12. Wilson, Humphrey and the "New Look"

Drawing on the results of a high-level strategy exercise dubbed Project Solarium, the group first sought to define the nature of the Soviet threat—was it primarily military or economic? The answer to that question mattered. If the threat was mostly military, it followed that America had to spend an increasing amount of money on defending the country, even if such spending required higher taxes and other sacrifices. But if the threat was primarily economic, defense spending could strive for adequacy rather than superiority, so as not to overtax and eventually exhaust the economy. The key to Humphrey's strategy was getting agreement on the latter definition.

As Humphrey launched his attack on Pentagon profligacy, Dulles reacted negatively and "with obvious emotion." If Humphrey was arguing that balanced budgets and tax cuts were more important than security objectives, Dulles said, he was strongly opposed. To insist on a completely balanced budget, he continued with growing agitation, was the "argument of a doctrinaire" and one that had caused the Hoover administration to "blow up."

Humphrey attempted to mollify Dulles, saying that he would be satisfied to work toward a balanced budget, rather than achieve one right away. But then Dulles reacted with suspicion to Humphrey's insistence that the country must "live within its means," fearing that the phrase would be interpreted as an "absolute commitment" to balance the budget—a commitment he felt would be "very dangerous." The president noted strong points on both sides, though at one point he said that over the long term he was "inclined to agree with Secretary Humphrey."

Secretary Wilson, on whom the burden of defense cuts would fall, took Dulles' side. Speaking also with "strong conviction," according to the minutes, he observed that "if we ever go to the American people and tell them that we are putting a balanced budget ahead of national defense, it would be a terrible day." With the standard of living at an all time high, he continued, "it is foolish to insist that we can spend no more." Humphrey again sought to reassure his critics. Of course we will not put a balanced budget ahead of national security, he said, but then added that "the military ought to be so damned dollar conscious that it hurts."

This discussion led to another defense spending issue—the continued deployment of American troops overseas. Seeing the problem from a financial perspective, Humphrey agreed with the judgment of many military leaders that American forces were overextended and that the troops should be brought home from Europe and Asia at the earliest possible time, with or without the consent of the countries where they were stationed. Admiral Radford had presented a redeployment plan to the N.S.C. a month before. Humphrey called it "terrific" and "the most important thing that had happened in this country since [inauguration day]." Eisenhower seemed to have some sympathy with that argument, noting that U.S. troops in Europe had always been a "stop-gap measure," there to give indigenous forces time to gain confidence and strength.

Dulles could not have been pleased to hear Humphrey question one of the fundamentals of American foreign policy. He knew that European governments were watching nervously as budget cutters in Washington pressed for reducing foreign assistance and cutting the size of the military—actions that could undermine America's commitment to defending the continent against Soviet aggression. The knowledge that serious consideration was being given to pulling American troops out of Europe, he felt, would send shock waves around the continent.

Dulles pretended to agree that redeployment was a desirable goal but then noted that, unless done with "the greatest delicacy," bringing troops home could "strangle N.A.T.O. in its crib" and result in the "complete collapse of our coalition in Europe." He even objected to any written account of the N.S.C. debate, for fear of leaks. Ike agreed with Dulles' note of caution, observing that U.S. divisions had done marvels in restoring Europe's faith in itself.

The discussion resumed on October 13. With Dodge's support, Humphrey continued his cost-cutting offensive. He urged the group to focus on what he considered the real objective of national security—the preservation of the American way of life. The first imperative was to resist spending pressures, which would lead to an inflation that would be "ultimately disastrous" for the country. Eisenhower replied to Humphrey's "forceful statement" by simultaneously endorsing and restraining him. He agreed on the goal of defining an "irreducible minimum" required to safeguard national security, while also declaring that "we can never under any circumstances say that we cannot afford to defend our country."[2]

To make spending reductions possible, Humphrey recommended changes in defense policy. The military cannot afford to prepare for several kinds of wars, as it had been doing, he argued. It must decide what kind of war it will fight and prepare only for that. Secretary Dulles brushed off this idea as "not quite as simple and easy as the Secretary of the Treasury had suggested." The cheapest kind of war might be an atomic war, but that would turn every little conflict into a big one and risk the loss of allies in the process. The national defense, he concluded, requires a good deal more flexibility than Humphrey's proposal allows.

Dulles went on to point out that the international situation hardly argued for spending less on defense. The Soviets were becoming bolder in both

12. Wilson, Humphrey and the "New Look"

Europe and the Third World. He believed that the United States was facing mounting rather than decreasing danger. Our peril would increase if our allies sensed we were sacrificing security for economy. Wilson previewed the coming defense debate by interjecting that any serious cost reduction program would have to anticipate the use of nuclear weapons. The discussion turned briefly and inconclusively to the conditions under which such weapons could be employed. Eisenhower avoided being pinned down on the issue—he pronounced the problem a tough one, with valid viewpoints on each side.

Humphrey then gathered himself for a final pitch. He declared, "with some heat," that 1955 was the critical year and that if we conduct business in the same way as in the past, "the American economy will go to hell and the Republican party will lose the next election." Humphrey pushed the service chiefs further on nuclear weapons: only their use on a "broad scale" would really change the Defense Department's program. Why can we not plan on using them? he asked. As one historian joked, the joint chiefs might have preferred to take on the Soviets than to fight Humphrey at N.S.C. meetings.[3]

Had Humphrey overreached? His comments on redeployment drew a rebuke from the president. The presence of American troops in Europe is the "single greatest morale factor" there, Ike pointed out. "You cannot therefore make a radical change so quickly." Further, the treasury secretary's injection of political considerations into the debate risked antagonizing Eisenhower, who was not about to make any decision based on its effect on an election.

But Eisenhower was just as determined as Humphrey to force cuts on the military. He was certainly aided in this conviction by Humphrey's arguments, but his own experience in the army had persuaded him that much money was wasted by inter-service rivalry and redundant weapons systems. At the N.S.C. session, Ike lectured Admiral Radford at length about the need for a complete review of defense requirements. "Can we not stretch out more? Do we need everything for our armed forces right now?" he pressed. He had not yet been convinced that the military needed all the money it sought, but he reassured Wilson and Radford that, once convinced of a reasonable figure, he would fight for it "with all the energy he could summon up."

The importance of Eisenhower's addition of the treasury secretary to the N.S.C. membership was apparent. Humphrey's aggressive presence was forcing national security policymakers to treat cost as a central issue in defense planning. In these two October gatherings, he had thrown down the gauntlet. Neither Dulles nor Wilson saw budget balancing as a central goal of this administration—not with serious foreign political and military challenges to meet. But Wilson now understood one reality—that the military would have to make do with less.

Pressure from the White House rattled the Pentagon brass. Defense planners knew that the president's budget targets could not be met by tinkering at the margins. It was true that redeployment, whatever the political impact of bringing troops home from overseas bases, promised eventual cost savings. But that action would make the United States reliant on U.S.-based air and nuclear forces to counter foreign threats. The result would be an enhanced air force and a diminished army and navy.

Maintaining the always sensitive balance of power among the services had long stood in the way of centralized management of the U.S. defense programs. Each service had its defenders in Congress, and any downgrading of the importance of conventional forces was bound to cause a firestorm, especially in army circles. Eisenhower realized the difficulty of such an undertaking. It was the main reason he told Wilson he would have to be the most unpopular man in government.

With its fixation on economy, the administration was moving in a politically vulnerable direction. Critics were already charging that the president was trying to establish a bottom-line for total military spending before deciding what an adequate defense was and what it would cost. Fiscal rather than military considerations appeared to be ascendant—a perspective viewed by many members of Congress as shortsighted, even dangerous. It seemed not only a curious position for a former army general to take, but it exposed him to attack from foreign policy hawks in his own party, as well as from Democrats looking to score political points.

The news media got wind of the internal disagreement. Unwisely, Wilson made a speech in November declaring himself "flatly opposed" to "sudden and radical changes" in defense spending, though he hoped overall expenditures would be somewhat less than in the current fiscal year.[4] *The Wall Street Journal* assumed that these comments would bring him into a collision with Humphrey.[5] The *New York Times* reported that the defense secretary and the joint chiefs were "in a lather" about Humphrey's reputed view that the defense budget needed to be cut another $6 billion.[6]

The president continued to believe that military cuts could be accomplished without bringing troops home or fatally weakening the country's defenses. Surely in a bureaucracy as large as the Defense Department, money was being wasted somewhere. Repeating his mantra that "the sound dollar lies at the very basis of a sound capability for defense," he again directed Wilson and the joint chiefs to develop a new policy, designed to deter aggression at the lowest possible cost. Their deliberations would soon produce one of the most controversial doctrines in American military history.

Wilson's Troubles Increase

In the last half of 1953, while the administration was wrestling with these issues, it was sometimes hard to imagine that Wilson could last into a second year. He had landed in the middle of a debate that encompassed not only military policy but strategic and foreign policy as well, and he was far from equipped to handle it. With Humphrey demanding budget cuts, Dulles fuming about obligations to allies, and the military services protecting their turf, Wilson was buffeted from one side to the other.

One of his most outspoken critics was the new chief of staff of the army, General Matthew Ridgway. Ridgway was a highly decorated and respected soldier, who had served under Eisenhower in the war, succeeded Douglas MacArthur as commander of American troops in Korea, and followed Ike as commander of N.A.T.O. forces in Europe. He also turned out to be a strong advocate for his service, despite the president's insistence that Pentagon leaders think corporately rather than parochially. Ridgway found Wilson's approach to management—in particular, his tendency to call meetings on the fly with no particular agenda—patronizing and a poor use of time. He perceived Wilson to be "rudely inattentive" when others were talking and overly fond of lengthy, fruitless, and irrelevant discussions.[7] Of course, Wilson had long been known for his meandering, leisurely style.

In addition, his relations with Eisenhower were becoming increasingly strained by his propensity for ill-considered remarks. The secretary's defenders considered his gaffes examples of "authenticity" and "Midwestern charm." One reason he was so quotable was that he liked to think aloud. "In the course of his explorations," explained one Washington journalist, "he may drop many a tentative sentence which, plucked later from its context, will give a quite false idea of his meaning."[8]

All too often, a Wilson comment at a Cabinet session provoked a stiff rejoinder from the president. On one occasion, according to Press Secretary Jim Hagerty, Wilson made some "rather elaborate points" about military resources. Ike seemed convinced that Wilson was trying to pull the wool over his eyes. "Charlie, don't tell me anything like that," the president responded. "I can tell you where every bald-headed major is in every armed service in the U.S. and throughout the world."[9]

Eisenhower's superior knowledge of the Pentagon and its problems meant that Wilson had to be careful before taking a strong position about internal issues, even relatively minor ones. A good example was his growing concern about the low reenlistment rate of men whose specialized training had cost thousands of dollars. But in November, the president told Wilson he was putting too much emphasis on raising military salaries and not enough on protecting "perks," such as health care for dependents.[10]

In his frustration, the president sometimes treated Wilson like a schoolboy in need of discipline. Administration official Arthur Larson was in Ike's office when Wilson made one of his frequent visits to discuss the defense budget. According to Larson, the conversation became a "one-way harangue," as Eisenhower lectured him on the need to stay under the targeted amount: "Not one penny over, do you understand? Not under any circumstances!" He heard Wilson make a solemn promise not to exceed the specified sum. A couple of months later, the defense secretary reappeared in Eisenhower's office. Coincidentally, Larson was again present. Wilson notified the "incredulous" president that he was already $2 billion over budget. Wrote Larson: "I shall never forget the protracted moment of blank silence that followed, while the two men stared speechless at each other, as if in the presence of some gigantic, unknowable, uncontrollable force of nature."[11]

At other times, to the president's chagrin, Wilson went "off message" in talking to groups outside the executive branch. When he told a congressional committee that the budget could not be balanced in 1954 and 1955, *Time* reported that Ike instructed him to leave fiscal policy to Humphrey and Dodge.[12] During an interview with the *Washington Post* in September 1953, Wilson made the same mistake again. He said that defense cuts would not be large enough to balance the budget and that, at any rate, "budget balancing is someone else's worry."[13] This comment incensed budget director Dodge. He wrote the president that he was "not only appalled but deeply discouraged" by Wilson's denial of responsibility for federal spending. "I know exactly what you mean," Ike replied. "I'll see what I can do." He added a P.S.—"Charlie Wilson says he was misquoted." The president then called Wilson to say that he had "stirred up a hornet's nest."[14]

Some of Wilson's careless comments reflected an incomplete understanding of the administration's foreign policy. In mid–1953, while the president was deliberating with his Cabinet on the subject of a negotiated peace with Korea, Wilson suggested that America recognize Communist China as part of a package deal that would "get the Far East issues settled." The group reacted in "shocked surprise," especially Eisenhower, who patiently explained why such a deal was both diplomatically and politically unrealistic.[15]

Wishing to improve relations with the press corps, Wilson began holding weekly "on-the-record" press conferences. He labored to give honest answers to all questions. "Often this is hard going for him," observed one Pentagon reporter. "He is not a facile man with words." As he struggled, his feet twisted and turned restlessly. When a correspondent wrote that he could tell Wilson's thoughts by watching his feet, Wilson draped a curtain over his legs at his next press conference with a sign on them saying "Top Secret." Later he told Eisenhower with a smile that he was making progress because "they're working on my feet now, instead of my head."[16]

At some of these press conferences, he had no message to deliver or new facts to impart, which raised the potential for embarrassment. Sometimes a clever reporter could trap Wilson into revealing sensitive information or appearing to be in the dark about internal matters. At one appearance, he replied, "I don't know" to a long series of questions, which made the White House wonder why the conference had been held in the first place. A memo from Ike to Wilson in early November warned him of the dangers of confidential revelations via his openness policy.[17]

That fall and winter, a flood of critical memos and calls from the president on various issues descended on the Pentagon:

- On October 14, Ike reminded Wilson to coordinate with Secretary of State Dulles on foreign policy matters before talking to Congress.[18]
- On November 30, he said he was "somewhat shocked" to learn that the proportion of general and flag officers was triple what it was in 1944. He told Wilson he should be focusing on reducing overhead.[19]
- On December 2, he noted that budget chief Dodge was "very much concerned—and rightly so" about Wilson's slowness in preparing the FY-1955 military budget.[20]
- On January 27, he expressed his unhappiness with the increase in overhead in the Army's reorganization plan and his "complete opposition" to one of the plan's initiatives.[21]

Eisenhower had not wanted to be his own defense secretary, but defense issues continued to take up far too much of his time. His memos to Wilson not only showed his displeasure but also a tendency to micromanage, despite his wish to do the opposite. In May he reminded Wilson that the commandants at the service academies should not exceed the rank of major general. A couple of months later, he wrote that he considered unwise any cutback beyond what was then planned in the combat strength of the armed forces.[22]

In the face of these reminders and warnings from his boss, Wilson fought to keep his sense of humor. "I remarked to a friend recently that I'm no politician," he said at a press conference. "He wanted to know why I insist on proving it over and over."[23]

Coming Up with the "New Look"

All the while, Eisenhower looked to the Pentagon for a military strategy that would adequately defend the country while saving money. The president's rejection of the redeployment plan had left the budget cutters frustrated. Humphrey continued to fume. Up to that point, he felt, the new leadership had not "done a damn thing but go along with the programs and policies of the last administration." In his anger, he warned again of political consequences: "Either do better," he had told the Cabinet, "or abandon all hope of being retained in office."[24]

One assumption seemed to hold the key to significant defense cuts. The cost of building and maintaining a nuclear arsenal was low compared with the manpower and financial requirements of recruiting, training, arming and supporting large conventional forces. In fact, the president had specifically urged the Pentagon to think along those lines. He had told the joint chiefs to emphasize the new technology in their search for a unifying concept. It was Admiral Radford who, in response to Humphrey's expressed horror at what he considered a bloated defense budget, first agreed that relying more on nuclear weapons would allow a less costly force structure.

When the president seemed receptive to the idea, Wilson pressed the full N.S.C. to come up with an agreed-upon definition of the circumstances under which such weapons would be brought into play, so that the budget could be designed around a formal doctrine. But Ike felt it best not to enunciate a policy—he would reserve that decision to himself. Rest assured, he added, that we would use them if our security was threatened.

This vague statement by the president did not help Wilson. He and Radford believed no further cuts were possible unless the United States committed to using nuclear weapons in both large and small conflicts. Without a formal change in strategy, they felt they had no choice but to seek an increase in the size of all the services, which would cost more money rather than less. Dodge and Humphrey were not pleased.

The division among N.S.C. members both angered the president and placed him in a bind. He was determined to carry through with his promise to reduce the size and cost of the military, and he knew that Wilson's resource request was too high to allow that. At the same time, he was sensitive to the charge of endangering national security. Finally, he ordered Wilson and Radford to return in December with a 1955 budget, planned "on an austerity basis," that reflected a greater role for nuclear weapons in American war planning.[25]

In carrying out this directive, Wilson and Radford decided to employ the services of a commission headed by an air force general. The commission was told to assume that nuclear weapons would be used in the event of war. In line with that guidance, it suggested a plan in which such weapons served both deterrent and offensive purposes. Implementation would require increased funding and responsibility for the air force, the logical home for a nuclear capability, as well as spending more money on nuclear research and development.

Force levels flowed logically from the new strategy. A massive cut—23 percent—in the size of the army and 13 percent in the navy would be required, while the air force would expand in line with its nuclear responsibilities from 39 percent to 47 percent of the entire services budget. One of the plan's fundamental assumptions was that our allies in Europe and Asia would provide the major share of ground forces for their own defense.

Of course, this was bad news for General Ridgway and the army. Ridgway protested he did not know how to reduce manpower further without compromising the army's ability to fulfill its commitments. Wilson suggested that he simply cut all combat divisions to 85 percent strength, an idea that Ridgway dismissed as naïve in the extreme. The general stood on principle, refusing to carry out any reductions unless convinced that they were militarily sound. In the end, it took a direct order from Wilson to get Ridgway's cooperation. He later wrote that Wilson and his staff had a "woeful lack of comprehension of the role the foot soldier must play in ensuring the safety of the country."[26]

Ridgway professed bewilderment that army reductions were considered necessary during an economic boom, with national production projected to increase by 50 percent in the next five years. He later "choked" when he read that Eisenhower's defense program for FY 1955 had been "unanimously recommended" by the joint chiefs of staff. Instead, he called it a "directed verdict."[27] Army secretary John Stevens publicly expressed his "grave concern" about the new direction. But the strategy solved Wilson's immediate problem. He and Radford decided to present it to the N.S.C. in December.

In this manner, the doctrinal underpinnings of what became known as the New Look were established. By sanctioning the use of nuclear weapons, the policy provided a way for the administration to address both spending and strategic issues in one stroke. Wilson told the N.S.C. that the 1955 defense budget, if based on New Look thinking, would save several billion dollars. This was music to Humphrey's ears. He fully agreed with the new program's assumptions—that to save money it was permissible, as he said on October 7, to employ nuclear weapons "on a broad scale."[28]

The president also acknowledged that the new approach meant nuclear weapons would be "as available for use as other munitions,"[29] a phrase that he insisted on adding to the new N.S.C. policy directive. In conversation, Eisenhower seemed convinced that any serious conflict with the Soviet Union would automatically escalate to a nuclear exchange—one which rendered

American conventional forces useless. To be coldly logical about it, he noted, "the money being spent for ground forces could be used to better advantage on new highways to facilitate the evacuation of large cities in case of an enemy attack."[30] Ridgway, he said, was "talking theory" while he was attempting to use "sound sense."[31]

Eisenhower's acceptance of the New Look and his often bloodless comments on the use of nuclear weapons did not mean that he was cavalier about the subject. On the contrary, he was well aware of their destructive potential, and he knew that no winner would emerge from a U.S.-Soviet nuclear exchange. He had already given serious thought to the workability of various international arms control mechanisms and to the possible outcomes of arms limitation negotiations with the Soviets. But Ike seems to have reasoned that the best way to avoid nuclear war while reducing the defense budget was to make it clear that the United States had the capability and the will to retaliate with all the force at its disposal if under attack.

Fully on board with his boss, Humphrey in November pressed for more drastic manpower reductions than even the president was willing to entertain, along with a rapid conversion to nuclear weaponry. He drew a direct connection between the billions that might be saved on defense and the amount of tax reduction that might be accomplished in 1954. It was still unclear whether the Pentagon believed the smaller military budget would adequately defend the country.

In several speeches during the fall of 1953, Humphrey reassured his audiences that the nation's security was not imperiled by the defense cuts he was advocating. Addressing the Union League Club in Philadelphia, he cleverly defined the new approach as a "middle way," which would preserve essential capabilities while avoiding reckless defense spending that would bankrupt the country.[32] In another speech, he extolled the economic benefits of a nuclear military. "The surest formula for defeat," he told the Economic Club of Detroit, "would be a static defense committed to an old-fashioned strategy, served by obsolete weapons."[33]

Humphrey continued to make pronouncements on defense policy. The secretary lavished particular praise on Dulles' controversial enunciation of a doctrine of massive retaliation. Later he maintained that the threat of nuclear annihilation was all that kept the Soviet Union at bay. "All the rest of these soldiers and sailors and submariners and everything else, comparatively speaking, you could drop in the ocean, and it wouldn't make too much difference."[34]

Administration spokesmen seemed confused about some details of the New Look policy. Wilson told the National Press Club that the policy would

12. Wilson, Humphrey and the "New Look"

allow withdrawal of some divisions from Europe. Secretary Dulles quickly reassured NATO countries that this was incorrect. The Office of Defense Mobilization announced an increase in the 1954 draft, only to be reminded by Wilson that the army was being reduced in size.

The New Look budget for fiscal year 1955 and its changed assumptions about war-fighting was the subject of hearings held by the Senate Appropriations Committee in March 1954. Wilson stressed the defensive and preventative role of nuclear weapons, but he had difficulty clarifying the conditions under which they otherwise might be used—not surprising in view of Eisenhower's refusal to define those conditions. He included a reference to Ike's belief that security took precedence over economy. If his presentation was less than totally reassuring, it represented accurately the division in administration councils.

The shock of the New Look forced leading Democratic senators into the unaccustomed role of supporters of increased military spending. Some of them were concerned about the increase in unemployment that would accompany force reductions, but others voiced national security arguments. All of them sensed the political potency of the issue. Former Air Force Secretary Symington expressed particular concern. He joined John Kennedy, Lyndon Johnson and Hubert Humphrey in calling the program risky and shortsighted, in view of growing turbulence in the Third World that could conceivably require the use of U.S. conventional forces. One representative stressed the need to prepare for more "brush fires," like Korea, but no one followed up on his comment. In their testimony, Pentagon officials hinted at internal dissent over the New Look. In 1953, at least, this dissent did not become widely known.

The key fact was that both houses of Congress were controlled by Republicans, and most of them were sympathetic to the administration's arguments. In fact, some members thought the Defense Department could get by with even less money. Few seemed inclined to question the New Look's assumptions. Public opinion was no help to the Democratic cause. Gallup polls revealed that Americans felt confident in the president's leadership and believed overwhelmingly that military spending cuts did not harm the nation's defenses.[35] Such polling data gave Humphrey and the president some cover in their defense of the new policy.

As a result, the administration submitted to Congress a defense budget for FY-1955 of around $37 billion, some $5 billion less than Wilson's initial proposal. Much of the savings came from a cut of 500,000 troops in the army. Ike had won the battle—the New Look was now Pentagon doctrine. But the war over the defense budget was far from over. The vulnerability of the New

Look was obvious. One army strategist called it the outcome of a political bargaining process unrelated to actual defense needs. A year later, Democrats would be in the majority, and their opposition would be aided by an increasingly outspoken military.

Military Dissent and Congressional Criticism

Budget chief Roland Hughes began the next round of the conflict with a gloomy report to the National Security Council in May 1954. He warned that unless spending was cut further, the 1956 and 1957 budgets would be several billion dollars in the red. Humphrey followed Hughes with an appeal to the president not to let this happen, not to succumb to pressures for "just a little inflation." It was also time, he said, to come to grips with the fact that the country could not afford to be "prepared to fight two or three or more different kind of wars."[36]

Leading military officers feared a different kind of disaster—one caused by reliance on weapons that could never be used. Ridgway assuredly advanced a parochial view, but his counsel to Wilson was that the New Look was strategic folly. He spoke critically about those who wished to rely on "new and untested devices, weapons, and equipment in the hope that these can substitute for men."[37] Once the Soviet Union had a nuclear arsenal, he also pointed out, neither side could escape the consequences of a general war.

Eisenhower was stung by Ridgeway's growing opposition. The president's disappointment was magnified by the realization that he would be a formidable adversary should he take his dissent to Congress or the public.[38]

Ridgway and Navy Chief of Staff Robert Carney had drawn an important lesson from the recent French defeat in Vietnam—that regional instability increased the importance of conventional forces. In fact, Ridgway had opposed helping the French because he felt the U.S. Army was not capable of saving the situation.[39] Without a strong army and navy, they both believed, the United States would be left with no option short of tactical nuclear strikes in countering developments where U.S. security was not directly at stake, such as Communist aggression in the Third World. Such strikes were certain to provoke international condemnation and cause unacceptable collateral damage.

Expressed today, these views would be considered unremarkable. But memories of the bloody and inconclusive Korean War were fresh in Eisenhower's mind. He had strong doubts about the wisdom of U.S. intervention in future Third World conflicts and saw no need to maintain large conventional forces. Ridgway's apostasy angered the president and doomed his chances for reappointment as army chief of staff.

But Secretary of State Dulles seemed as troubled as Ridgway. He told the N.S.C. that America could not risk nuclear Armageddon over every small conflict, arguing that the Pentagon needed to meet each challenge with a response appropriate to its importance to U.S. security. Taking aim at the budget-balancers present, he noted that with the international situation worsening, it would "increase our peril if either our allies or our enemies concluded that we were sacrificing security to economy"—exactly what Democrats in Congress were already charging.[40]

Humphrey returned the fire with his by now familiar argument that excessive spending would jeopardize the "American way of life" and "a strong and free economy." When the two antagonists finished sparring, Ike again appeared to lean in Dulles' direction. The "American way of life" was important, he agreed, but so was "physical survival."[41] Thus Ike continued a pattern of agreeing with defense hawks in group sessions and encouraging budget hawks in private.

The military sufficiency issue continued to simmer throughout 1954. The Pentagon bureaucracy mounted a powerful display of its ability to influence the policy debate independent of the secretary of defense. A series of alarmist papers from the J.C.S. planning board assessed the Soviet threat as growing "exponentially," requiring an immediate expansion of American conventional forces, budget increases, and the jettisoning of the New Look. It also noted that several money-saving actions posited by the new strategy—for example, the redeployment of some American forces abroad and the augmentation of allied defense forces—had not taken place.[42]

The strength and frequency of Pentagon complaints showed that Wilson was powerless to bring the defense apparatus to heel. In fact, his support for further reductions in the defense budget seemed to wither in the face of these warnings. He told the *New York Times* in April that the dangerous international situation "may force a soul-searching review of our specific policies, plans, objectives, and expenditures."[43] One observer said he had evidently been brought "under the spell of the Pentagon expansionists."[44]

Many defense analysts of the period concluded that the U.S. policy of massive retaliation using nuclear weapons was simply not credible—not to our allies, our enemies, or even the American public.[45] No one doubted that the country would meet an existential threat using all means at its disposal. But would a Soviet incursion in a far-off corner of the world merit a nuclear response? In *Nuclear Weapons and Foreign Policy*, the young Henry Kissinger argued that relying on strategic forces made the United States vulnerable to lesser challenges. Conventional forces were still needed, perhaps more than ever.

In November 1954, the J.C.S. planning board went too far and wound up hurting its own cause. One of its papers declared that America had been overly passive on the international stage and predicted a "doomsday" scenario in which growing Soviet power would increase the danger of an all-out war. Secretary Dulles was quick to challenge the characterization of his foreign policy as "passive," while Humphrey was angry at what he considered a transparent attempt to frighten the administration into increasing the Pentagon budget.[46]

The flap reinforced Eisenhower's support of the New Look's assumptions. The argument that America would need stronger conventional forces for local conflicts did not impress him. The responsibility for preventing Communist aggression overseas, he believed, belonged to the ground forces of those countries, rather than the United States. "We must make plans to use the atom bomb if we become involved in a war," he declared in December, no matter what the other side did. In fact, the main role he saw for the army was not fighting conventional wars but helping to preserve order in a country devastated by Soviet nuclear strikes.[47]

Many senior officers continued to underestimate the president's resolve. Under the mistaken assumption that growing tensions with China over the Taiwan straits would cause him to abandon the New Look, they pressured Wilson and Radford to brief the president on a tentative plan to increase the size of each armed service for fiscal year 1957. The fact that Wilson agreed to do so suggested that he was completely unmoored in the debate and was becoming merely a transmission belt for the views of those above and below him.

Predictably, the briefing did not go well. Ike not only rejected the proposal but ordered additional cuts in the 1956 budget. The next day, while announcing this decision to the N.S.C., the president said with a fierce smile that "he did not know if Radford went along with this idea, but that he'd better."[48] A chastened Wilson then sat down with budget director Hughes to work out the details.

Wilson's Request for Guidance

Wilson was in a quandary. He wanted to serve the president well and was willing to defend the unwelcome directives he was obliged to carry back to the Pentagon. But his main problem was to determine from whom the budget pressure was really coming. Many Washington political observers assumed that Humphrey, behind the scenes, was the "architect" of the defense budget.[49] In one of his columns, Joe Alsop worried that Humphrey's counsel on defense and foreign policy counted for more than the rest of the Cabinet combined, even though his only concern was money.

Once Wilson was certain he was receiving orders from the top, he was faced with the counterarguments of career military officers, whose informed perspectives on war-fighting doctrine were difficult for a civilian to refute. These men felt that Wilson did not argue hard enough with the president before agreeing to his demands, especially since he often confided some sympathy with their views.

For his part, Wilson was dismayed by the inter-service strife he was forced to put up with. He once joked he could not "understand it, unless the Army and Air Force plan on fighting each other."[50] He tried without much luck to find common ground between the experienced soldiers both above and below him. Wilson was a man who tended to worry anyway, and many of his days must have been an ordeal.

Bewildered by the twists and turns in the president's thinking and anticipating a struggle with the newly Democratic Congress over the fiscal year 1956 budget, Wilson took a curious step. He sent a note to Eisenhower in January 1955 asking for detailed guidance on the issue of force levels. "I have found so much value in the views underlying your decisions as to the personnel strengths of the Armed Services that I wonder if you would give me the gist of them in written form," he wrote.

Coming as it did a full two years into the president's first term, Wilson's request risked making him seem too dependent and hesitant to make independent recommendations. But Ike responded immediately with a detailed memo that emphasized the importance of incorporating new technology in America's military posture.[51] It was, in other words, a vigorous defense of the New Look's cuts in conventional forces.

Wilson seemed enormously relieved to have a written expression of the president's views at hand. Such a document, he undoubtedly hoped, would act as a brake on Eisenhower's tendency to tack left and right in response to pressure from both sides of the budget battle. Wilson referred to it many times at congressional hearings throughout 1955 to bolster his public defense of the New Look.

Shortly after the exchange of memos, Ike formally asked Wilson to reduce the armed forces from 3.2 million to around 2.8 million troops. General Ridgway was quick to warn Congress that the order would jeopardize American security, and he again criticized Wilson for failing to stand up to the president.

Many members of Congress backed Ridgway and launched an attempt to pass a measure that would do the opposite of what Ike wanted—increase the armed forces. Though it failed, it was indicative of the gulf separating administration thinking from that of the senior Pentagon brass and Democrats in Congress. "Nothing Wilson has said so far has changed my opinion that these heavy cuts in our armed forces are not justified from the standpoint of national security," said Senator Symington.[52] Other congressmen expressed similar concern. Wilson responded that "so many people worship things as they are, and they don't want to change anything."[53]

By early 1955, Eisenhower's irritation with Ridgway and Navy Secretary Carney had reached the boiling point. The president decided to replace Carney, though he had not embarrassed the administration by going public with his opposition to the New Look as Ridgway had. As a replacement for Ridgway, Wilson had in mind Maxwell Taylor, the commander of U.S. forces in the Far East. He asked Taylor to come home for a job interview in February 1955. When they met, Wilson began with a "long, rambling discussion" of problems in Asia and then cross-examined Taylor on his commitment to carrying out orders from his civilian superiors. "After thirty-seven years of service without evidence of insubordination," Taylor later wrote, "I had no difficulty of conscience in reassuring [Wilson], but I must say I was surprised to be put through such a loyalty test."[54]

Wilson's caution was justified. It turned out that Taylor held views similar to Ridgway's, and he would be equally protective of the army's role and budget. Like his colleagues and predecessor, he viewed the New Look with alarm. Even at a time when America had nuclear forces superior to those of the Soviet Union, Taylor believed that "such a doctrine offended the common sense of many thoughtful people and aroused their skepticism as to its practicality."[55]

In August 1955, Eisenhower surprised a Cabinet session by announcing that a balanced budget for FY-1956 was attainable if each department took a further budget cut of 3 percent (details in Chapter Fourteen). The person upon whom this cut would have the greatest impact sat in stunned silence for a while. Then Wilson complained of the many "special difficulties" that would make additional defense cuts impossible. He was already undertaking to make a 5 percent cut—the new order would raise that to 8 percent.[56]

Eisenhower was unmoved. He took the opportunity—for the umpteenth time—to encourage Wilson to search for "luxuries and non-essential practices—perhaps in some of the military schools, perhaps in an over-abundance of storage depots, etc." that would not interfere with all-important weapons programs. Wilson had heard all this before.

In the end, he promised to do his best. Eisenhower and Humphrey assured him that was good enough for them. Wilson had a final plaintive comment: "I have so many people in my department who keep putting off decisions until only the wrong thing is left to do."[57] Following the session, he announced that he had re-estimated defense expenditures at around a billion dollars less. When Democratic senator Lyndon Johnson confronted him with rumors that the additional cut would translate into an army cutback of 80,000 troops, he reassured Johnson that national security had in no way been harmed.

Despite assuring Wilson that he would respect civilian control of the military, Maxwell Taylor was outraged at the steady erosion of army strength. Later he looked back on "turbulent years fraught with well-nigh continuous conflict with my colleagues of the J.C.S. and [the defense secretary]." Taylor judged the president sincere about not wishing to weaken the economy with excessive defense spending, "but he had no way of determining the needs of a sound economy other than through the acceptance of the personal, unsubstantiated views of advisers such as the Secretary of the Treasury, George Humphrey, a conservative banker with an overpowering manner in Cabinet debate."[58]

In defending itself, Taylor believed, the Defense Department was held to a different standard than other parts of government. Whereas the military had to prove its needs, there was no such procedure for examining civilian requirements. By objecting, Pentagon officers risked being called "parochial." Finally, he charged that the question "How much is enough?" for the military was never answered except "by the money finally allocated to it in the annual budget."[59]

A Partial Success

While the 1956 defense budget was working its way through Congress, unwelcome new intelligence findings roiled the Senate. The Soviets were said to have developed a long-range bomber similar to the American B-52, capable of delivering nuclear weapons. Also, an administration committee estimated that the U.S.S.R. was farther along in missile development than previously thought. Senator Symington used these discoveries to lash out at the defense secretary. "Throughout his tenure of office, Mr. Wilson has underestimated the strength of the Communists and their ability to produce modern arms, nor has he taken the steps necessary to obtain adequate arms for this country,"[60] he charged, though blaming Wilson was not quite fair. The senator pressed for a congressional investigation of the B-52 procurement program.

Despite the turmoil, Wilson was able to reassure enough congressmen that the B-52 program was soundly administered to secure passage of the FY-1956 budget, with only minor amendments. The administration agreed to allocate a half billion dollars to a crash program in missile research and development, but in absolute terms, defense expenses were projected to remain roughly the same as in FY-1955. With the gross national product steadily growing, defense spending was now a smaller percentage of GNP—something to which Eisenhower could point with pride. Though forces in opposition to the New Look were gathering strength on Capitol Hill, two consecutive budgets based on this thinking had now passed Congress.

An account of Wilson's Pentagon years credits his political skill and determination for this accomplishment, though the author admits that "conservative political realities" in Congress were also responsible.[61] Senators like Symington were vocal but did not have the support to vote down the administration's military budget. For his part, Eisenhower never believed in the existence of a "bomber gap"—and he was later proved correct. Still, toward the end of 1955, even stalwart administration supporters like Senators William Knowland and John Stennis began to express concern about the adequacy of American defenses.

In late 1955, Eisenhower gave in slightly to arguments for higher military spending. In internal talks on the fiscal year 1957 budget, he agreed to a $3 billion increase over what Congress approved for 1956. In making this concession, he assumed—or at least hoped—that Pentagon officers would refrain from public criticism during the upcoming election campaign. Wilson guaranteed him that the program "would be fully supported by the services."[62]

But 1956 would prove to be another year of bruising conflict.

13

1956: Wilson's Troubles Worsen

Before leaving his job as army chief of staff in the summer of 1955, General Ridgway bared his soul on the subject of the New Look in a final report to Wilson. Fearing its effect on Congress and the public, Wilson classified the memo, but it was later handed over to the press by a staff officer.

Ridgway remained convinced of the folly of proposed reductions in the strength of army combat divisions, which left them insufficient to carry out their assigned missions. The possibility of military action in Vietnam and confrontations with mainland China over offshore islands belonging to Taiwan seemed to bolster his argument. Going public with his criticism, he told the House Armed Services Committee that the United States was in no position to defend the islands militarily.[1] Eisenhower again dismissed his remarks as parochial.

Missteps Continue

Wilson's relationship with the president remained troubled. In his third year of service, he was still making occasional remarks that blew up in his face. At one press conference, he was asked to comment on the wisdom of targeting defense contracts to areas of heavy unemployment in order to put more people to work. Wilson seemed uninterested in doing the unemployed any favors. "I've always liked bird dogs better than kennel dogs myself," he said. "You know, one who will get out and hunt for food rather than sit on his fanny and yell."[2]

Eager reporters besieged Sherman Adams for his interpretation of Wilson's colorful metaphor. Adams chose not to comment. In private, he reasoned that Wilson's remark might have sounded more clever in a corporate board room than before a media audience. Wilson's supporters may have found his "candor" refreshing, but most people considered the comment politically insensitive. It so inflamed United Auto Workers president Walter Reuther that he called for Wilson's resignation. Milton Eisenhower quipped that "the only thing CW does worse than putting his foot in his mouth is taking it out again."[3]

In an October 1955 meeting in which Wilson again asked for suggestions about where to make budget and personnel reductions, Ike protested that he could not form a judgment about what could be cut or assess the usefulness of every division. He reminded the defense secretary that he had to be tough.[4] As such occasions became more numerous, Ike reacted with increasing irritation. After a phone call from Wilson, Ike told Ann Whitman that he needed to "hold his hand."[5]

Whitman, Eisenhower's perceptive—and protective—secretary, could see that Wilson's continuing visits to the White House were a drain on her boss' time. In a mid-1956 diary entry, she described these meetings as "more for the purpose of bolstering Mr. Wilson's ego than anything else."[6] Ike's brother Milton, concerned about the president's energy level, particularly after his September 1955 heart attack, asked Whitman what she thought he could stop doing. "I can't always see why some of the inter-service problems cannot be resolved before they come to the Pres.," she wrote to Milton, "but apparently, as matters stand, they cannot. Budget, manpower, etc., take an enormous amount of time, either with the Chiefs of Staff, or with the chiefs and their civilian superiors."[7] In other words, Wilson's dependence on Eisenhower was becoming a permanent feature of his tenure.

Despite Ike's detailed memo of the year before, Wilson complained, even in public, about a lack of guidance from the White House. Appearing on the interview show *Face the Nation* in 1956, he was asked how much direction the president gave him on budgetary matters. "I sometimes feel like not enough," he admitted.[8]

One area in which Wilson had performed well was in defending the military from Senator Joe McCarthy's infamous search for communists in government. To his credit, he did not join the right-wing hysteria that McCarthy's efforts unleashed. He took reasonable steps to tighten security-clearance procedures at the Pentagon and approved some investigations but never bought into McCarthy's dark assumptions about employee disloyalty.

In the middle of the furor, however, without informing the White House, he took it upon himself to give a luncheon for the senator at the Pentagon. Hearing about it, Ike expressed a wish for "acute politicians" in positions like defense secretary, since "they are the only ones who know how to stay out of traps."[9] Wilson had again demonstrated his unenviable ability to undermine his instances of good judgment.

Eisenhower continued to caution him in the strongest terms about casual statements he was "constantly making" in press conferences and elsewhere "which sometimes cause very definite embarrassment to the administration." These statements often interfered with American diplomatic strategy. For example, in 1955 Wilson offered the view that the loss of Taiwanese islands Quemoy and Matsu to the mainland Chinese would make little difference in the long run.[10] This comment infuriated Eisenhower and Dulles, who were trying to keep China guessing about America's commitment to help defend them. In a memo for the record, the president wrote: "While I think that [Wilson] considers himself a master of public relations, he seems to have no comprehension at all of what embarrassment such remarks can cause the Secretary of State and me in our efforts to keep the tangled international situation from becoming completely impossible."[11]

Wilson also went off message during the Suez crisis of 1956. He referred to the crisis as a "relatively small incident" in front of the British ambassador, who was said to be horrified. "I had to tell my Defense Secretary he shouldn't deride its seriousness," the president later wrote.[12] The error may appear insignificant in retrospect, but the fact that Eisenhower chose to recount the incident in his memoirs says otherwise.

For his various errors of judgment, the press frequently criticized Wilson, and some columnists were not above using sarcasm in doing so. *Time* magazine noted in 1956 that his relations with Congress had improved—now they were merely poor. His answers to questions used to land him in hot water—now they are merely uninformative.[13] The *New York Times* observed that he has a hard time freeing himself from his pre-Washington experience—"a difficulty which tends toward a certain dogmatism in fields foreign to his talents."[14]

Eisenhower's personal domination of defense policy making invited ridicule of the circumscribed nature of Wilson's duties. Secretary of State Dulles quickly learned that neither Humphrey nor Wilson were well enough informed to threaten his primacy in national security policy. While he retained a certain respect for Humphrey, he once cruelly referred to Wilson as a "glorified office manager."[15]

Wilson's news conferences continued to draw unwanted publicity. In June 1956 he managed to offend leading senators with another careless comment. When asked what he thought of the legislature giving the air force money the administration had not requested, he responded: "If Congress wants the Air Force to spend more money, he said, it should raise taxes to pay for it."

The Senate promptly overreacted to the remark and rained down abuse on Wilson. "In my humble judgment—and I said this more than three years ago," said Senator Henry Jackson, "he should no longer serve as Secretary of Defense." Echoing Milton Eisenhower, he opined that Wilson's "latest comment has demonstrated his ability to keep his foot in his mouth most of the time. The rest of the time, he is trying desperately to take his foot out of his mouth." Influential Senator Richard Russell commented that Wilson's "arrogance and vanity" were exceeded "only by his ineptness." He accused Wilson of trying to intimidate military leaders into suppressing their real views and suggested that he take "a short course on the American constitution."[16]

Wilson's Defenders

Throughout his service at the Pentagon, Wilson had a small but loyal and sometimes influential following. They admired his outwardly cheerful manner and his willingness to work hard and dig into the issues. Overall, they considered him an asset to the administration. Attorney General Herbert Brownell, one of Eisenhower's brightest and most effective Cabinet members, observed, mostly from afar, that he was managing the Defense Department with skill, despite his impolitic remarks. Brownell wrote later that the two men thought alike on most issues. He and his wife became good friends with the Wilsons because protocol sat them next to each other at state dinners.[17] Even Sherman Adams, who experienced first hand Ike's immense frustration with Wilson, called him a "smart cookie," especially in the area of labor relations.[18]

Other senior officials appreciated Wilson's contributions. Presidential aide Bobby Cutler had the impression that the Pentagon seemed to baffle him at first, because it was so full of "intangibles," but that he soon "got used to paddling his own canoe and enjoying it."[19] Press Secretary Jim Hagerty offered the view that once people became accustomed to his peculiarly Midwestern way of expressing himself, they began to like having Wilson around. Hagerty was impressed with Wilson's "education" in the ways of the Pentagon and believed that he made a generally successful transition from life in the private sector.[20] All in all, Wilson had enough support from his boss and others to last five years in a complex, difficult, and often thankless role.

The few people in Wilson's corner believed that Senate Democrats were being less than fair to him. The *New York Daily News*, in a June piece entitled "Oh, Let Charlie Talk," admitted that Wilson "acts like a bull in a china shop now and then. But he is an ace executive and has done an excellent Defense Department job up to now.... What's wrong with having at least one Cabinet officer who always says what he thinks?"²¹ Other columnists agreed that Wilson's main problem was his style rather than his substantive views. *Newsday* editorialized that "Wilson's manner is the root of more trouble than any real ineptitude.... Some of the biggest bobbles he has made have been tactless—but they did express the truth as he saw it."²² Congressman Gerald Ford objected to General Ridgway's criticisms of Wilson and commended the secretary's concern for American servicemen.²³

Sadly, Wilson would continue to fall short of Eisenhower's expectations, despite the four and a half years he spent at the Pentagon. Cliff Roberts reflected the president's thoughts and words when he mentioned Wilson's "great anxiety and hesitancy in the absence of a specific order from the president to do this or that." Ike told Roberts that he felt he had completely failed to get Wilson to assume more responsibility.²⁴ Yet he could not bring himself to let him go.

New Look Debate Intensifies

Wilson presented to Congress the administration's third New Look budget—for fiscal year 1957—at the beginning of 1956. It continued the reductions in army capabilities, which were compensated for by accelerated production of the air force's B-52 bomber. By now the air force budget was more than twice that of the army.

After two years of going along with the administration's New Look program, its opponents in Congress were resolved to mount a stronger offensive. Their resolution had been strengthened by the Soviet unveiling of a new intercontinental bomber the year before, which seemed to heighten American vulnerability to attack. The difficulty, as always, was challenging Eisenhower's authority as a military leader and planner. The fact that 1956 was an election year increased the political appeal of the issue for Democrats. In truth, they had little else to run on—the economy was buoyant and international tensions had temporarily abated.

The serialization of General Ridgway's memoirs in the *Saturday Evening Post*, beginning in January, gave Democrats potent ammunition—dramatic evidence of Pentagon dissent. In his new book, Ridgway criticized the phenomenon of "civilian secretaries making military decisions on a basis of political considerations." He recalled exchanges of views with Wilson from which he "came away convinced that either the Secretary was a man who operated on a level of genius so high that I could not grasp his meaning or that considerations beyond the ken of a soldier's logic were influencing his thinking."²⁵

Senate critics pounced. Estes Kefauver said it was "wonderful for the country to have [Ridgway] speak up."[26]

Wilson's reaction to the criticism was muted. "I have no quarrel with General Ridgway and I am sure he is a dedicated officer that has done a great deal for his country," he said at a press conference. "I don't expect any of my associates to polish the apple by seeming to agree with me when in their hearts they don't."[27] The president was much more angry than Wilson with Ridgway's disloyalty, but he limited himself to denying that politics had in any way interfered with his military decisions.

Only a few weeks later, the assistant secretary for R&D of the air force, Trevor Gardner, suddenly resigned over what he considered inadequate funding for missile development. He then wrote an article for *Look* magazine calling budget cuts in that area "short-sighted." In his memoirs, Sherman Adams recalled that "everybody who left the Defense Department after a battle with Wilson seemed to write a magazine article about the fight later."[28] An irate president privately endorsed "a new type of oath, to be taken by all military and civilian officials who served in the Pentagon" pledging non-disclosure of security information after their tours ended.[29]

The Gardner resignation fed the fears of conservative columnists like Joe Alsop that the Russians were ahead of the United States in the development of ballistic missiles. In an open letter to Wilson, Joe Alsop accused him of "ignoring all the unpleasant facts reported by the intelligence services and faithfully following your own natural instincts (with some help from the budgetary policies of your friend, George Humphrey)." Sarcastically, he thanked Wilson for allowing the Russians a path to nuclear superiority.[30]

Even the president admitted that a Soviet breakthrough in this area would be psychologically harmful to the nation. He authorized additional funds for missile research and development, but he told Wilson that he did so with great trepidation. All three services would be involved in the missile program, and he anticipated problems of coordination and duplication of effort.[31]

The concern for the adequacy of the American missile program spread to Congress, where Democrats began to argue that a "bomber gap" had opened up between Soviet and U.S. forces—a charge that the air force was only too willing to confirm in public testimony. The result, to the administration's chagrin, was a formal Senate investigation of American air power, headed by Senator Symington.

Throughout the spring, Wilson dutifully continued to defend the New Look in congressional hearings and public speeches. He held a press conference in March to address public concern about American air power, saying

13. 1956: Wilson's Troubles Worsen

he did not wish to get into a "numbers game" with the Russians and try to match them plane for plane. He pleaded for the trust of the public. "I do wish that some folks would get away from the theory that [the Pentagon] is made up of brass, bunglers and bureaucrats," he said, "because that is not what it is."[32] A few weeks later, Wilson described the Symington hearings as partisan politics and predicted that the senator would find out that "he doesn't know as much as he thinks he knows."[33]

Ike's refusal to be stampeded into unwise spending by congressional criticism reflected not only his knowledge of the true state of Soviet air strength (thanks to intelligence reporting) but also his resistance to political pressure. The problem was that the issue loomed large in the 1956 presidential campaign, and Republicans were nervous about being seen as overly complacent.

Despite all Eisenhower had done to ensure a unified perspective on the part of the service chiefs, by early 1956 the air force and army were openly promoting their separate views via public relations campaigns and selective leaks of classified information. Though by now tired of having to repeat himself on this subject, the president gathered the joint chiefs in February and tried to impress upon them their responsibility to set aside service loyalties and think only of the national interest. He hammered home the same point two months later—the services should be talking to each other and deciding how each can help the other. "If they are not doing this kind of thing," he asked in frustration, "what in the world are they doing?"[34]

Pressure from Congress did nothing to dissuade Eisenhower from continuing to look for ways to cut the military. In a contentious meeting with Admiral Radford and budget officials in March 1956, he echoed Humphrey's primary talking point—that a sound economy was an essential component of national security. He wondered aloud why no one from Defense could say: "Let's get rid of something." People he had known all his life, Ike complained, were asking for more and more—a comment that seemed to reveal a sense of betrayal. The Defense Department had not yet made a strenuous effort to achieve a "Spartan defense structure." Extravagance and waste were still on his mind: "I say the patriot today is the fellow who can do the job with less money."[35] When budget chief Brundage proposed an orientation course for new officials who would be joining the administration if Ike were reelected, Wilson quipped that he needed a course on how to save money.[36]

In support of Ike's demands for spending restraint at the Pentagon, Humphrey put the generals on the spot by insisting that they relate their resource demands more clearly to budgetary limitations. He understood the importance of new missile programs, but he felt older programs should then be eliminated and some troops brought home from overseas to keep expenses steady. Maxwell Taylor, for one, felt overpowered by the relentless pressure, which placed him constantly on the defensive.[37]

Eisenhower's memos to Wilson during the spring reflected his increased impatience. In March he expressed doubt that much progress had been made in cutting civilian personnel in each of the services, as had been promised. He continued: "There is one disappointing feature about my three years' experience in dealing with the Defense Problem. It is that every recommendation made by the military authorities seems to be for an increase in strength or in money or both. It seems odd that such recommendations are so rarely accompanied by a suggestion that money could be saved in some of our great and complex logistic or administrative operations."[38]

At about the same time, the J.C.S. issued another paper declaring that the influence and relative strength of the United States were on a steep decline. Once again, it criticized American foreign policy as passive and ineffective. To avoid the "great jeopardy" in which the country would soon find itself, it advocated a substantial increase in the military budget in the years 1958 through 1960. The president told Radford and Wilson he would not accept the "dark picture" drawn by the joint chiefs. If they were correct, Ike added scornfully, "we should go to field conditions, declare an emergency, increase the military budget and even go to a garrison state."[39]

In an attempt to press his view that more spending was needed, as well as to take the wind out of the Symington air power hearings, Wilson submitted a supplemental budget request of $550 million for 1956 to buy more intercontinental bombers. In April, Ike accepted this idea and used it in talks with air force leaders to secure their buy-in for an otherwise spare budget. Wilson begged for their support, telling them that he would be unhappy "if all top people do not battle it out on this basis."[40] At this meeting, Humphrey suggested that the Defense Department review American security commitments worldwide—obviously with a view toward eliminating those deemed least important.

The increasing contentiousness of defense spending drove Wilson's frustration to new heights. One day he was on Capitol Hill defending its adequacy, and the next he was at the White House trying to explain why the Pentagon could not cut more. The dissatisfaction with defense policy apparent in congressional testimony by Taylor and General Nathan Twining in March only added to the credibility of the president's critics.

Until 1956, at considerable cost to his reputation at the Pentagon, Wilson had conscientiously implemented Eisenhower's orders to hold the line. By the spring, however, even Wilson seemed to have stopped believing that further defense cuts were either possible or desirable. Research and development, upgrades to older equipment, multiple commitments, and inflation were pushing costs up. "Simply to carry out current national security policies is certain to cost billions more over the next few years," he told the president. Budget Director Hughes called Wilson's air of resignation a signal of a "complete change of atmosphere" in Washington.[41]

Wilson's burdens were increased when his army chief of staff took up where Ridgway, his predecessor, left off. In a May 1956 meeting, General Taylor told Wilson, Humphrey and the president, that reducing the size of the army would prove to be a fatal strategic error. He argued with what today would seem like irrefutable logic that an overemphasis on nuclear weapons would "freeze out" the conventional forces required to handle "small-war situations." It made no sense to him that the military would have only a nuclear option in a low-level regional conflict. A flexible response was needed to suppress local aggression while making sure that hostilities did not escalate into general war.[42]

Younger officers in particular were attracted to the "flexible response" doctrine that Taylor had articulated, not least because it seemed to them the only way to guarantee the army's future. Soon this movement was being termed the "revolt of the colonels." Army officers provided the *New York Times* with studies supporting their view, and the newspaper added fuel to the fire by inviting the air force to publicly rebut army arguments.

But Ike held firm. He declared it "fatuous" to believe that the two superpowers, once involved in a local conflict, would not use the most powerful weapons at their disposal. Tactical nuclear weapons, he told Taylor, had "come to be practically accepted as integral parts of modern armed forces" and the military should plan "on the basis of the use of tactical atomic weapons against military targets in any small war in which the United States might be involved."[43] To both Eisenhower and Humphrey, flexible response seemed likely to lead to another Korean War.

In July, Humphrey, Radford, the president, and budget director Hughes again went to the mat over the numbers. The J.C.S. was determined to uphold the preeminence of military strategy over fiscal restraints. Leaks from their planning sessions that huge defense increases would be required in FY-1958 elicited the usual furious response from Eisenhower. After weeks of discussions, despite time-consuming crises in Hungary and the Suez, a total defense budget of about $38 billion was hammered out. It was more than Ike wanted, but he hoped thereby to deter future "end-runs" by the services to Congress.

People around Eisenhower believed that Wilson had lost control of Pentagon finances. In her diary, Ann Whitman noted the growing gulf between Ike and the military. "I gathered that Wilson and the others simply do not see the president's point of view, whether willfully or not I do not know."[44] Part of Wilson's problem was that many of the preconditions for the New Look policy had yet to be implemented, or perhaps never would be. American forces had not been drawn down in Europe and Asia, army resource demands continued to have high-level support in Congress and elsewhere, and nuclear weapons had yet to be integrated with conventional arms as envisioned. The new doctrine would probably not be able to reduce defense costs significantly until the long process of force restructuring and mission redefinition was completed. Wilson admitted his frustration, saying he felt "like a frog trying to jump out of a well."[45]

The response from the budget cutters to Wilson's perceived surrender to the uniformed military was to double down on their demand for more internal discipline. Roland Hughes proclaimed that the administration had "reached a vital crossroads." To George Humphrey, it meant no more balanced budgets until "a basic review of our troop deployments and ... our national security policies" was undertaken.[46] He feared that the country was headed for a "warfare economy," sustained by high taxes and defense spending.[47] The unpalatable alternatives, they agreed, were a tax increase or a budget deficit.

In April, Senator Symington had begun holding his air power hearings. Their timing and focus strongly suggested that their primary purpose was to influence the November elections. Called to testify, air force brass were unable to pass up the opportunity to complain about perceived inadequacies in every relevant war fighting category. The hearings received a good deal of public attention, even though much of the testimony was based on estimates of Soviet activity and strength that turned out to be incorrect.

Wilson testified before the Symington committee in late June and early July. Little new substantive ground was broken, and the main feature of his appearance was sharp conflict with several senators, especially Sam Ervin and Henry Jackson. Wilson sparred repeatedly with Jackson:

> JACKSON: I just want to say this, Mr. Wilson, that the difficulties you have had with the Congress have stemmed from your own statements and when not a single member of your own party stood up and defended you, I think that speaks for itself.
> WILSON: I might tell you a story. This is what the mama whale said to the baby calf.... "Son, always remember that is only when you are blowing that you are liable to be harpooned."
> JACKSON: I think the public knows who has been doing a lot of blowing.[48]

In the end, the Democrats (and the air force) achieved a limited victory. The 1957 defense budget contained a billion dollars more than the adminis-

13. 1956: Wilson's Troubles Worsen

tration had requested—the only time since Eisenhower had become president that Congress had done that. The president signed it without comment.

But his anger at the air force's complaints to Congress surfaced when he met with his civilian military chiefs in July for preliminary discussions of the 1958 budget. He was in no mood for pleasantries. When Wilson remarked that the services seemed to have goals of their own, Ike spoke with disdain about military "requirements." "I have listened to the term all my life," he said. "You people never seem to learn whom you are supposed to be protecting. Not the generals, but the American people."[49]

Ike's continuing frustration was revealed in correspondence with his old friend Swede Hazlett. "Merely 'getting tough' on my part is not an answer. I simply must find men who have the breadth of understanding and devotion to their country rather than to a single Service that will bring about better solutions than I get now," a sentence the president set down in italics.[50]

In an attempt to demonstrate that the services were now on the same page, Wilson held a joint press conference in May 1956, with all the top Pentagon officers in attendance. Wilson read a stern statement that acknowledged "honest differences" and "reasonable competition" among the services but asserted the primacy of his office and the J.C.S. in assigning roles and missions.

The press conference came across to the media as the staged event that it surely was. *Time* magazine called it "mock solidarity."[51] On the positive side, Wilson's intervention set in motion administrative actions that resulted in the punishment of the "colonels" and kept the army from challenging Wilson again. But the air force continued to undermine the administration's budget on Capitol Hill.

By now, Eisenhower's patience was nearly exhausted. He denounced the inter-service feud, especially the inevitable release of classified information in support of each side's views. Wilson was equally appalled by the lack of internal discipline. "There's a bunch of eager beavers down in the Army staff," he said. "If they stick their heads out again, I'll chop them off."[52] Appalled though he might have been, it was his job to see that sniping and public relations wars between the services did not happen. His bluster did little to hide his failure to rein in the embarrassingly public dissent and reduced still further his usefulness to the beleaguered president.

With the greater importance of missile development, Admiral Radford noted that the roles and missions of the services relating to missiles were yet to be resolved. This was a task for which Wilson had neither the knowledge nor the credibility. He issued occasional rulings that he hoped would put a stop to inter-service sniping about their separate responsibilities. It seemed sensible, for example, to stop or limit the development of an aviation capability within the army. Accordingly, he prohibited most army work on missile systems and aircraft, but his edict was met with determined opposition from army planners. Wilson then told the president that separate missile programs would produce beneficial competition, a conclusion that Ike questioned. Over the course of Eisenhower's two terms, the army nearly doubled its number of airplanes.

Wilson continued to ask the president to make his decisions for him. In a meeting held the day after the November election, he raised several unresolved disputes that needed settling before the 1958 budget could be put in final form. These disputes ran the gamut from research and development priorities and overseas deployments to force levels and military assistance programs. Ike looked over the list and called the issues "largely technical, and would require his getting back into the whole atmosphere of military planning," which of course he was not willing to do.[53]

Late in the year, under tight constraints laid down by the president—a defense budget of around $38 billion, which was at least $10 billion less than the services had previously requested—Wilson and his senior officers looked over the numbers for fiscal year 1958. The services again used external events to argue their case for more resources, citing the recently ended Middle East crisis and Soviet invasion of Hungary. Ike was unmoved. He confronted the joint chiefs with a request that they support the budget he was demanding, and they reluctantly agreed.

So 1956 ended unhappily for all the major players in the defense debate. No solution to the budget impasse had emerged. Raymond Saulnier, who replaced Burns as head of the C.E.A., saw "no substantial outlook for improvement in the balance of receipts and expenditures," even assuming continued economic growth. At the Pentagon, Wilson described expenses as spiraling out of control, with the only options for meeting the president's demands being the phasing out of entire programs and large-scale reduction of forces. He began planning force reductions after another appeal to Ike for more budget flexibility was again denied.

Eisenhower felt that his attempts to reform the military establishment and rein in defense costs were going nowhere. After the year-end confrontation over the defense budget, Wilson informed him that a rebellion was brewing. It was apparent that the service chiefs had merely acquiesced in, rather than accepted, the president's budget dictates.

The only hopeful conclusion that could be drawn by the White House was that if budget cutters and budget enhancers were equally dissatisfied, then the course being pursued must be very close to Eisenhower's preferred middle way. But the president was not drawing that conclusion. The best news was that the federal government's 1957 budget ended up in the black, thanks to the rise in tax revenue caused by a booming economy, but Ike felt an opportunity for a more healthy surplus had been lost.

The constant pressure from the White House ensured that Wilson would never achieve a meeting of the minds with the career military. Even the praise from Pentagon subordinates that occasionally made its way to the press had an obvious down side. "Wilson was one of the greatest guys I ever worked with," remarked one subordinate. "Most bosses want you to come in, sit down, say what you've got to say and get out. He wants you to sit back, relax, and have a thorough visit."[54]

As Wilson's difficulties mounted, a well-meaning colleague, presidential aide Bernard Shanley, offered him some candid advice. The secretary came out of a meeting with Eisenhower one day and decided to pay Shanley a visit. "Do you think I should quit? he asked. "I'm going to give you the answer in all honesty," Shanley replied. "You're not going to like it ... but I mean this very sincerely. You should have gotten out a couple of years ago." According to Shanley, Wilson looked as though he had been hit in the head with an axe.[55]

The Wilson-Humphrey Relationship

Along with the institutional struggle among government agencies on spending issues, Wilson and Humphrey had to manage their antagonistic official relations. The two men held equal rank, but Humphrey's demands for budget cuts felt like orders, and often were. Some Washington observers assumed that Wilson was Humphrey's agent at the Pentagon, bent on cutting the military budget to Humphrey's specifications, but the record suggests otherwise.

They entered the administration as friends and allies and attempted to remain so. Humphrey was often angry at the way Wilson was treated by the media and Congress. The 1954 "bird dog" flap, in which Wilson implied that he had little sympathy for the unemployed, disturbed Humphrey so much that he met with Republican party leaders to discuss the situation and then boarded a plane to Chicago, where Wilson was making a speech. As he was preparing to go on stage, Humphrey arrived, patted him on the back, wished him good luck, and then returned to Washington.[56] The sequence of events also suggests he was worried that fallout from the incident might affect Republican candidates in the November elections.

Humphrey's budget-cutting ardor was, of course, not personally directed at Wilson. He was honestly upset by what he viewed as the maddening opacity of the defense budget. He marveled at what he viewed as the Pentagon's misleading estimates of the operational effects of various budget cuts. If you ask "these military people" to make reasonable reductions in specific programs, "they have to cut the whole heart out of their entire activities," he wrote to Budget Director Brundage in frustration. "I have never seen anything quite like it in my life, and I hope that somebody someday will be able to figure out how to really get at it."[57]

Humphrey's noisy exhortations to Wilson as early as 1953 on budget cutting were bound to raise the defense secretary's hackles during a time when he was still trying to assess military requirements. That summer, Humphrey urged Wilson to expedite a J.C.S. study of defense strategy geared toward saving large amounts of money. Wilson apparently dragged his feet on this "order" until Eisenhower expressed his own interest in the study.[58]

As we have seen, their Cabinet relationship began with Humphrey's surprising tongue-lashing of the defense secretary in 1953 about the importance of not just "patching up the old jalopy" and Wilson's negative reaction. Drew Pearson was not wrong when he wrote that the debate "puts in direct opposition to each other two of the ablest and biggest businessmen in the Eisenhower Cabinet."[59]

When Humphrey spoke on budget issues, he noted the importance of a strong military but always with a reminder of the larger budgetary task at hand. In a talk to a C.I.O. conference in May 1954, he admitted that assuring national security was expensive but that it had to be funded intelligently. "We have to be sure," he added, "that what we do will enable your old friend, Charlie Wilson, to get us more security for less money and greater efficiency."[60]

Wilson's growing unease with Pentagon cuts as time passed was sometimes displayed in angry responses to questions about Treasury's influence on the defense budget. He told *Fortune* magazine that the defense budget needed to increase by at least $5 billion in fiscal year 1956. He was asked what his "good friend" George Humphrey would say about that. "I don't care what he says," was Wilson's testy response.[61] His irritation was increased by the knowledge that Humphrey had the distinct advantage in their relationship, because he knew what he wanted and Wilson was usually conflicted.

Along with influencing the Defense Department budget, Humphrey even made his influence felt in high-level Pentagon personnel decisions. Cliff Roberts recalled that Eisenhower was upset when Robert Anderson, who Ike admired greatly, decided to leave his post as deputy defense secretary. The president asked Humphrey to figure out a way to persuade him to stay. But

Humphrey, with some embarrassment, told him that it was too late—he and Wilson had already agreed on a successor to Anderson.[62]

Coordinating with Humphrey on a defense appointment added credibility to the frequent charge that Wilson was the junior member of the relationship. Some journalists came to the same conclusion. Conservative columnist Joe Alsop wrote that Wilson "in effect operates as a Treasury representative within the Department of Defense" and that he had a "working partnership with Humphrey in which Humphrey is the guiding spirit." As such, continued the columnist, his first duty is to think about tax cuts, his second, balancing the budget and, "as a very poor third," defense needs.[63] In a sarcastic note, he said that Wilson must sympathize with Humphrey's view that budgets were more important than defending the country from the Soviet military.

Wilson's penchant for impolitic remarks kept him in the doghouse with Eisenhower throughout his term of office. One of his defenders, in an article titled "Oh, Let Charlie Talk," acknowledged his "bull-in-a-china-shop" style but pointed out that he was always willing to express the truth as he saw it (1957 Herblock Cartoon, © The Herb Block Foundation).

The theme of Wilson as Humphrey's puppet, as his "faithful crony," and as Treasury's "spy" at the Pentagon made a regular appearance in Alsop's columns. If Wilson was not upset by these inferences, it was because he believed that Alsop's real goal was to raise doubts about the wisdom of Ike's defense cuts rather than to portray Wilson as weak.

Wilson's difficulty in staying the budget-cutting course was due to his daily exposure to the counterarguments of military experts. As he became more knowledgeable about the trade-offs involved in eliminating programs and forces, he tried to balance presidential concerns with those of the career officers he represented. He wound up with a clearer view of the issue than Humphrey, who heard no such dissent at Treasury or from the White House. He began to resent Humphrey's disinterest in the details of how budget cuts affected military readiness. But Eisenhower and Humphrey were more inclined to believe that Wilson was too easily persuaded by the arguments of his generals and admirals.

At a press conference in October 1955, only a few days after Eisenhower's heart attack, Humphrey chose to address speculation that he was feuding with Wilson. He assured the public that efforts were continuing to eliminate wasteful spending. Then he said:

> Now, there has been a good deal of conversation about the situation between Mr. Wilson and myself.... There is no controversy or problem between Mr. Wilson and myself at all. We had lunch together yesterday. There never has been any time when I wanted to or thought that there should be any change in the program of defense.... I don't have anything to do with it.
>
> Mr. Wilson, on the other hand, has assured me ... that he is doing everything that he can do to try to eliminate unnecessary expenditures.... Now, that's all I can ask. It's all I want. And I have known Mr. Wilson for a great many years—we have been associated for a long time, and I have a lot of confidence in him and his ability to get things done.[64]

These words concealed the true state of affairs. Wilson's separate institutional perspective inevitably led him to resist Humphrey's pressure. The title of a *New York Herald Tribune* piece—"Rise in Arms Spending Blocks Economy Drive"—aptly summarized their intensifying conflict. The author described the budget as "being blown to bits" by the unexpected increases in defense spending. Humphrey was said to have expressed his ire to Wilson in frequent face-to-face conversations and phone calls. Wilson did not like the trend either, but he professed helplessness—prices were simply going up, he said with an air of resignation.[65]

The one factor that kept a lid on this and other conflicts across the administration was shared loyalty to a president who was admired and respected by everyone who worked for him. For the most part, this loyalty transcended the differences between Humphrey and Wilson. They were always on the same team.

The Draft-Dodging Flap

After the discouraging year of 1956, and considering Wilson's well-known proclivities for overwork, his health and psychological well being were increasingly at risk. He worked so hard on the 1958 defense budget that Budget Director Brundage said: "You could actually see him sweat."[66] Before the 1956 presidential election, rumors circulated that he would not serve in a second Eisenhower term. Asked about his plans on a television news program, he said: "When I took the job on, I made no time commitment and I haven't established any in my mind yet." After Eisenhower was reelected in November, Wilson remained at his post. He decided tentatively that the fiscal year 1958 budget would be his last.

He made yet another unfortunate public comment as 1957 began that caused him renewed difficulty. The subject this time was the National Guard.

Alone among the so-called reserve forces, Guard members were not required to take six months of basic training. This feature of Guard duty was very helpful in its recruiting efforts, and Guard officers wished to protect it. But in January Wilson decided that uniform standards for all reserve units were needed. He directed that all National Guard recruits would henceforth undergo the same six-month program required of other reservists. During his congressional testimony on behalf of the new policy, he also expressed the view that "the Guard was a sort of scandal during the Korean War, a draft-dodging business. A boy seventeen to eighteen and a half could enlist in the National Guard and not be drafted to fight in Korea."[67]

The "New Look" gave Defense Secretary Wilson the thankless task of altering the delicate resource balance among the services. As Pentagon brass squabbled over their budgets and missions, Wilson said he "could not understand it, unless the Army and Air Force plan on fighting each other" (1956 Herblock Cartoon, © The Herb Block Foundation).

There was some truth to Wilson's comments—many young men had joined the Guard during the war for that very reason. But the Guard had many defenders, some of them in Congress, and the infelicitous phrase "draft dodging" struck a nerve. Amid the storm of criticism were more calls for Wilson's resignation. Senator Morse said: "Wilson was never qualified for the job and he is not now."[68]

The defense secretary met with the press a few days later as he was leaving a meeting with Eisenhower. He insisted that his sole aim was to improve National Guard training. "The people who are trying to perpetuate the inefficiency," he maintained, "are doing the Guard damage." A moment later, Wilson again put his foot in his mouth. When asked what he had been discussing with the president, he declined to answer. "This is not my dunghill," he replied. "Anything to be announced, somebody else [at the White House] ought to announce it."[69] The comment caused some critical headlines, but Wilson was innocent of any malicious intent. The word "dunghill," as used long ago by a Roman philosopher, was not meant to be pejorative—it was synonymous with bailiwick or turf.

A day later, Eisenhower prepared to meet the press, which immediately asked for a comment on the National Guard controversy. Publicly, he agreed

Defense Secretary Wilson and his wife, Jessie, in a light moment with the president. Jessie Wilson became so upset by public criticism of her husband that she told a reporter in early 1957 that she was "disgusted" by it. "You reach a point sometimes and this was it" (National Park Service/Eisenhower Presidential Library and Museum).

with Wilson that new Guard recruits needed "at least six months of good, hard, basic training," but he admitted that the Secretary was "short-cutting and making a very, I think, unwise statement."[70] Relieved not to be facing a repudiation from the president, Wilson decided to stick to his guns and ask Congress to approve the revised Guard training.

At this juncture, there was an unexpected development. Jessie Wilson, the secretary's wife, had endured enough criticism of her husband. She told a *Washington Post* reporter that the president's remarks were unwarranted and that she was recommending that he quit his job. The *Post* quoted Mrs. Wilson as saying: "I know the President means to be fair but once in a while a slap on the back would be helpful to one who is doing a good job. I know he [Wilson] speaks bluntly, but it takes courage to do it.... I know he is unpredictable, but maybe some people would have a different view if they were working seven days a week at a job like he has. I've stood back and listened to criticism until I'm disgusted of it. You reach a point sometimes and this was it."[71] Along with the mounting strain of living vicariously through five years of constant controversy, or more likely because of it, Mrs. Wilson had developed ulcers and had just undergone treatment for them.

The public responded with an outpouring of sympathy for the couple. Hundreds of letters agreed with Wilson that the National Guard was not well trained and praised his candor for saying so. The White House received some correspondence that admonished Ike for failing to give Wilson more encouragement. Moreover, the public flap inaugurated a sharp debate in Congress and among National Guard leaders about the need for better training. Sensing the public mood, several Republican senators actually expressed the hope that Wilson would continue in office. The Guard matter was resolved in February with a compromise measure that made most of the training improvements while delaying their implementation.

Again, Eisenhower gave the embattled Wilson his full support while confessing serious doubts to those around him. On a human level, the National Guard "fracas," as Ann Whitman described it, caused Ike considerable discomfort. He was moved to write a note to Mrs. Wilson regretting that his comments had been misinterpreted as a rebuke.[72] He also wrote to Wilson expressing his "astonishment, not to say chagrin" that the newspapers were furthering this misperception. He continued in a labored fashion: "If my mere observation that I thought your particular words of description concerning the Guard were unwise seemed to you to be a 'rebuke,' then all I can say is that I hope you will realize that such was not my intention." In conclusion, he expressed thanks for all Wilson had done for the administration and the hope that he would stay on for as long as he liked.[73]

Privately, Ike confided to Ann Whitman some very different sentiments. Wilson can do more to ruin himself than any man, he told her in astonishment over the Guard controversy. The reason for his difficulties, he believed, was that he fancied himself a "sort of homespun philosopher."[74] The episode underlined the existence of a persistent and troublesome issue—judgment—that time and experience would not resolve.

14

The Price of Prosperity

Eisenhower's war on spending and the debate over the New Look took place against a background of unparalleled prosperity. As the recession of 1953–54 faded into the rear view mirror, the economy shifted into high gear, powered by a low jobless rate, a vast increase in consumer goods spending, and low interest rates. The mid-1950s saw sizeable gains in the average American's standard of living, leading to the era's gauzy reputation as a golden age of middle-class contentment. Manufacturing companies in the United States employed millions of workers who, backed by strong unions, were paid generous wages. Coupled with a less threatening international environment, the widespread good times gave Eisenhower a commanding advantage heading into the 1956 presidential election.

At the same time, the strong economy highlighted unresolved issues that dimmed the administration's satisfaction. Higher American incomes increased the amount of tax revenue flowing into Washington, but differences of opinion existed on what to do with that money. On the one hand, an array of unmet national needs brought pressure from within and outside of government for spending hikes on both defense and social programs. On the other hand, if expenses could be held down, the long-sought goal of a balanced budget, or even a surplus, would be attainable.

Humphrey had a game plan for the final years of the administration. He would continue to demand a squeeze in federal spending until enough money was saved to finance a sizeable tax cut in 1956—in time to guarantee Ike's reelection. He could then return to private life having accomplished his most important goals. He anticipated opposition from several strong voices in the Cabinet, but as long as he had the president's support, the odds for success seemed to be in his favor.

Spending Pressures Mount

The administration had been successful in bringing government spending down—from $74 billion in fiscal 1953, to $68 billion in fiscal 1954, and then to $65 billion in fiscal 1955—but by 1956, the rapid growth of the country had created needs that were difficult for the federal government to ignore. Domestic programs, such as Social Security, unemployment compensation and farm subsidies, were becoming more expensive. The government was also undertaking other important initiatives—a modernization of the country's civil aviation facilities, a program of small-business lending, medical and atomic energy research, an upgrade of the postal service, the construction of an interstate highway system, and an expansion of Export-Import bank rescue operations abroad. As Wilson had long been arguing, the costs of defense technology were rapidly growing. After adding in rising inflation, the impact of higher interest rates on debt, and foreign aid commitments, holding the line on the federal budget was becoming nearly impossible.

Humphrey courted increasing criticism by citing "pressure groups" as the cause of bigger budgets, as though the demands stemmed from ordinary selfishness. With exquisite sarcasm, one economist noted that the airlines, "with their deplorably selfish opposition to accidents" were "no doubt a pressure group too."[1]

The strongest domestic spending pressures came from within a Cabinet department subject to Humphrey's constant harangues and headed by a former Humphrey appointee. Marion Folsom had served as deputy treasury secretary for two years, but he adopted a different perspective after he was appointed secretary of health, education and welfare in August 1955. He was persuaded of the importance of his new agency's social and educational programs and became an advocate for more spending in these areas. He found it "natural that [federal] programs would cost more, not to mention the new needs developing." This was the same man who had helped to create the Social Security system in the 1930s, so it was not surprising that he came to champion additional social services.

Folsom was persistent and persuasive, and Ike often gave in to his eloquent pleas for increased resources. "I felt the need for many of these [H.E.W.] programs," Folsom recalled. "Especially when they were trying to hold expenditures down, I was arguing with the budget people all the time."[2] Humphrey was so irritated by Folsom's small victories that he directed some of his anger at the president. "They've got to cut out all this welfare nonsense," he complained to a columnist with a wave toward the White House. He noted with alarm that two-thirds of federal budget increases in 1956 were for non-defense

14. The Price of Prosperity

related programs. "Those people across the street," he noted, "never had to meet a payroll." A journalist reported that Humphrey told the president "in vigorous, unvarnished language just how he felt," but Ike had smiled and said nothing.[3]

As we have already noted, the president was deeply conflicted. Of course, he saw the world differently than Humphrey—he was a self-described liberal when it came to satisfying human needs—but that did not mean he easily gave in to Folsom's arguments. According to an Eisenhower aide, Folsom would keep after him until "finally in desperation the President would throw up his hands and say 'okay,'" later claiming that he had not meant to do so.[4] Some other Cabinet members also found that persistence and good timing would sometimes be rewarded.

One reason for Eisenhower's ambivalence was that he saw political benefits to a slightly higher level of spending. He had long been trying to gain acceptance for his "modern Republican" philosophy among party loyalists, seeing it as the best way to compete with Democrats in national elections. He also calculated that his approval of selected budget increases might win support from congressional Democrats for other programs he valued, such as foreign assistance. Going in this direction, however, risked antagonizing increasingly vocal conservative Republicans, many of whom thought the president was giving up the fight against big-government liberalism.

Another problem for Humphrey was that, by 1955, he was often outnumbered by more pragmatic Cabinet officials, such as Vice President Nixon. In a January session, Humphrey questioned the wisdom of a school construction program, to be run with federal grants, and asked that it be submitted to his department for review. Ike agreed, but lest Humphrey consider the referral a license to suggest cuts, he went on to say that, in his view, the program did not go far enough. Nixon chimed in with praise of the "moderate and progressive character" of the school proposal. The discussion ended with Humphrey in retreat.

At the same Cabinet meeting, Nixon complimented the annual Economic Report of the president for its effective presentation of the administration's economic philosophy. This was the same report that Burns had drafted and that Humphrey had strongly criticized for its allegedly socialist content. Ike had pronounced it a "magnificent document."[5] Humphrey said nothing.

Humphrey and Budget Director Hughes fumed at the Cabinet's lack of resolution and the drift toward increased spending. "The direction must come from the top," insisted Hughes. "The staffs want to do it. [But] they're still going in the wrong direction."[6] But Ike refused to give Humphrey a blank check. When the treasury secretary urged Eisenhower to order strict limits on departmental budgets for fiscal year 1956, the president declined, in view of the uncertainty of defense needs.

Despite his customary opposition to expensive government programs, Humphrey seems to have been a supporter of the one for which Eisenhower is best remembered—the interstate highway system. In fact, Gabriel Hauge called him "one of the principal agitators for the whole idea."[7] Humphrey believed not only in its usefulness to the country but that the spending would offset any tendency toward recession that might follow the Korean War. The key was to find a way of financing the project without budgetary distress. "The only way it can be done," he said to Sherman Adams in 1955, "is on some combination of direct road tolls as security for special bonds and increased taxes levied for this purpose."[8] Ultimately, it was mostly financed "off budget," in much the manner he suggested.

Humphrey also seems to have favored a long-overdue pay raise for Federal government workers. Burns argued that it would fuel inflation and lead to salary demands from other sectors of the economy, but Humphrey countered that national increases in productivity would allow such an increase without inflation.[9] He may also have seen a political upside to the raise.

Campaigning for Tax Cuts

The issue of spending cuts, of course, was closely related to the purpose of those cuts. For Humphrey, the goal was to reduce taxes. The president understood the political attractiveness of tax cuts, but he always tried to take the long view and do what he felt was right for the country, rather than what would poll well.

Humphrey argued—in a manner similar to a later generation of "supply-siders"—that tax cuts would stimulate economic activity and bring in more rather than less revenue. At his insistence, Ike agreed to add a sentence to the January 1955 budget message mentioning the desirability of tax cuts. The president did this even though he had a strong feeling that a balanced budget might not allow tax reductions. He confided to Chief of Staff Adams that Humphrey was "too quick to recommend tax reduction on the basis of anticipated savings in expenditures that might not necessarily materialize."[10]

Humphrey remained unapologetic about his role as the Cabinet nag. Some aspect of the budget was discussed at every meeting, "and if somebody didn't bring it up, I did—because we just had to drive and drive and drive every minute to hold expenses down.... It had to come up every day. You just had to keep working at it all the time."[11] Later in 1955, he told the group that if a balanced budget could not be achieved by the following June, "we ought to hang our heads and put our tails between our legs."[12]

At a May budget review, the president served notice that cutting taxes was not his first priority. He said emphatically that he would fight a tax cut if achieved at the expense of a balanced budget "as long as I am here."[13] He suggested that any surplus in fiscal year 1957 might instead be applied to a reduction of the national debt. This was not what Humphrey wanted to hear. He responded that he did not think the economic boom could continue without a tax reduction. He urged the president to aim at even lower expenditures so that both a balanced budget and a tax cut could be achieved at the same time.

Adams recalled that Humphrey's comment started an "outburst of arguments around the table."[14] Ike said he did not see how additional reductions in spending could be made. To Secretary Wilson's chagrin, Humphrey countered that another $2.5 billion in defense cuts were attainable. The president cautioned against expecting much more savings from the Pentagon—only "small amounts of fat" would probably be found.

Finally, Ike's temper flared. "Look," he responded, "we started from $40.6 billion," meaning that his administration had already brought down spending significantly. But before he could finish, Humphrey interjected "And pick another $2.5 billion out, if [you're] devoted to it." He then pled with the other Cabinet members for one more campaign to save money. "Really go after it," he said encouragingly. Ike had the final word. Until he saw a balanced budget in "black and white," the issue of tax cuts was "one place I'm going to get stubborn."[15]

The tax cut issue continued to fester. In a story related by Ike staff member William Ewald, Humphrey confronted Burns later in 1955 when Burns announced his conclusion that tax reductions might spur inflation. "Arthur, the President can't have two advisers on taxes," Humphrey exclaimed. "He'll just have to choose between us." Burns accepted the challenge, and soon they were on Eisenhower's calendar. Ike greeted them effusively. "Boy, am I glad to see you fellows," he said. "I've just had a damn fool businessman in here, and you know what he wants? He wants me to *cut taxes*! And with inflation starting up again!" According to Ewald, Burns "almost choked with repressed laughter."[16]

Under what conditions might the president support a tax cut? The press would ask Eisenhower this question again and again during the surplus years of 1956 and 1957. Each time, he would say that balancing the budget came first. And if a surplus did materialize, he would be inclined to use it to reduce the national debt, not to reduce taxes. He reasoned that with budget cuts becoming next to impossible in the current political climate, revenues must be held steady. Tax cuts again would have to wait.

When Humphrey's exhortations to the Cabinet did not result in significantly less spending, he was not above seeking allies in Congress who might be willing to help institute reforms that would have the effect of reining in his own executive branch. Such reforms included a ceiling on supplemental appropriations and a constitutional amendment requiring balanced budgets, as well as a line-item veto for the president. This kind of maneuvering was not only irregular but naïve for its presumption that a Democratic Congress would come to the aid of a Republican administration.

Stymied on Capitol Hill, Humphrey redoubled his efforts in the executive branch. One of the most dramatic Cabinet sessions took place on August 5, 1955, during which Eisenhower surprised the participants with an "off-Agenda" subject—the FY-1956 budget. Following advice given him earlier by Humphrey, he told the group that with the administration just shy of bringing that budget into balance, he now wanted to make a "real attempt" to finish the job. If each department cut its spending by another 3 percent, that mission would be accomplished. (Humphrey had suggested 5 percent.) Adams called it a "rare command decision from Eisenhower, and he made it plain that it was to be obeyed."[17]

Before anyone else could weigh in, he emphasized "very strongly" that this push to cut agency budgets was not intended to cripple essential programs. If any Cabinet member felt that a 3 percent reduction was going to do that kind of harm, he should notify the president at once. In the end, he felt sure that there were "wasteful practices of one sort or another" that could be rooted out without damage to the national interest.

Reactions around the table were predictable. Agriculture Secretary Ezra Benson welcomed Ike's renewed commitment to frugality. Humphrey enthusiastically urged the president to consider the 3 percent cuts *already made* and to announce them as a fait accompli. A chorus of objections greeted this idea, which moved Ike to say: "The reduction is not yet a reality. It's still only an objective. We can't claim it now as an accomplished fact."[18] Humphrey replied that it was "better to do that than to have to admit another expected deficit." With Ike unyielding on the issue, he finally had to settle for a declaration that each department would "aim" for the 3 percent cut. He added a statement at end of the budget report emphasizing his view.

As a way to cut the budget, Ike's 3 percent order lacked coherence or a sense of priorities, but making across-the-board cuts of a fixed percentage was no doubt the easiest way to cut expenditures. As the president well knew, every Cabinet member was subject to tremendous pressure from below to maintain and expand his agency's programs. After absorbing multiple demands to cut expenses since 1953, the departments were unlikely to admit that another one of their programs was unnecessary and put its budget on the chopping block. Humphrey and budget director Hughes gathered the media a few days later to make a promise that "every effort will be made by everyone in government service to accomplish this result."

Eisenhower's presentation placed Cabinet members in a familiar dilemma. On the one hand, Ike was demanding a sizable cut; on the other hand, he wanted nothing "essential" eliminated. In the past couple of years, the departments had already gone a long way toward eliminating "wasteful practices of one sort or another." Who could guarantee that each department's definition of "essential" was the same? In the end, it came down to whether a given Cabinet member had the courage to press his case with a skeptical president.

The following week, Burns expressed strong support for Eisenhower's budget goal, and then went a step farther. The economy now had such a strong foundation, he noted, that merely balancing the budget would not be much of an achievement. "If we cannot produce a surplus under conditions of such unprecedented prosperity," he continued, "a question can be raised as to whether we can really manage the fiscal affairs of the country."[19] He concluded that federal expenditures must be cut without delay, while the economic expansion continued, rather than in six months or a year, when conditions might change.

Humphrey was at first delighted with these comments, but then Burns made it clear that he did not advocate a tax cut. If Eisenhower was going to demand further cuts to put the budget in balance, giving in to a tax cut would place the main goal in jeopardy while risking more inflation. Humphrey promptly countered that a tax cut would stimulate growth. Looking ahead to FY-1957, he asked the president if he would reconsider tax cuts if the surplus that year exceeded $1.5 billion. Ike again said no.

Ike's Heart Attack and After

Momentum on all of Eisenhower's goals came to an abrupt halt with his heart attack in September 1955. The event stunned the nation and the world. For several weeks, Americans held their breath, not knowing if the president would be able to return to work. It was widely assumed that, even if he did, he would not run for reelection the following year.

The administration's senior officials kept the country running smoothly in his absence. A triumvirate of Vice President Nixon, Chief of Staff Sherman

Adams, and Humphrey was steering the ship, but the entire Cabinet came together and worked harmoniously under stressful conditions. Nixon's calm and confident behavior during the crisis inspired confidence and was widely praised.

But without a strong executive presence, Humphrey's agenda suffered. He could exhort the Cabinet to cut spending, and he did, but to have the desired effect, the president had to be there to back him up. The fall of 1955 was consequently a time of drift in fiscal policy.

Eisenhower had said repeatedly in the months leading up to his illness that a tax cut was out of the question, at least until a balanced budget was an accomplished fact. But Humphrey took advantage of his absence to keep the issue open. In October, he and Hughes pressed the Cabinet to finish the 3 percent cut the president had ordered two months before. To Wilson, he remarked: "Time is of the essence, because Congress won't let us balance if they can help it."[20]

In November, with the president still absent and unable to object, Humphrey tried to persuade the Cabinet that a tax cut could not wait. Tax rates, he insisted, were higher than the economy could long endure. He drew a dark picture of a nation reduced to a dictatorship and a garrison state as an ultimate consequence. Some debt retirement, such as the president had advocated, should come but only after defense costs were further reduced.[21]

Perhaps Sherman Adams anticipated Humphrey's low-key rebellion, because he had suggested to Eisenhower that Burns might be useful in keeping Humphrey in check while he was convalescing. After listening as Humphrey harangued the Cabinet, Burns stated his own preference for debt reduction only. Perhaps a larger surplus in FY-1957, he offered, could make tax cuts possible then. At that point, Adams entered the discussion to remind Humphrey of the president's views on the issue. Humphrey bluntly disagreed. He called debt reduction "window dressing" while tax cuts were necessary for the country to grow and prosper. Without the president to referee the discussion, it ended inconclusively. But it was apparent that Humphrey would take matters into his own hands given the chance.

In December, Humphrey provoked a confrontation with the Cabinet's more moderate members on the content of the January State of the Union speech. He accused each department of packing the draft text with proposals for new programs, in order to counter promises being made by the Democratic Congress. Humphrey saw this as evidence that all fiscal discipline had been lost. "I'm going to be brutally frank," he said. "It is pie-in-the-sky.... A campaign piece."[22] He then ordered a redraft that emphasized principles and objectives, rather than new spending.

There was a murmur of dissent. Dulles, Stassen and Burns took the floor to defend the appropriateness of discussing program needs in the State of the Union speech. Besides, they countered, it was totally unrealistic to continue to try to hold spending at 1955 levels indefinitely. Vice President Nixon, who was presiding, tried to be conciliatory. He defended the draft text as consistent with previous messages of its kind, but he agreed to try to tighten it up.

Economic Impact of Ike's Return

By November, it was apparent that Eisenhower would be able to resume his duties. An event took place that month that affected his views on fiscal matters. Secretary Dulles reported that the Geneva Foreign Ministers conference had failed to reach an anticipated agreement that promised to reduce Cold War tensions. This meant that further savings on defense might not be possible. The news reinforced Ike's support for paying down the national debt before giving any consideration to tax cuts, a conviction he repeated in a December meeting with Republican legislative leaders.[23] Consistent with his distaste for political considerations, he also told them that he would veto any tax reduction enacted during the election year of 1956.

Eisenhower's focus upon his return was on making sure the 1956 budget wound up in balance. At a January Cabinet meeting, he reminded Humphrey and Hughes to act as watchdogs on revenues and spending and to regularly nag the department heads—a reminder that they surely did not need. "We've got people in our own shops who aren't interested in balances," he stressed. He also warned Wilson to not "get tricked" by the service chiefs. Humphrey and the president hoped to announce prior to the 1956 elections that both the 1956 and 1957 budgets were on track to be balanced. To make that happen, Humphrey warned the Cabinet, "everyone in this room is responsible."

Humphrey could not resist an oblique reference to his favorite subject. He noted that Democrats would probably attack the administration for having a hidden "nest egg" in the budget that would allow a tax cut. The comment drew Ike's fire. He "just did not see any desirability of talking about tax cuts at this time." Playing politics with the issue would be wrong, he said, when there is such a great need for debt reduction.[24] Humphrey managed to hide his disagreement and again resolved to be a team player.

But Humphrey was nothing if not persistent. During a March 1956 Cabinet discussion, he felt compelled to predict a period of severe competition with foreign firms because of high taxes, which were "changing our whole way of life." No other country, he continued, depends so much on taxing profits for its income. Unless the "spirit of 1953" was recaptured, the administration would have to raise taxes and American credit would "go to hell." Agriculture Secretary Benson, who shared Humphrey's outlook, expressed regret that the administration was "doing no better than breaking even in a period of great prosperity." His implied wish was for a huge surplus, most of which could be used for tax cuts. The president did not take the bait—he simply agreed that taxes were too high and let it go at that.[25]

Humphrey searched for bureaucratic ways to ensure compliance with orders to cut spending. He proposed to Budget Director Hughes the introduction of an expense monitoring system at each federal agency. Such a system, he pointed out, would identify budget excesses in time to allow corrective action. "I will be glad to carry the laboring oar in trying to effect reductions," he wrote, "if you will take the responsibility of getting me the information on which to act." Hughes wrote back in agreement: "I have gone over this with Ike and he heartily endorses it."[26] The idea was apparently never implemented.

The booming economy led to an ironic budgetary outcome. Despite the administration's best efforts to contain expenses in fiscal year 1956, by April they were running $4 billion higher than expected, leading the president to feel that he had failed. But good news overcame the bad. As national income and corporation profits grew, federal tax receipts were climbing even faster than expenditures. In this way, a balanced budget became a reality.

Humphrey's enthusiasm for the FY-1956 balance was dampened because, despite all of his efforts at economy, inflation again became a source of concern in early 1956. After almost three years with little change, prices rose 5.3 percent in only fifteen months. All the major conditions for price stability seemed to be present, including a steady series of interest rate hikes by the Fed and two consecutive balanced budgets. Humphrey counted escalating federal expenditures among the main causes of the trend, even when covered by increased revenue. (Later, many economists would agree in principle.[27]) But other factors were in play. Generous labor settlements had caused some wages to outpace productivity increases, and a sharp increase in consumer credit had created more demand. Humphrey surely knew that cutting taxes and putting more money into circulation risked adding more fuel to the fire.

Humphrey and Eisenhower tried to pressure industry leaders into assuming joint responsibility for controlling inflation by keeping prices stable—probably a naïve hope. They both expressed disappointment with the reaction of business to their entreaties. In a memo to the president, Humphrey complained about the "increasing number of executives who believe a little continuing inflation is essential to full employment" and who were "not too thoughtful about the future so long as their current quarterly statements look good."²⁸

By mid-1956, most leading officials in the administration considered more spending inevitable. Wilson's pessimistic statements, noted earlier, made him one of the first to throw in the towel. The defense budget was soon running 5 percent more than expected. Budget Director Hughes agreed with Humphrey that "the zest for the crusade is gone." He accused the department heads of clientitis—being "married" to their programs.²⁹

The election campaign season in 1956 brought another irony. As Eisenhower's popularity surged and his reelection looked increasingly likely, he and Humphrey were gripped with a sense that their economic policy was failing. Humphrey wrote to Ike in September: "We made a big step forward when we first arrived. For the last two years, we have been going backwards … and I think it is essential that we change the trend.… I do not believe we can control inflation and continue any reasonable stabilization in our cost of living unless we can reverse the present upward trend of government … expenditures."³⁰ Equally unhappy, Rowland Hughes left the administration in April, predicting that pressures for budget increases would become irresistible. Critics would be justified in calling the trend "New Dealish," he concluded gloomily.³¹

In the fall, Gabriel Hauge tried to rein in Humphrey's more aggressive policy statements, fearful of their effect on the election. The treasury secretary had asked Hauge to comment on some of the bullet points of his recent speeches, which included his familiar themes: cutting foreign aid, reducing the number of American troops abroad, eliminating the balance-of-payments deficit, monetary restraint, and cutting further the overall cost of government. Hauge cautioned him about his overuse of "hard-boiled language," advised him not to pressure the Federal Reserve, and suggested avoiding entirely any discussion of balance of payments, which would be an intrusion on foreign policy turf.³² But Humphrey was rarely deterred from speaking his mind.

Ike professed helplessness in the face of overall spending pressures. "Over the past five years, it seems to me that I have put in two-thirds of my time fighting increased expenditures in government," he said, "yet … we find that the 1957 expenditures for every single department of government exceed comparable ones in the year 1956." After Humphrey left the administration the following year, Ike wrote to him in frustration: "I have already approved bills which I personally considered as imposing unwarranted drains on the Federal Treasury."³³ Even more galling, congressional conservatives were blasting the president as a hypocrite for espousing economy yet enabling extravagance.

Many economists later criticized Ike's constant agonizing about what in retrospect was a relatively modest upward trend in expenditures. Because of rapid economic growth during the mid-1950s, federal spending as a percentage of the gross national product actually declined. His treasury secretary seemed fixated on nominal increases year over year, regardless of inflation or the growing capacity of the economy to absorb additional spending. But Eisenhower accepted Humphrey's thinking and felt guilty about the spending he could not stop.

This performance would be repeated in 1957—a balanced budget with a small surplus. But Eisenhower would never again consent to tax cuts. He would grudgingly agree to a slight increase in government spending to address the most important national needs, while applying the remaining surplus to a reduction of the national debt. By satisfying neither the spenders nor the tax cutters, Ike had again found a middle way, though not one he was especially proud of. Humphrey's failure fully to convert the president to his way of thinking was one of his biggest disappointments.

The Boom and the Federal Reserve

Because Federal Reserve Chairman Martin was an inflation hawk like Eisenhower and Humphrey, some observers viewed the Fed during the Eisenhower years as a "White House appendage," so closely did it appear to hew to the administration's line. It lowered interest rates in reaction to the downturn of 1953–54, and when Humphrey and Burns began worrying about "irrational exuberance" caused by the upturn in 1955, they looked to the Fed to apply the brakes. "If we don't slow the economy now, we will pay for it in a year or two" with higher inflation, Humphrey told the Cabinet in March.[34] Though some of Martin's colleagues were worried about the opposite—that the rally would be nipped in the bud by a hike in interest rates—the Fed approved several rate increases as the year progressed.

But the administration's relations with the Fed became strained later in 1955 and into 1956 as their short-term interests diverged. One issue was the Treasury Department's occasionally erratic management of the national debt. Twice in 1955, Treasury asked the Fed to help the government finance its debt by making adjustments to monetary policy, which ran contrary to the anti-inflation policies the Fed was then pursuing. Each time, Martin deferred to Humphrey, saying it would be "irresponsible to ignore the Treasury's problem."[35] When a congressman asked him why he yielded, his reply reflected his view of the Treasury-Fed relationship: "I have served faithfully and con-

14. The Price of Prosperity

scientiously with Secretary Humphrey, and have had to say 'no' to him on a good many occasions, but I also want to work with him. The Treasury and Fed are partners. We are trying to achieve the same general ends and we each have a 50% interest."[36]

As the 1956 election loomed, Humphrey, and to some extent the president, became concerned that the Fed's efforts to rein in the booming economy were becoming too aggressive and might lead to a slump that would cost the Republicans votes in November. (Tightening credit never enhances the popularity of the party in power.) Humphrey was especially upset when the Fed raised interest rates by a quarter of a percent in the spring of 1956.[37] He called the raise untimely and followed up with a note in April to Martin, citing his fear of growing unemployment, which "will be widely discussed if we don't begin promptly to do what we can now to prevent it."[38]

Eisenhower did not want to be viewed as interfering with Fed prerogatives, but now he seemed uncharacteristically bothered by the potential political impact of tight money. He became so irritated at Martin that Humphrey had to advise him not to publicly criticize the rate increase. "[T]o go further," he counseled, "would have put the story on page one if we had openly broke with the Fed."[39] Hearing of Ike's anger, Martin offered to resign, but the president chose not to contest Fed policy and, in effect, reaffirmed Fed independence. He even made a series of speeches defending the interest rate hike as a necessary tool in the fight against inflation, and he begged American business to do what it could to cool off the economy before it overheated.

Treasury continued a low-level campaign against the Fed's mind-set through 1956. Humphrey kept trying to get Martin to liberalize credit. Other Treasury officials charged the central bank with an "ivory tower" attitude and a disregard for how higher rates affected small business. The Fed countered by faulting the administration for not controlling spending, but the pressure achieved limited results. By mid-summer Humphrey could report to the president: "Bill Martin is performing nicely and the extreme pressure is abating."[40]

The wrangling with the Federal Reserve showed that Humphrey was willing to sacrifice principle for political gain and that he was able to get the president to back him up. During 1956, in fact, Martin appeared to be a far more zealous inflation fighter than the economic policy makers in the executive branch. Martin certainly understood that higher interest rates might lead to economic inactivity and unemployment, but he felt that some unemployment was a tolerable price to pay to wring inflation out of the system. In time, Ike would fully agree.

Neither the debate over military readiness nor persistent inflation affected the American public's affection for its president. The country was prosperous and at peace. In November, Eisenhower was returned to office in a landslide.

But Humphrey considered the victory bittersweet. His agenda seemed to be foundering. Federal spending and inflation seemed unstoppable. Cabinet members who were willing to curtail their departments' spending had either left the administration or succumbed to pressure from liberals in Congress or their own bureaucracies. The president seemed willing to court Democratic support for his favorite programs by agreeing to spending increases.

As 1957 began, Humphrey was about to make a last-ditch effort to turn things around.

15

Humphrey for President?

Most historians consider Richard Nixon the administration's most politically-minded official and most energetic campaigner for the Republican ticket. But George Humphrey was every bit as partisan and as committed to his party and to Eisenhower's reelection. While the president was still recovering, he made speeches at several Ike rallies and held a series of fund-raising dinners. His addresses listed the accomplishments of the administration, ending with the rhetorical question "Do you want to go back?" In December 1955, the president having returned to work, Humphrey was the keynote speaker at a huge "Salute to Ike" dinner in New York City.

These events raised millions of dollars, and the enthusiasm they generated may have influenced Eisenhower's February decision to run for re-election. At a minimum, they convinced him that others would be more than willing to campaign on his behalf in order to help him conserve his energy.

The fall of 1955 had been difficult. In the two months following Eisenhower's heart attack, panicked Republicans had been forced to consider who they might nominate for president in 1956 if Ike could not run. Even if healthy, he would have had serious doubts about seeking a second term. In mid-1955, with the economy in good shape and a thaw underway in relations with the Soviet Union, Ike concluded that he had done his duty and thought seriously about retiring from office.

As he surveyed the field of possible alternatives to himself, however, he saw no one with the ability or support necessary to succeed him. He was often heard lamenting the lack of attractive younger candidates who were committed to his centrist philosophy. He joked to Arthur Larson he was afraid the party might have to go back to the Spanish-American war in its search for potential leaders.[1]

Some prominent moderate Republican leaders were still around, but they were judged either unsuitable or unavailable. The day of Tom Dewey, the party's standard bearer in 1944 and 1948, had passed. The president would have gladly supported Earl Warren, the liberal Republican former governor of California, who he had named chief justice of the United States in 1953, but Warren showed no signs of wanting to give up his guaranteed lifetime appointment. Nixon, in Ike's view, was not ready. The question was: if not Eisenhower, then who?

Eisenhower's main concern, as he looked ahead to 1956, was keeping the conservatives from regaining control of the party. He had already had several run-ins with congressional "Neanderthals," as the termed them, about foreign and defense policy. Bob Taft, long the main rallying point for conservatives, had died of cancer in 1953. Another popular figure in right-wing ranks was California senator William Knowland, who coveted the presidency, but Ike considered him a rigid ideologue.

In private discussions with friends, Eisenhower had often mentioned several men who he felt would make good presidents. Because he was a shrewd judge of people and understood the importance of leadership skills and character, his views carried considerable weight. In order to make Ike's list, a candidate had to lean toward his "middle way" philosophy and take a larger (i.e., relatively nonpartisan) view of national issues.

Despite his skill in evaluating others, Ike's frequent musings on the subject were startlingly naïve. The men for whom he had the most enthusiasm may have had the intellectual capital to be president, but they were unlikely to appeal to political kingmakers and voters. For example, he praised the undeniable talents of his brother Milton, though Milton's chances for the Republican nomination, as a college president and the president's brother, were nil.

Another example of the kind of man Ike preferred was Arthur Larson, a bureaucrat, intellectual, and workman's compensation specialist who was serving as undersecretary of labor. Larson was an admirer of the president and an articulate spokesman for modern Republicanism—he even wrote a book on the subject. He had no background in politics, was virtually unknown to the public, and had no support for high office within the Republican party, but Eisenhower sought ways to raise his public profile and make him more competitive. Being a better judge of his chances for electoral success, Larson declined to make the effort.

Ike reserved his greatest enthusiasm for Deputy Secretary of Defense Robert Anderson, a mild-mannered, scholarly-looking Texan. Anderson had many necessary attributes—a belief in Eisenhower Republicanism, strong character, and a record of quiet efficiency—but he had little charisma and no interest in politics. Though Ike actively promoted his candidacy, Anderson would have been an unexciting and unsuccessful nominee. He went on to replace Humphrey as treasury secretary and continued to be a favorite of the president's throughout his second term.

15. Humphrey for President?

There were other men who Eisenhower could imagine as president, but who also had little chance. Among them were Attorney General Herbert Brownell, ex-soldiers and former associates Al Gruenther and Lucius Clay, and Gabriel Hauge.[2] He later admitted that the problem of "making [these men] better known and appreciated by the public proved troublesome." The only genuine politician on Ike's list was Henry Cabot Lodge, a U.S. senator, who had "the greatest amount of personal charm and persuasiveness."

In February 1956, at a crucial juncture in his presidency, Eisenhower repaired to Humphrey's estate in Thomasville to decide whether to pursue a second term. As he rested in this tranquil setting, his vigor gradually returned, while Humphrey helped him resolve his doubts about running for reelection. According to journalist Marquis Childs, Humphrey assured other Republicans that, at a minimum, Ike could continue in office as a kind of chairman of the board without undue strain on his health.[3] Upon returning to Washington, Ike sent Humphrey a warm note, punctuated with inside jokes and intimate references, expressing gratitude for good times shared.

With such a close bond between the two men, it was perhaps not surprising that Eisenhower had long considered George Humphrey presidential timber. In a wide-ranging conversation with Sherman Adams about the succession issue in 1955, Ike unexpectedly threw out Humphrey's name. Adams suppressed what must have been his immediate negative reaction and commented that while Humphrey had the requisite vitality, Adams "doubted he could liberalize himself."[4] Ike replied that Humphrey was "deceptively flexible."[5] He had particularly in mind Humphrey's support of the administration's federal highway pro-

"Bring Me the Black Ink!" Humphrey achieved one of his most important goals when he oversaw the balancing of the 1956 budget (Berryman in *The Washington Star*. Provided by Western Reserve Historical Society, Cleveland, Ohio).

gram in 1955 and 1956—a program that, though expensive, promised to stimulate the economy.

The thought continued to intrigue the president. Impressed with Humphrey's recent success in building enthusiasm for Republican candidates, he toyed with the idea of a George Humphrey-Milton Eisenhower ticket. He even believed that Humphrey would receive more support from the general public than from Republican voters. But Ike admitted that neither man had much of a political following and that Humphrey would have a difficult time getting nominated.[6]

That summer, the *Pittsburgh Press* reported that Humphrey was Eisenhower's first choice as the Republican nominee for president if he did not run himself. At that time, three California politicians—Nixon, Knowland and Warren—were considered serious candidates. The article suggested that Humphrey would be a good alternative for Republicans "who don't like the Californians," but conceded that he would be hard to elect.[7] At about the same time, rumors swirled that Ike planned to replace Nixon with Humphrey as his vice presidential candidate in 1956.[8]

The Humphrey boomlet gathered some steam after Ike's heart attack. Several journalists speculated about his candidacy because of his Cabinet prominence, his fund-raising abilities, and his friendship with the president.[9] Marquis Childs, who was writing a book on Ike's first term, saw him as a viable alternative by virtue of his good political instincts. He was undeniably conservative, Childs admitted, but his ideology was leavened by his good will and geniality.[10] A Midwestern newspaper reported the formation of a "draft Humphrey" movement.[11]

All speculation about Humphrey as a presidential candidate turned out to be pointless, because he took every opportunity to deny any interest in the position. When asked at a press conference whether he would run if Eisenhower asked him to, he dismissed the idea as nonsensical and "out of the question," which indeed it was.[12] Perhaps the most accurate reflection of Humphrey's standing as a Republican presidential candidate was provided by a January 1956 Gallup Poll of 1,692 party county chairmen. Only seventy of that number considered Humphrey the best choice to succeed Ike.[13]

On the last day of February 1956, Republicans breathed a collective sigh of relief when Eisenhower announced his decision to run for reelection. According to Ike intimate Ellis Slater, the president did not agree to do so until Humphrey ruled himself out as a candidate.[14] Ike confirmed this story later. "I tried to get George to run for president," he told Ann Whitman in mid-1957.[15]

Humphrey did agree to give the opening speech at the 1956 Republican convention. He also played a key role in the fall campaign, not only in support of Ike but by raising funds for senatorial candidates. Several of the president's friends revived Citizens for Eisenhower, a group that had played an important part in his 1952 victory. One of its goals was to attract younger Republican candidates by giving the party a broader-based, progressive orientation. Humphrey served as the president's liaison to this organization.

But running for office was the farthest thing from his mind. Within six months of the election, he would be back in Ohio for good.

16

The "Battle of the Budget" and Its Aftermath

Though Eisenhower's reelection was cause for celebration, other developments deepened Humphrey's pessimism about the country's fiscal future. The president's coattails were not sufficient to give Republicans a majority in either the House of Representatives or the Senate, and Humphrey expected Democrats to try to sabotage his cost-cutting efforts by expanding many domestic programs. All around him, in fact, he saw a growing acceptance—both in government and among the public—of the need for additional spending and of small amounts of inflation as an inescapable accompaniment to economic growth. Something had to be done, he believed, to shock people out of their complacency. He told the president that he viewed himself as an evangelist whose mission was to guide the modern Republicans back into the fold.[1]

The Metastasizing of the 1958 Budget

After the election, Arthur Burns left the administration. He was replaced as head of the Council of Economic Advisers by Raymond Saulnier, a leading official of the National Bureau of Economic Research. Saulnier posed no threat to Humphrey's plans to reinvigorate the administration's commitment to fiscal prudence. He was viewed as somewhat more conservative than his predecessor, an inflation hawk and balanced-budget proponent. His first report to the Cabinet, in December, predicted a continuation of growth during 1957, though at a less rapid rate. But economic forecasting was temporarily eclipsed by a public relations fiasco early in the year that damaged and embarrassed the president.

The episode that came to be known as the "battle of the budget" was the direct result of Eisenhower's unresolved ambivalence about economic policy.

16. The "Battle of the Budget" and Its Aftermath

Of late, he had had little time to think about budget matters. He had been campaigning for reelection throughout the fall, all the while preoccupied with the Suez crisis and the Soviet invasion of Hungary. Now that he could focus on the fiscal year 1958 budget, then nearing completion, he saw that his pleas for restraint had had little effect. It would total almost $72 billion—a $3 billion increase over the year before. Unless revised, it would be the largest peacetime budget in American history. Though social and educational programs accounted for a large part of the increase, military spending, as usual, was a major contributor.

Deeply concerned, Humphrey set down his thoughts in a long memorandum to the president, outlining a political strategy in which the administration might succeed in lowering taxes in 1958. The key to this plan was overcoming "all those who have a vested interest, either politically or financially" in military spending, which was "all cost with no effecting gain."[2] He told the Cabinet in January that a $5 billion surplus would allow a $4 billion tax cut.

Humphrey reminded whoever would listen that weapons contributed little to the national well-being: "You can't eat them; you can't use them; they aren't tools to make any new jobs for anybody."[3] To the Cabinet, he complained that "we're throwing away $40 billion in capital every year.... [It] serves only our security for that year, then on the dump heap."[4]

Similar frustration drove Budget Director Brundage to fire off a memo to Secretary Wilson, expressing his and the president's concern about the increases in the defense budget. He pointed out what Wilson already knew—that the administration was trying to avoid additional spending at a time when business activity was at a high and adding to inflationary pressures. Only essential projects should be funded, he concluded.[5]

The budget dilemma brought back into focus Eisenhower's longstanding inability to resolve his economic views. Being returned to office in the November election had prompted him to brag that the electorate had approved of modern Republicanism, which posited an acceptance of the government's responsibility to spend more money on domestic programs. The president believed that his relatively liberal philosophy reduced the political appeal of Democratic promises, but conservatives saw it as an abdication of principle. Senator Barry Goldwater chose the occasion to launch his ultimately successful struggle for control of the Republican party.

Objectively speaking, the increase in the 1958 budget hardly qualified as a capitulation to liberalism. Moreover, it made sense as a step toward the kind of Republican party Ike had always favored. Now that he saw the sum total of what he had agreed to, however, his basic frugality—and ambivalence—reasserted itself. He was having buyer's remorse.

An Ill-Advised Scheme

Humphrey reflected on the budget mess during an informal dinner party at his home in February 1957. To Ike's buddy Cliff Roberts, he confessed ruefully that the process had "slipped up on us and got out of hand, and we fumbled the ball." But for this outcome he blamed his Cabinet colleagues, who were busy helping in the reelection effort and did not "do their homework as thoroughly as they might have." While campaigning for Ike, they "pulled out all the stops" by promising more money for Social Security, schools, farmers, and so on. These promises had "come home to roost" in the budget.

He found particular fault with Wilson and even his ally, budget director Brundage. Wilson, he said, had given him a personal commitment to hold military spending to $36 billion, but then he "made the mistake" of asking each service what they needed, and the cumulative answer was $46 billion. So now, he said, Wilson was fighting to get back to the lower number without much hope of success.[6]

Wilson's efforts in this direction were probably lacking in conviction. He had gone over the numbers many times, had brought spending down "billion by painful billion," and considered all remaining spending essential.[7] He met with Brundage and the president, who reluctantly agreed to Wilson's bottom line of $38 billion. Learning of the meeting, Humphrey turned on Brundage, charging him with lacking the spine of his predecessors, Joe Dodge and Rowland Hughes. Cliff Roberts regarded Brundage as "not too strong a character" who had not done a good job of "shaking down" Wilson's budget request.[8] The *New York Times* got wind of the dispute and in March again assessed that Humphrey's budget crusade was being "blown to bits" by defense costs.

It seemed that Humphrey's best efforts to keep the 1958 budget lean had failed—he had been let down, he felt, by men who could not say no. He believed the final document would be severely criticized and bring political problems in its wake. If implemented in full, he was certain it would lead to further inflation. Further, it seemed possible that the Congress would succumb to end-runs by Pentagon officers and add to an already bloated defense budget.

But he still had a few cards to play. First, he decided to lay out a case for a final round of budget cuts in a series of memoranda to the president and the Cabinet. He wrote in December of the consequences of failing to "put our house in order," which would "shake the confidence of the great mass of thinking Americans."[9] He warned of "false prophets" who advocated spending to stimulate the economy. Finally, he called for a four-year budget plan that would lay the groundwork for a substantial tax cut.

In January Humphrey told the president and the Cabinet that $4 billion could still be shaved off the 1958 budget. With a hint of desperation, he suggested that Eisenhower assess every Cabinet department a further 5 percent cut. Nobody in the room agreed to this. Folsom and Stassen objected that defense spending had actually declined as a percentage of GNP and was easily sustainable. The president seemed unmoved by Humphrey's argument.

Seeing that changes to the budget at this stage were unacceptable to everyone, Humphrey came up with an audacious scheme that, if successful, might unravel the budget strategy of the Democrats in Congress. Perhaps he could induce Congress to make the necessary cuts.

"I wouldn't worry. You can be sure George Humphrey won't let this dip go any further."

This *New Yorker* cartoon strengthened the impression that George Humphrey's priority as treasury secretary was reassuring the business community rather than helping ordinary Americans. A Democratic senator charged that Humphrey "judges the prosperity of the nation by the condition of the wealthy" (Alan Dunn, *The New Yorker* Collection, The Cartoon Bank).

His idea was to write the president an open letter in which he would defend the administration's budget while decrying extravagance in government in general and suggesting that defense spending could be cut even further.[10] Then he would invite Congress to join the administration in looking for additional economies. His implied message was that even though 1958 spending levels might seem excessive to some Republican congressmen, the executive branch was still deeply committed to frugality.

Humphrey knew that it would be tricky to do this without giving the impression that he was breaking ranks with the president. He probably also doubted that he could sell the idea, but he felt he was well positioned to take a risk, because he planned to return to Hanna in a few months anyway. The draft letter was discussed at a Cabinet meeting on January 9. Secretary Dulles, and even budget director Brundage, immediately raised objections, fearing the negative consequences of public grumbling by the Treasury Department.[11] Attorney General Brownell called it misguided. Eisenhower himself was lukewarm at best. If he had believed further cuts were possible, he would have made them already.

To everyone's surprise, including Humphrey's, Eisenhower finally agreed to the plan, or rather decided not to oppose it. Later Humphrey spoke of Ike's consent to Cliff Roberts, who expressed disbelief. It's "a literal fact," Humphrey told Roberts. "It's what happened."[12]

Humphrey read the letter to a crowded press conference at the Treasury Department. It did indeed sound like criticism of his administration. "The overall net results [of the 1958 budget] are not sufficient," he wrote. "Only the most drastic action will suffice."[13] It was now up to Congress to save the situation. He encouraged the legislature to "find ways to cut and still do a proper job with respect to our security and with respect to proper services to the republic."[14]

Two minutes before the press conference ended, he uttered the words for which he would primarily be remembered. He told the assembled journalists that, unless expenditures were reduced and taxes lowered over the next several years, "I predict that you will have a depression that will curl your hair."

Despite Humphrey's intentions, the media interpreted his remarks precisely as Dulles and others had feared—as a rejection of the budget he had just helped to formulate and as evidence of a serious rift with the president. Ike's "gang" made fun of this interpretation. "When we read that headline, we all laughed," said Ellis Slater, "I said if there is a rift it is because of that stupid club lead George had made the night before."[15]

But the result of this ill-thought-out strategy was a public relations disaster and a budget that was dead on arrival on Capitol Hill. Questioned about

Humphrey's open letter, the president took pains to point out that no rift existed. "I not only went over every word of it, I edited it," he said. "It expresses my convictions very thoroughly." Was he really hoping that Congress would cut the budget further? a reporter asked. "It is their duty to do it," Ike replied. Alarmed at the fix Eisenhower was getting himself into, Sherman Adams used a New England expression—"gumming up the sapworks—to describe the result of these attempts at clarification.[16] Ike later admitted that his "invitation to Congress to do its Constitutional duty had better been left unsaid."[17]

According to both Arthur Burns and Milton Eisenhower, the president had to resist the impulse to fire his treasury secretary.[18] In reminiscing years later about the crisis, Burns recalled that he "tried to calm [Ike] down. He was so angry with Humphrey, and rightly so."[19] The president decided not to act precipitously—he was reluctant to fire anybody, least of all Humphrey—but many columnists saw Humphrey as the inevitable scapegoat and called him an isolated figure in the Cabinet.

Loss of Credibility

What followed was a chaotic spring in which the president was continually asked to defend the government's handling of the matter. He found himself upholding a budget he wished were smaller while insisting that further fiscal discipline was necessary. Quizzed about the wisdom of new domestic spending, Ike replied: "As long as the American people demand, and in my opinion, deserve, the kind of services this budget provides, we have got to spend this kind of money." Such comments seemed to expose him as more liberal than Humphrey on the budget issue and left him vulnerable to attacks from conservative Republicans, such as senators Goldwater and Knowland, who considered the administration's 1958 budget reminiscent of New Deal excess. Ike's denial that his stance was a departure from modern Republicanism did nothing to reassure these men.

For their part, Democrats were leery of being tarred as the party of extravagance. Reacting to recent polls that had shown growing public support for economy in government, they decided to appropriate the spending issue for their own political purposes. In a role reversal, congressional liberals proceeded to accept Humphrey's suggestion that they cut the budget, and did so "with a vengeance,"[20] calculating that the administration would bear the blame for reductions in popular programs. Democratic congressmen were also quick to propose cuts in areas that the president felt were sacrosanct, such as foreign aid.

Having encouraged Congress to act in this manner, Cabinet officials now had to decide whether to accept the targeted cuts or appeal for restoration of selected funds. Wilson was in a mood to fight any cuts in defense, while the president recommended that Cabinet members tell the public precisely who might be victimized by congressional reductions in services. But Humphrey disagreed. He conceded that they all had worked hard to develop the budget, but they should be "delighted" with any suggestions Congress makes.[21] Publicly, he challenged Congress to step up to the task. "If you've got the nerve and the votes," he exclaimed, "we'll take the cuts."[22]

Cabinet meetings in March reflected considerable frustration with the budget situation. Administration officials continued to wrangle over the document they had already submitted to Congress. Again, Humphrey chastised the Pentagon for not winding down conventional programs, but Wilson had drawn a line in the sand against more defense cuts. He pointed out that rising prices and world developments gave no basis for any more economy moves. H.E.W. Secretary Folsom strongly agreed—a higher rate of federal spending, he predicted, would sustain prosperity into 1958. Humphrey could not believe his ears. "All the wonderful influence of the Treasury has rubbed off on Marion," he joked. Adams warned the Cabinet in March that continuing to look for ways to cut the budget tended to undermine the budget submitted to Congress just two months before.[23]

Taking advantage of its upper hand, Congress toyed with the administration. The finance committees reduced the operating budgets of several Cabinet departments, including Treasury. This move forced the affected departments to return to Congress hat in hand to request that the money be reinstated. Eisenhower kept his sense of humor, telling Humphrey he could not believe newspaper accounts that his most fiscally-minded adviser had requested a supplemental appropriation—one intended to restore his own budget. He advised his treasury secretary to sue the newspapers for libel and defamation of character.[24] Humphrey was not amused.

To counteract persistent rumors that the two men were estranged, Ike suggested that Humphrey make a speech to dispel any public misperceptions. This he did at a Republican fund-raiser in May, noting that "no man has worked harder than President Eisenhower" to lower budget expenditures.[25]

Humphrey had planned to resign his post in mid-summer, but the serious illness of Hanna board chairman Ernest Weir convinced him that he would have to return to his old company ahead of schedule. The timing was unfortunate, because it suggested that his departure was due to disagreement with the president. Though he submitted his resignation in late May, he did not behave like a lame duck. He spent most of the month promoting administration frugality and assuring adequate revenue to keep alive the possibility of tax cuts in 1958 or 1959.

The president's fought to rescue his budget and repair the damage with several speeches and appearances in May, culminating in an address to the nation. Meant to influence votes in Congress, it largely fell on deaf ears. Congress cut the overall 1958 budget by $4 billion but not in ways that the administration would have wanted. Funding for economic development abroad, for example, took a sizeable hit.

Eisenhower had lost the initiative in fiscal matters. Adams called the episode a "serious and disturbing personal defeat."[26] The fallout from the failed Humphrey ploy caused media speculation that the "strong man of the Cabinet" had lost out to his internal opponents. Drew Pearson wrote that some of the president's economic advisers disagreed with his insistence on tight money and increasingly had Ike's ear.

This view was correct as far as it went, but Humphrey's problem was not just his colleagues—it was the president himself. More than ever, Eisenhower's two minds about spending had forced him into espousing two contrary positions simultaneously. He complained that he was helpless to keep the budget in check, but he was not helpless—he had been talked into approving the increases.

Most revealing—and confusing—were two remarks he made at the height of the budget mess. "The fellow who caused us more trouble than anyone else in the past four months is George Humphrey," he admitted. "And yet," he continued, indicating a space of one inch with his fingers, "he and I are no further apart than this."[27] At about the same time, with little apparent awareness of his own inconsistency, he said: "Frankly, I would rather see the Congress cut a billion off the defense [budget]—as much as I think it would be a mistake."[28] Eisenhower was a man divided against himself.

As Humphrey's term of office wound down, the president renewed his attempts to control future spending by asking Brundage to come up with a four-year budget plan that aimed at holding total spending at FY-1957 levels. Humphrey declared that Brundage's plan would be six months too late to do any good, but it did seem to address Humphrey's main concern. He had predicted that military spending would reach $42 billion by 1962. To reverse this trend, Brundage suggested establishing a spending ceiling for defense at $39 billion a year. At a Cabinet meeting called to discuss this idea, Wilson objected strenuously. Ike's response showed his irritation. "[I'm going] to fire every official down to colonel," he raged. "I'll turn in my suit of we can't do it better than that."[29]

In late June, Eisenhower approved the Brundage plan and ordered all departments to freeze their commitments and obligations for FY-1958 at FY-1957 levels—effectively impounding the funds at a time when Congress was still discussing and authorizing the 1958 budget. Congressional Democrats retaliated by taking money out of foreign assistance and moving it to housing programs, an action that led to a presidential veto. H.E.W. Secretary Folsom, noting that Congress had increased his agency's funding, told the president that he feared the administration would expose itself to criticism by insisting on lower numbers. Characteristically, Ike replied that he was quite used to criticism and it would not bother him.[30]

Prelude to Recession

Through 1956, the administration had done little thinking about how to combat a new recession. The problem of the day seemed to be preventing the strong economy from overheating rather than making plans for when bad times returned. As long as the boom continued, the government's promise to intervene if necessary to counter negative trends became less explicit in administration speeches and planning documents. The recession of 1957–58 turned this lack of foresight into a major error.

One reason for complacency was the administration's belief that the 1953–54 recession had largely corrected itself. Aided by previously scheduled tax reductions and a liberalization of money and credit by the Federal Reserve, the economy had snapped back. Ike's Cabinet had considered actions that would have resulted in deficit spending but backed away from most of them. This experience shaped its view of any new recession that might appear. A combination of marginal tweaks and monetary adjustments, it was felt, would work again.

But effective countermeasures, even minor ones, required thinking ahead—creating a "shelf" of options from which policymakers could quickly draw in the event of a sudden downturn. A decision to pursue tax cuts, for example, required a long lead time—the 1954 tax package had taken a year to get through Congress. As Herbert Stein has written: "[The administration had] no advance plan, no strategy for relating anti-recession fiscal policy to the longer-range financial prospect and program, no decision on the conditions in which taxes should be cut, on whether the cut should be permanent or temporary, or on the form of the cut.... All the important decisions still had to be made, under fire as it were."[31]

While the administration was dealing with the fallout from the budget fiasco, signs of economic trouble began to appear. In the spring of 1957, C.E.A.

chief Saulnier expressed concern about a loss of momentum and suggested that a recession might be on the horizon. As had been the case four years before, Eisenhower's economic team looked to the Federal Reserve for help. Calling the situation "extremely delicate," Saulnier complained to Martin that monetary policy seemed "excessively tight," but Martin was more focused on breaking the back of the persistent inflation than on arresting a downturn. By July, interest rates were at postwar highs.

Humphrey, too, was exercised by Martin's obduracy. As interest rates rose, the Treasury Department had a harder time financing the country's debt. The conflict with the Fed again revealed Humphrey's tendency to browbeat his opponents, even in the waning days of his tenure. He put pressure on Martin, until the Fed chief admitted in his typically understated manner that his people "might not approve the way in which the Treasury was running its affairs."[32]

Humphrey would not be around when the recession of 1957–58 roiled the economy and raised again the question of government intervention. But by then, the president had memorized the Humphrey playbook. The treasury secretary was gone, but his influence lived on.

The Changing of the Guard

Wilson and Humphrey had served in the Eisenhower Cabinet since early 1953. They were increasingly anxious to take up the life of leisure they had postponed five years earlier and felt they had more than earned. Both had delayed their departures in order to help with the 1958 budget. Humphrey resigned his office in July 1957 after many rounds of celebratory good-byes. Wilson departed the Pentagon three months later.

Humphrey left office on a low note, amid the shambles of a six-month fight with Congress, far short of his goal of restoring the fiscal discipline of 1953. His exodus was hard on Eisenhower. "The President hated to see Mr. Humphrey go," wrote Ann Whitman, "and I think Mr. Humphrey himself was close to tears."[33] In a final note of levity, at the Secretary's last Cabinet meeting on July 24, Eisenhower invited him to "make a speech on the economy." Humphrey replied that he did not think he had left anything unsaid.

To replace him, Ike selected Robert Anderson. He was just as conservative as Humphrey but, as one colleague put it, his views had a firmer intellectual foundation, and he was less motivated by partisanship. Saulnier contrasted him to his predecessor, calling him "a distinctly reflective sort of person, a person at home in a discussion, including discussions in depth on an economic or financial question."[34]

As a result of Humphrey's resignation, relations between the Treasury and State departments improved. As Humphrey admitted in introducing his successor, Robert Anderson: "Don't be misled about him just because he doesn't shout and pound the table the way I do."[35] Douglas Dillon, the assistant secretary for economic affairs at state, immediately noticed the difference, finding Anderson more flexible and pleasant. He followed the conservative Treasury "line," recalled Dillon, but "it wasn't with the same violence or vigor." Dillon found that he could take spending initiatives to the president and prevail at times: "Well, Bob," Ike might say, "I think you've got to let these poor [folks] have their money, it won't break the U.S."[36] Dillon also managed to get Anderson to reverse Humphrey's demand that all State Department cables dealing with money be cleared by the Treasury Department.

The new economic team believed that the Cabinet was too large and diverse a body for detailed economic policy making. As the economy worsened, a group was organized at Hauge's suggestion that included only the president and his key economic advisers—the treasury secretary, the C.E.A. head, the chairman of the Federal Reserve. Known informally as the "little four," the group provided a way for Eisenhower to be more regularly and deeply involved in fiscal and monetary matters.

The timing of its creation and the identity of its creator suggest that Humphrey would have opposed it, on the grounds that it diluted his control of economic policy. Chairman Martin immediately approved the idea, recalling that he had been "seriously handicapped by being unable to talk directly with the President, as happened during April 1956," when Humphrey encouraged him to resign unless he could support administration policies. One analyst called the genesis of the "little four" a "watershed in the coordination of economic policy making in the United States."[37]

Humphrey and Wilson departed before new foreign and domestic challenges accelerated Eisenhower's transformation from "modern Republican" to staunch fiscal conservative. In 1958, two leading believers in Eisenhower-style moderation—Gabriel Hauge and Arthur Larson—left the administration. Hauge's replacement was agricultural economist Don Paarlberg, who lacked his rapport with the president and usually went along with Anderson's conservative views. Hauge's steadying hand would be missed. From the sidelines, Humphrey kept his reservations about modern Republicanism to himself and urged party unity under Eisenhower's leadership. The more dangerous and politically damaging of the administration's two recessions officially began the same month Humphrey departed.

16. The "Battle of the Budget" and Its Aftermath

Dispiriting developments after Humphrey and Wilson left office probably made them glad to escape the Washington pressure cooker and would have tested them severely had they remained. In October 1957 came news that the Soviet Union had orbited an artificial satellite, an event that rattled the American public and fundamentally altered the defense budget debate. The Sputnik shock derailed the four-year budget plan devised by Brundage and approved by the president. From that moment, the political pressure on the administration for an adequate response was unrelenting. Dealing with the challenges of the recession and Soviet technological prowess would fall to Robert Anderson and the new defense secretary, Neil McElroy.

Before leaving Washington, Humphrey did what he could to help his successor achieve tax relief. He pushed hard for a 1959 budget so much in surplus that it would not only make tax reduction possible but strike a blow against inflation. (Humphrey's goals and methods were nothing if not consistent.) However, the Soviet satellite and the economic downturn sent budget planners back to the drawing board. In November 1957, Humphrey wrote to Eisenhower, reminding him of his 1952 pledge to cut spending. The president sadly responded that in the new political environment, he could make no guarantees.

Early in 1958, as he was deliberating with his aides over how to address worsening economic conditions and public concern about rising unemployment, Eisenhower left Washington for a ten-day vacation at Humphrey's Georgia plantation. The timing of his trip was unfortunate—the media speculated on how his increasingly questionable health might be affecting the strength of his leadership. Adlai Stevenson commented that Ike's visits to Humphrey's estate facilitated the former treasury secretary's Svengali-like influence over the president, even after leaving his job.[38]

Humphrey had been asked in late 1957 if he thought the administration would take strong action to combat the sagging economy. "I don't think so ... no," he replied. "I will put it this way: we didn't do it last time, did we? Pressure was brought on us to do it. We didn't do it and it worked."[39]

Years later, Eisenhower explicitly confirmed that Humphrey had taught him an important lesson. "From the outset of the [1958] recession, my associates and I took the same view as we had in 1954 that we should prepare strong programs to prevent a serious and lengthy decline but should never be swayed from reason by purveyors of gloom."[40] Hoping to duplicate the apparent success of the 1953–54 recession fighting strategy, Anderson and the president adopted a Humphrey-like stance, relying on automatic stabilizers, rejecting tax cuts, and avoiding any action that might "frighten the country."[41] It was again a policy of watchful waiting.

Complicating economic decision making at this time was concern about the growing U.S. balance of payments deficit and the potential effect of an inflationary fiscal policy on international confidence in the dollar. Eisenhower took this problem very seriously, as did his new advisers. As the brief recession deepened, Ike seemed willing to accept its negative consequences in the interest of preventing deficits and inflation. "We watched with concern the increase in unemployment," he later wrote, "but we refused to take action that would fail to cure unemployment and cause more acute trouble later on." In the absence of anti-recession measures, unemployment rose to 7.6 percent, the worst since 1941. Between August 1957 and April 1958, industrial production fell 14 percent and business profits declined by 25 percent.

Arthur Burns, now a private citizen, wrote to Eisenhower as conditions worsened. Liberated from the need to be even-handed, Burns strongly recommended increases in defense spending, coupled with some cuts in civilian programs in fiscal year 1959, and urged him to consider a tax cut—the combined result of which would be a small deficit. He argued that the deficit would be in a good cause—showing the country that the administration was serious about the Soviet threat while "help[ing] materially to check the gathering forces of business recession."[42]

Ike's response to Burns has often been quoted. The president admitted that he might be a "reactionary, unsympathetic fossil," but he was determined to oppose "wild-eyed schemes" and "vast and unwise public works programs ... as well as the slash-bang kinds of tax cutting" done only for political advantage.[43] Ike denied that a tax cut would be good for the country, saying he was "quite sure its future would be inflationary." Vice President Nixon, for one, disagreed. "In supporting Burns' point of view," he later wrote, "I must admit that I was more sensitive politically than some of the others around the Cabinet table."

Ike's letter to Burns showed that he had resolved his painful ambivalence. The "battle of the budget" had turned out to be a clarifying experience. The embarrassment of being accused of abandoning his principles drove his well documented turn toward the right in fiscal matters. He would double down on fiscal restraint over the remainder of his term.

The 1957–58 recession was sharper than the earlier one but also shorter— with eight months of economic contraction instead of thirteen. But the political timing could not have been worse. The fears of Richard Nixon and others were realized when dozens of Republican candidates went down to defeat in November 1958. As one historian points out, "virtually every study of voting in 1958 reads the outcome as a rejection of administration economic policy."[44] To many political scientists, Eisenhower's refusal to stimulate the lagging economy with an election approaching made him a rare exception to the "rational politician" theory.[45]

Asked why his administration did not act at the time, Ike replied in character: "You know, the same thing happened in the war. Whenever a crisis occurred, some interested but excitable people began screaming for action. And when they did, I had only one answer. 'I guess I'm just too stubborn to act fast until all the facts are in.'"[46]

The developments of the next two years gave Nixon, who was preparing a presidential run in 1960, an additional source of concern. The administration's economic policy makers, alarmed by continuing inflation even as the economy slumped, resumed budget tightening as the economy began to recover in 1958 and precipitated a new spike in unemployment. As economist Milton Friedman concluded: "That interruption [in the recovery], I conjecture, is the accident of a nonpolitical President, Dwight Eisenhower, who was willing to sacrifice his party's and his vice president's presidential prospects in order to cut short the inflationary process."[47] Another scholar called it the worst fiscal error committed by any administration between 1945 and 1970.[48]

Humphrey did not formulate or implement Ike's economic policies in the late 1950s, but those policies were a continuation—and, in many ways, an intensification—of the Humphrey approach and constituted his most important legacy as treasury secretary. "George Humphrey is the most powerful man in town," said Senate Majority Leader Johnson two years after Humphrey's resignation. "And he lives in Ohio."[49]

17

Ike, Humphrey and Wilson in Retrospect

Humphrey and Wilson were not quite ready to retire to their country estates. Humphrey returned to the M.A. Hanna Company as honorary board chairman, while Wilson went home to Michigan to chair a state advisory committee on civil rights. But these pursuits turned out to be brief transitions into the lives of leisure they had postponed.

The two men showed no interest in reflecting for the record on their recently completed service. Neither elected to write memoirs, reminiscences or rationales for their various actions. Neither sat for detailed interviews with the oral history projects that documented the Eisenhower years. They had gone to Washington to "do a job for the country," and now they were finished. That chapter of their lives was closed.

How well had they served the president and the nation?

Humphrey in Hindsight

Humphrey fared much better than Wilson in an environment neither of them found congenial. He departed to general praise from commentators and journalists, as well as most of his colleagues. The *Washington Post* wrote that he would be "affectionately regarded even by those who have disagreed with him."[1] Newsman Eric Sevareid said he would miss Humphrey's avoidance of "cautious doubletalk."[2] Most of his Cabinet colleagues and other members of the Eisenhower team, whatever their policy views, had genuinely enjoyed his company over the years and treated his departure as a major event.

As measured by the condition of the economy during the first five years of Eisenhower's presidency, Humphrey's stewardship can be viewed as creditable. Conservatives in particular regarded the tight lid on spending as a welcome return to fiscal sobriety, particularly after years of activist government in Washington. Humphrey's supporters could point to steady, sometimes rapid growth, without serious or prolonged economic downturns, which seemed to dispel any lingering fear that Republicans could not manage the economy successfully. The period also included two balanced budgets, in which he and the president took considerable pride.

The failure to halt persistent inflation and to keep federal expenditures under control greatly reduced their sense of satisfaction. Humphrey also fell short of his ambition of using budget surpluses as a springboard to tax reduction. The prosperity and explosive growth of those years called into question the importance of this goal, but lower federal income taxes in 1956 and 1957 might have mitigated the economic (and political) damage caused by the 1957–58 recession. Looking down the road a bit, they also might have bolstered the balance sheets of American business sufficient to stave off the arrival of competition from countries like Japan, which eventually seized market share in a number of key industries.

As we have seen, Humphrey's influence went far beyond economic policy. Eisenhower wanted "broad-gauged" Cabinet officers—assertive, independent actors who would advise him on "the total national welfare, not merely the concerns and needs of one segment of society."[3] Humphrey filled that role to perfection. Ike was not only prepared to defer to his judgment on most economic issues, but he also gave him the most running room of any Cabinet member. Humphrey made pronouncements on nearly every aspect of administration policy. He fought for a defense structure determined more by cost than capability. He tussled with Secretary Dulles over foreign assistance and, more generally, on the importance of balanced budgets. He used back-door channels to Congress to generate pressure on his own administration for budget cuts. He brought an element of political calculation into executive branch decision making that did not reflect Eisenhower's priorities. All the while, his close relationship with the president created the illusion that he spoke for both of them. (Of course, at times he did.)

Humphrey's personal style was an important ingredient in both his successes and failures. His quick intelligence, charm, and powers of persuasion helped him carry the day on many occasions, but the very quality he was most proud of—his diligent collection of all relevant facts—was rarely in evidence. Instead, he doubled down on his experience as a corporate titan, conceding that he could do no more than view policy through "business eyes." That experience made him suspicious of government "meddling" in the economy, in the likely vain hope of curing a recession.

In his articles and public appearances, he claimed to understand that business and government were very different, but he did not use that knowledge to his advantage. His policy views were based on instinct and gut feeling rather than data. He expressed disdain for people who knew more about economics than he did. As one historian put it, he knew "only enough [about economic theory] to pronounce it useless."[4] It seems remarkable that a U.S. treasury secretary could be so closed minded on a subject central to his job.

Humphrey's white-shoe background also tended to constrict his understanding of less fortunate people and their problems. His belief in self-reliance, which had made him wealthy, caused him to disparage government programs for individuals who were not as "electrically charged" as he was and who had not been able to build as charmed a life. While he worried about upsetting the confidence of his fellow businessmen by sanctioning aggressive government action during a recession, he seemed far less concerned about the primary victims of recession—the poor, those in debt, the unemployed. An associate's comment that he would fire his own grandmother (but do it gently) suggested that Humphrey's head always ruled his heart.

Eisenhower and his other advisers recognized Humphrey's limitations. His dogmatism and unwillingness to explore an issue in depth before pronouncing an opinion clearly bothered people around the president. They assumed that exposure to new people and ideas would broaden his perspective but, as many reporters pointed out, he was making the same points and espousing the same policies in 1957 as he was in 1953. Four years after praising his apparent flexibility, journalist Stewart Alsop was struck by how little his basic views had changed.

But Ike usually went along with his thinking. Because he wanted the defense establishment reduced, he shared Humphrey's enthusiasm for the New Look which, if fully implemented, would have saved money but also would have increased the danger of nuclear war. As scientists began to develop and publish scenarios describing the amount of death and destruction that would result from such a war, Americans recoiled in horror. U.S. defense policy struck many at the Pentagon as "apocalypse management." Ike was equally distressed by the prospect of nuclear conflict, but he often seemed reconciled to its inevitability.

Humphrey later denied the danger. He wrote that the New Look prevented rather than courted mutual annihilation and that the nuclear standoff rendered the army and navy close to obsolete. Massive retaliation, "and that alone, I am sure is what kept peace in the world," he reflected years later. "And all the rest of these soldiers and sailors and submariners and everything else, comparatively speaking, you could drop in the ocean, and it wouldn't make too much difference."[5]

Gabriel Hauge was one of several people who tried without success to persuade Humphrey that the country could easily spend more money on defense, which would have made the New Look unnecessary. During the administration's first month, he wrote Humphrey that "we cannot enter [the Eisenhower] era with what appears to be a retreatist mentality."[6] He played down the importance of a balanced budget—"I think seizing the initiative from [Soviet leader] Malenkov and his gang outranks it." He believed that the president need not worry about a fragile economy, which "can support whatever he thinks he needs as he undertakes to [go on the offensive] against Communism." These arguments did not carry much weight with either Humphrey or his boss.

In reflecting later on Humphrey's tenure at Treasury, Hauge was struck more by his problems than his successes. His primary goal—dealing with the deficit—was "a task he ultimately found more difficult than he ever dreamed."[7] Hauge partly faulted Eisenhower for believing that the experience of businessmen was easily transferable into government. The president, in his view, failed to understand how much more complicated and frustrating a Cabinet position could be, especially for a man like Humphrey, who was used to complete personal control over the decision making process. These differences gave Hauge "the feeling that [Humphrey's] service in Washington was a rather trying experience."[8]

The Eisenhower-Humphrey Relationship

Despite their occasional and serious differences, it is apparent that Humphrey's views greatly influenced Eisenhower. Ike admitted that he consistently agreed with his treasury secretary, even when he did not follow his advice. Moreover, he internalized Humphrey's zeal for frugality and returned to it again and again after Humphrey had departed.

During the 1950s, there was growing acceptance of the view that deficit spending had a role to play in leveling out swings in the business cycle and softening economic downturns. Arthur Burns brought this thinking into the administration's policy debates, but Humphrey assailed it as "extremely radical."[9] Eisenhower understood its implications, and even teased Humphrey for being an economic curmudgeon, but he almost always sided with his treasury secretary when faced with a decision.

In fairness to the president, Humphrey's assumptions about budgets and deficit spending were widely shared in Republican circles, and sometimes even among conservative Democrats.[10] Non-economists, probably including Eisenhower, found the presumed value of spending more money than the government takes in counterintuitive. Since then, of course, ideas about fiscal policy have changed. Balanced budgets, for example, are no longer seen as necessary for strong economic growth, and the economic history of the last twenty years has not demonstrated any necessary connection between deficits and inflation.

In order to win debates on the importance of budget balancing, Humphrey had to either convince Dulles and Wilson to support him or somehow reduce their influence in administration councils. In early Cabinet sessions, the two men had attacked Humphrey when he had the temerity to suggest that the country might not be able to afford high levels of defense spending. Dulles even called his thinking "doctrinaire" and "dangerous." They continued to grumble in the years that followed but without much effect once they realized that Eisenhower had been won over by Humphrey's arguments.

Some members of the administration downplayed Humphrey's influence on Eisenhower's economic views, including his budget-balancing goals. In an oral history interview, Arthur Burns judged that his impact on the president in the economic sphere had been "greatly, greatly overestimated." On balance, however, it is not credible that an inexperienced president who believed in delegating authority and badly needed economic advice would reject the policy prescriptions of a man he so obviously liked and admired. Humphrey's outspoken conservatism reinforced Eisenhower's instinctive beliefs, and those beliefs eventually came to dominate his economic perspective.[11] Professor Edward Flash has argued that Ike may have welcomed Arthur Burns' briefings and asked him to coordinate anti-recession policies, but he did not attempt to place Burns between himself and Humphrey, nor did he directly overrule Humphrey in favor of Burns on important issues.[12] (Burns would have disagreed with this assessment.)

A notable example of Humphrey's clout was his shunting aside of Nelson Rockefeller, who served as an adviser to Eisenhower on security policy. In late 1955, Charles Wilson suggested to Rockefeller that he move to the Pentagon as deputy defense secretary. Feeling that his influence at the White House was on the wane, and hoping to succeed Wilson eventually, Rockefeller jumped at the chance. He even talked it over with Ike, who seemed agreeable to the idea. But a week later, Rockefeller learned that Humphrey had blocked the appointment. "George told the president I'd wreck the budget with my spending," he later said. "That settled that. George had a lot of influence in those days."[13] The incident showed not only that he could turn Eisenhower around on a personnel issue, but also that he could affect Wilson's choice of a subordinate in his own department.

The first wave of Eisenhower scholarship, which characterized Ike as a passive and disengaged figure, identified Humphrey as the power behind the throne on economic policy, just as it believed that John Foster Dulles made foreign policy and that Sherman Adams kept the president insulated from tough domestic issues. Journalists charged that Ike took advice from his treasury secretary on "matters as remote from currency and tax collection as mine inspection and atomic research, both of which Humphrey has favored less of."[14]

But we have found firmer support for the revisionist picture of Eisenhower as fully in command of his administration's agenda. A weaker president might have been overwhelmed by Humphrey's sense of certainty and endless advocacy (for example, of tax reduction), but Ike was able to reject his counsel when it seemed to reflect a limited view of the issue at hand. During his first five years in office, his broader perspective made him the "modern Republican" he aspired to be. He decided that he could live with Humphrey's biases and liabilities—partly because he assumed they gave him an insight into the thinking of the American business community, and partly because he had more liberal voices in his immediate circle.

The president was especially unwilling to substitute Humphrey's judgment for his own on foreign policy issues. Eisenhower could rarely count on Humphrey for a recommendation based on a nuanced understanding of conditions overseas and U.S. national interest, rather than on budgetary considerations. This weakness showed in his reflexively negative attitude toward foreign assistance and foreign lending, in exchange for which he sought ironclad guarantees of repayment from underdeveloped and frequently unstable Third World countries. His resistance to aid for India and Egypt created unnecessary difficulties for the president. In all, Humphrey was often an impediment to the foreign policy Eisenhower and Dulles wished to pursue.

Less difficult to measure was the direct impact of their close personal relationship on economic policy. As one historian wrote, it was "hard to pin down because it was exercised in private, directly with the president."[15] We will never know what they discussed at the bridge table or over a round of golf. But Cliff Roberts, a member of Ike's gang, told an oral historian that he rarely saw Humphrey and the president "talking shop" during their vacations together.

A big problem with their relationship was its exclusivity. The other members of the Cabinet knew that Humphrey was Eisenhower's only close friend among top administration officials. Did that knowledge cause anyone second thoughts before arguing against Humphrey in Ike's presence? At times, Arthur Burns seemed to be pulling his punches when summing up the case for government action during the 1953–54 recession. By allowing himself a special friend among his top advisers, the president may have created a dynamic that inadvertently deprived him of the candid counsel he needed. It might not have been clear to the other members of the Cabinet that Eisenhower could carry on a close friendship with Humphrey even while disagreeing with him.

Eisenhower was frequently unsuccessful in reconciling the conflicting views of Humphrey and his more liberal advisers. His uncertain grasp of economic complexities, though a common deficiency of new presidents, gave him little foundation to push back against parochial advice. He probably understood that Republican thinking on the subject had to be revised, but during his first five years in office, he could not decide in which direction he wanted to go.

Until he could resolve his internal conflict, he used Humphrey and his other advisers in a way that was consistent with his management style. He balanced Humphrey's recommendations against those of Burns and Hauge. They each made their case, and the president sometimes tacked left and sometimes right, or when he could not decide, he drifted.[16] He kept control of the debate by measuring the advice from both sides against the practical requirements of the situation as he saw them.

In an oral history interview, Raymond Saulnier charged that Humphrey "clearly did some things that were imprudent and unhelpful"—for example, in the 1957 budget crisis—and that such actions undermined his relationship with Eisenhower.[17] But after that trauma, Eisenhower opted for the approach to economic matters Humphrey had been urging on him for four years. By then, several of his more liberal advisers had departed, and Humphrey was soon replaced by another fiscal conservative, Robert Anderson.

An intriguing question surrounding Humphrey's relationship with the president is the extent to which his own impatience with the relentless growth of defense spending shaped Eisenhower's famous farewell speech. In it, Ike counseled the nation to "guard against the acquisition of unwarranted influence, whether sought or unsought, of the military-industrial complex." The Pentagon's resistance to budget cuts had stirred him against the "incompetence, disloyalty, and outright insubordination" of military officials under his command.[18] His and Wilson's efforts to rein in the services and trim their budgets, while sometimes successful in the short term, had failed to meet Ike's expectations.

No doubt Humphrey strengthened the president's convictions on this matter. In a tone strikingly similar to Ike's in his later speech, he wrote a letter to the new defense secretary, Neil McElroy, in November 1958, a year after leaving the administration. "The country has never before had an enormous entrenched military bureaucracy," he began. "The longer this military bureaucracy continues, the more entrenched it will become and the more impossible it will be ever to bring it to manageable proportions."[19] He ended by advising McElroy to resist this trend. Humphrey sent a courtesy copy to Eisenhower, who proclaimed the letter a "masterpiece."[20]

Despite Humphrey's flaws, Eisenhower felt that he had been well served, and it is easy to see why. The president valued independence and conviction in his immediate subordinates, and Humphrey exhibited both in spades. In contrast to Wilson, he did not bring his problems to the White House. While some administration officials pursued their goals only sporadically or lacked the talent to make those goals attractive to others, Humphrey knew what he wanted and had powers of persuasion to match. To Ellis Slater, the difference between Humphrey and John Foster Dulles was that Dulles went to Ike for decisions, while Humphrey made many of them on his own, later telling the president what he had decided "and then only on matters of high policy."[21]

The fact that Eisenhower considered the dogmatic Humphrey flexible and amenable to persuasion shows how masterfully Humphrey managed his relationship with the president. "Now George isn't really a conservative," Ike told Press Secretary James Hagerty earnestly, "because every time we have an argument ... and the facts are presented to him, [he] usually ends up going along with the liberal point of view or my point of view, which I think is fairly liberal."[22] He believed that Humphrey came to respect his conviction that military cuts had to be gradual and that foreign aid was not always the wasteful giveaway he had thought it was. On another occasion, Ike maintained that no one in his administration had changed as much as Humphrey.

Convincing evidence for the liberalization of his economic views is in short supply, however. If anything, Humphrey's insistence on those views grew stronger with

"It won't be the same without you, George!" By the time Humphrey resigned as treasury secretary in mid-1957, both he and Eisenhower bore wounds from their long struggle to keep government spending within limits (Western Reserve Historical Society, Cleveland, Ohio).

time. When he was outnumbered or out-argued, he might concede defeat on an issue, but he rarely changed his mind.

Ike's perception that Humphrey was flexible, whether correct or not, undeniably raised his stock with the president. He was certainly loyal. Though he never signed on to modern Republicanism, he remained a member of the team and decided to tolerate the president's more liberal inclinations. Once he had his say, he could usually be counted on to defend administration policies he disapproved of. According to Sherman Adams, Humphrey understood that Eisenhower accepted Dulles' assessments of foreign dangers. When a conservative senator asked him about the prospects for tax reductions, Humphrey suppressed his own enthusiasm for them and took the administration line. He "indignantly reminded the senator of 'the atomic Pearl Harbor hanging over our heads,'" which might require more defense spending.[23]

In taking stock of his impact on the Eisenhower administration, the power of his personality stands out. Peerless social skills not only enabled his successful business career but maximized his effectiveness in Eisenhower's Cabinet. He had bitter disagreements with John Foster Dulles, Gabriel Hauge, Charles Wilson and many others, yet these men almost unanimously reported that they had amicable working relations with him. Humphrey's high spirits and good humor seemed to cast a spell that neutralized his opposition. He disagreed regularly with Hauge, the man who best articulated Ike's philosophy, but his charm and "magnificent smile" helped make their relationship work. He even offered Hauge the job of assistant secretary for international affairs at Treasury, although it may have been an attempt to remove him from his close proximity to the president. (Hauge turned it down.)

In the end, it would be unfair to criticize Ike for appointing a treasury secretary with an outlook typical of a conservative corporate executive. He had appropriated business views of the economy during his postwar years of close association (and fascination) with the nation's corporate elite. He took office worried about the rise in inflation during the Roosevelt-Truman years. He signaled his intention to balance the budget, cut taxes, and bring back "sound money." Humphrey reflected and embodied these views as well as anyone. And the president was obviously satisfied—in the end, he called Humphrey his best Cabinet choice.

It is a bit easier to find fault with Lucius Clay, the man who took the lead in selecting Humphrey. He bragged that Eisenhower's Cabinet selection process was not burdened by committees and detailed investigations, because he knew all the candidates personally. He was certainly aware of Humphrey's high intelligence, conservative views, and dynamic personality. Perhaps he even sensed that Humphrey and Eisenhower would enjoy each other's company. Finally, he understood the value of membership on the Business Advisory Council, an organization that accepted the changed landscape brought about by the New Deal.

Even so, he might have cast a wider net. His main problem was that the field of available candidates had been narrowed by the scarcity of Republicans with public policy experience. The range of options was further circumscribed by Eisenhower's known preference for a businessman in the post. But with a little more digging, Clay might have learned of Humphrey's headstrong nature, his tendency to browbeat those who disagreed with him, and his naked partisanship. Eisenhower had to keep these tendencies in check if Humphrey was going to be a useful addition to the Cabinet.

Consequences for the Party and the Country

Most historians believe the economic policies of the Eisenhower administration were appropriate for the times. Ike and his colleagues still receive credit for achieving two balanced budgets and keeping military spending roughly level in real terms. Ike has also been praised for imposing fiscal discipline on the government during his second term sufficient to create the conditions for the boom of the 1960s—a boom over which Democrats would preside and for which they would receive much of the credit. In so doing, the president showed less concern for a Republican victory in the 1960 presidential election than for what he thought was best for the country. His focus on the national interest regardless of the political consequences was a quality still sadly lacking in most American presidents.

A common observation about the administration's domestic policy, and a frequent criticism by the era's Democrats, was that it was bereft of new ideas and burdened with the "tranquilizing effects" of Ike's leadership.[24] To the extent that this was true, an important reason was the constant pressure to cut costs. With the support of the budget chiefs and the president, Humphrey exhorted his colleagues to rein in their budgets at nearly every Cabinet meeting. The targets of his lectures could be forgiven for believing that Eisenhower cared more about saving money than the substance of their programs. The message they carried back to their departments was that expensive initiatives aimed at solving national problems were likely to be rejected. Only those Cabinet members who were prepared to go to the White House and battle it out with the president had any chance of increasing their budgets.

In time, many Americans began to feel as though the country was drifting. Eisenhower's health problems, his preference for behind-the-scenes management, and his well publicized golf vacations contributed to this perception. Especially after the Sputnik shock of 1957, the administration's critics charged that caution and conservative fiscal policy were exactly wrong at a time the American economy needed to compete successfully with the Russians. Democrats argued that the administration should have opted for a higher growth rate, requiring more vigorous federal interventions and looser monetary policy.

Political consequences were inevitable. The recession of 1957–58, lengthened by Eisenhower's reluctance to countenance strong federal action, either resulted in or worsened Republican losses in the off-year elections of 1958. In its aftermath, many Americans believed unemployment persisted longer than necessary.

In the presidential election of 1960, Democrat John Kennedy struck a responsive chord among voters with his promise to get the country moving again. In speech after speech, he lambasted the administration for giving short shrift to the needs of ordinary Americans in a misguided attempt to adhere to fiscal principle.[25] Democrats also cited Sputnik and the collapse of May talks with the Russians as evidence that Eisenhower had allowed the U.S.S.R. to gain the upper hand in the bilateral relationship.

Given the narrowness of Kennedy's victory over Vice President Nixon, it is likely that the Humphrey economic legacy played a role in the outcome. Nixon certainly believed this. He complained in a letter to a supporter as early as 1958 that Eisenhower economics was outdated and that Republicans needed to come up with new ideas.[26] In the 1960 campaign, his moves in this direction were limited by his wish not to alienate the president. Even so, it was clear from his campaign statements that he had a more positive view of the role of government than did Eisenhower.

Wilson's Unhappy Tenure

Saying goodbye to the amiable Wilson occasioned some regret among Washingtonians. He had been a fixture in the capital for several years and had shown an appealing resilience in the face of controversy. More important, despite the constant complaints of Humphrey and the directors of the Bureau of the Budget, he and the president had managed to reduce defense spending as a percentage of the federal budget—from 70 percent in 1953 to only 60 percent seven years later. This was a significant accomplishment, in view of the constant scare-mongering by Congress and the Pentagon. But Wilson would be remembered more for his frustrations than his successes.

17. Ike, Humphrey and Wilson in Retrospect

At the beginning, Lucius Clay considered Wilson an even better choice for the Cabinet than Humphrey. Not only did the former G.M. president have a history of dealing with defense issues and relevant management experience, but he also had made speeches about the relationship between defense and economics that dovetailed nicely with Eisenhower's views.

A little more diligence on Clay's part might have uncovered evidence that Wilson would be a poor fit in a hierarchical, rank-conscious, rule-bound organization like the Pentagon. At G.M. he claimed to have learned that organizations should not follow rigid rules, but rather should be adapted to the abilities and personalities of the people who staff them. The Pentagon's culture was alien to his previous experience. Information about Wilson's informal management style was probably available to Clay, had he sought it. His breezy comment that if Ike was going to hire a businessman as defense secretary, "why not go to the biggest business we have?" reflected poorly on his thought process.

Clay admitted later that Wilson had not worked out as well as he hoped. He believed that Wilson had made a serious mistake in not becoming more involved in foreign policy as a representative of the armed services and that "he was never quite able to live down his maladroitness with his tongue" at his confirmation hearings. But he noted that Wilson was "a hell of a lot better than his successor from Ford (Robert McNamara)."[27]

Wilson's longevity was astonishing, in view of his almost constant failure to measure up to the president's expectations and his penchant for politically embarrassing remarks. He failed at his most important tasks—asserting control over the Pentagon's sprawling bureaucracy, dealing with inter-service rivalry and competition for resources, and persuading the military to accept reductions in spending.

Little by little, it became clear that Wilson was not only ill suited to his duties at the Defense Department but temperamentally mismatched with his boss at the White House. If Humphrey had a long leash, Wilson had a very short one. Ike fumed and fussed about Wilson's shortcomings, both to his staff and to Wilson himself. Yet he could not face facts, realize he had made a mistake, and cut Wilson loose. He took pride in his ability to select good people and saw value in creating and maintaining a harmonious team. He would work with Wilson and deal with his failings rather than start from scratch with someone else.

As we have seen, Eisenhower was frequently and openly disappointed by Wilson's need for constant guidance and his unwillingness to use the authority he had. Some of this was Ike's fault. Because he constantly overruled Wilson, he never developed trust in his judgment. Wilson did his best to understand the legitimate needs of the Defense Department, but when he finally decided that many of the demands of the services had merit, the president assumed he was being duped. Ike's frequent micromanagement and strong views about defense reform made it almost impossible for Wilson to fulfill the expectation that he act autonomously.

At the same time, Wilson was not up to the challenge of dealing with fierce inter-service rivalries or stubborn service heads. He was too much of an outsider to gain the confidence of his subordinates, and he did not push back hard enough when generals and admirals tried to protect their pet programs from the budget axe. Ike demanded that he be the "most unpopular man in government" in order to bring the Pentagon under control, but the main result of his unpopularity was to cause men like General Ridgway to undermine administration policy by going public with their complaints. Wilson was in a no-win situation.

Wilson's five years in office are mostly remembered for his handling of the budget and his personal foibles, but his primary charge from the president was to use his experience as leader and manager of a large organization to reform the Pentagon's management structure and bring the services more firmly under civilian control.

No prospective defense secretary would have found these tasks easy, as the experiences of his predecessors had shown. As might have been expected, Wilson attempted to transfer many methods and organizational forms into the Pentagon from G.M. Assistant secretaries for the army, navy and air force, became analogous to corporate vice presidents. The overall management goals, described in jargon-laden language, were to "clarify ... policy and simplify the administration, fix responsibilities and delegate authority [and make] the boss responsible in the final results of every activity."[28]

Though Wilson made incremental progress throughout his tenure, the services mistrusted and resisted this effort from the start. Many of the same problems remained for the next administration to tackle. Early in President John Kennedy's term, the service heads were reported to be anxious and angry, with some in "a state of near rebellion" about losing their decision-making prerogatives and having their budgets cut by Defense Secretary McNamara. It seemed that little had changed.

Along with G.M. management principles, Wilson brought along his own personal leadership style, which de-emphasized written memoranda and relied on prolonged discussion. Depending on the complexity of the issue, his decision-making process could last for weeks or months. As we have seen, many senior officers chafed under this approach.[29]

But others applauded his desire to hear the full range of opinions on a problem and to get all the facts. A future defense secretary, Thomas Gates, noted approvingly that Wilson "ran the Department of Defense by the human, as opposed to the machine method."[30] It is also true that his engineering background increased his credibility in a few areas. On visits to defense manufacturers, he sometimes recommended improvements to detailed production processes and once suggested a completely new method of internal factory organization, evoking the comment from one observer that it was the "most marvelous exhibition of plant analysis he had ever seen."[31] Wilson's vast experience in procurement matters led predictably to improvements in Pentagon procurement processes.

Wilson might have had greater success by mounting a genuine effort to adapt to the unique "culture" of the military, in order to establish relations of confidence and trust with senior officers. Instead, Wilson clung to his meandering and digressive leadership style in an environment where hierarchy and tradition demanded crisp orders and a command presence.

Caught in the Middle

Wilson's gaffes and his tendency to speak out of turn wasted the president's time, caused him embarrassment, and sometimes gave the impression of an administration in disarray. His public disagreement with Humphrey about the military budget reflected the considerable stress under which he operated and gave the media its occasional field day. But faulting Wilson too much for his natural outspokenness seems unfair. He was unused to reading every careless word he uttered in the newspaper the following morning. Again, it would have helped if Ike were aware what kind of man he was hiring.

Instead of Wilson, Ike needed a civilian with a strong military background, a thorough understanding of how the Pentagon worked, the trust and confidence of the senior officers in each service, and a clear vision of how to begin the process of unifying the country's air, land and sea forces. Membership in the Republican party was not a strict necessity. Such a person could have saved the president and administration countless hours of frustration and wasted effort. Wilson was a good and decent man, but he was one of Eisenhower's most costly mistakes.

If Ike was going to replace him, he should have done so early in his first term, before the high cost of bringing a new defense secretary up to speed would outweigh any potential gain. As with Humphrey, the president reasoned that his performance would improve with time. On a personal level, he understood that he had put Wilson in a tough spot and felt some obligation to honor the diligent effort he was making. So he retained a man in whom he had little confidence, charged him with implementing a controversial military strategy, and overruled most of his budget requests. As one journalist summarized, Ike opted for smoother operations through prolonged personal intimacy at the cost of confusion and policy contradictions.³²

Wilson's frustration was compounded by his inability to please anyone, either above or below him. At the Pentagon, he was known as the man who cut the defense budget by billions of dollars and the size of the armed forces and civilian staff by thousands. The president and George Humphrey viewed him in the opposite light—as having succumbed to the budget demands of an insatiable military, even though defense spending never exceeded $40 bil-

Eisenhower's leadership team and his wife, Mamie, present the president with a birthday gift (left to right: George Humphrey, Vice President Richard Nixon, Secretary of State John Foster Dulles, Mrs. Eisenhower, Ike, and Charles Wilson). The three Cabinet officers had their differences but were united by their loyalty to a president they admired and respected (Western Reserve Historical Society, Cleveland, Ohio).

lion in constant dollars after 1953. When he gave in to White House pressure for cuts, the Washington media criticized him for being under Humphrey's thumb. It is a wonder that the hopelessness of his situation did not drive him to resign earlier. A less dutiful man would have.

Eisenhower, Wilson and Defense Policy

One of the main tasks before Eisenhower and Wilson was to decide how much defense the country needed. In those days, defining an adequate force structure was not easy. Ike was the first president who had to grapple with the question of how nuclear weapons might fit into America's war-fighting strategy. Looking back from the twenty-first century, with a sixty-year record of restraint by the nuclear powers, we are apt to forget that the world of the 1950s was still making up the rules. In 1953, for example, Eisenhower briefly floated the idea, later considered naïve, of turning over all nuclear weapons to an international authority.

Even so, Ike's decision to rely on nuclear weapons, or the threat to use them, in any conflict in order to save money does not look wise in retrospect. Pentagon planners correctly anticipated an era of low-intensity struggles in Africa and Asia in which conventional forces would do most of the fighting. Seen in this light, the Pentagon's strong opposition was inevitable. Humphrey's enthusiasm for this approach may have helped Ike overlook or minimize the danger it posed.[33]

In his defense, Eisenhower had little doubt that competition among the services for resources was wasting millions, or perhaps billions, of dollars, and he was determined to put an end to it. At the time, almost 70 percent of the nation's budget was directed toward military and related activities, compared to only 22 percent today. It is no wonder that he thought an alliance of aggressive Pentagon officers and money-hungry defense contractors was becoming a problem of special concern in America.

In fact, Wilson joined Humphrey in expressing great concern about the many individuals and organizations whose livelihood depended upon high defense budgets. "One of the serious things about this defense business is that so many Americans are getting a vested interest in it; properties, business, jobs, employment, votes, opportunities for promotion and advancement, bigger salaries for scientists and all that," he told a Senate subcommittee in 1957. He found the trend "troublesome."[34]

Wilson's problems did not deter John Kennedy from choosing a defense secretary who had also been president of a major American automobile manufacturer, the Ford Motor Company. McNamara's style was vastly different from Wilson's, but he committed many of the same errors. According to a biographer, he "made precious little allowance for the possibility that the military as an institution, whose ultimate work is the willed risk of human life, was different from Ford or any other large organization."[35] Though the president was new, he had the same blind spot as his predecessor.

A full year after Wilson had left Washington, Eisenhower still felt obliged to defend him. In response to an August 1958 newspaper column containing familiar criticisms of the former defense secretary, Ike took up his pen to soothe Wilson's feelings. "If you have seen the thing, I know that your good sense won't allow you to become upset over [the] senseless diatribe," he wrote. The president went on to call the columnist a person of "low character" who needlessly "deprecate[s] the abilities and dedication of one that we admire, respect and like."[36] Eisenhower may have been a tough and demanding boss, but he remained loyal to a man who had been an important and hard-working member of his team.

Eisenhower's choice of businessmen for two of the most important domestic roles in his administration was, at best, a partial success and at worst a drag on his agenda and a political liability. By succumbing to Humphrey's blandishments, he dashed any hopes of building a centrist movement that would attract enough votes to win future presidential elections. And Wilson forced the president to be what he swore he would not be—his own defense secretary.

Even so, President Eisenhower emerges from this analysis as a sympathetic figure and a highly effective manager. What he lacked in preparation for high office he made up for with a quick mind, personal magnetism, contagious conviction, and skill in handling the tensions and conflicts among the strong personalities around him. He was a perceptive student of human nature who extracted the most out of his subordinates by tapping their strengths and working around their weaknesses. In return, they extended him absolute loyalty—a precious commodity.

Ike's ability to screen out political considerations in making decisions made him a unique president. Instead of viewing policy through an ideological lens, he used and trusted his common sense and his comfort with middle ground. Today's polarized political environment can only increase nostalgia for his style and approach.

At the same time, his oft proclaimed belief that the solution to all complex problems was roughly midway between the two most extreme positions contributed to his troubling tendency to "split the difference." This made him more of a custodian than a leader, especially in domestic affairs. A president

17. Ike, Humphrey and Wilson in Retrospect

Eisenhower presents Charles Wilson with a service medal upon his retirement in October 1957. Wilson survived more than four years as defense secretary, despite his inability to satisfy either the president or the Pentagon brass he supervised. A friend told him in 1956 that he "should have gotten out a couple of years ago" (National Park Service/Dwight D. Eisenhower Presidential Library and Museum).

who all too clearly saw both sides of an issue was especially vulnerable to sustained argument, as George Humphrey well knew. Eisenhower was correct to be concerned that his centrist philosophy might be perceived as "namby-pamby." All too often, the economic result was failure to satisfy either the spenders or the savers.

The service of Humphrey and Wilson did little to reinvigorate the Republican party or further its electoral success, and caused the president some serious problems. But the innate moderation and qualities of intellect and temperament that Eisenhower brought to his job were a good fit for a nation that had recently undergone twenty years of wrenching struggle and change. They made him one of America's most popular presidents.

Chapter Notes

Introduction

1. Related in Herbert S. Parmet, *Eisenhower and the American Crusades*, New York, Macmillan, 1972, p. 150.
2. Joseph and Stewart Alsop, "The Man Ike Trusts With the Cash," *Saturday Evening Post*, May 28, 1953.
3. *Indianapolis Star*, November 29, 1953.

Prologue

1. The phrase is David Halberstam's (*The Fifties*, New York, Villard Books, 1993, p. 236).
2. Cited in William A. Arnold, *Back When It All Began: The Early Nixon Years*, New York, Vantage Press, 1975, pp. 40–41.
3. Quoted in Halberstam, *The Fifties*, p. 312.

Chapter 1

1. See, for example, Joseph Satin, ed., *The 1950s: America's "Placid" Decade*, Boston, Houghton Mifflin, 1960.
2. Maxwell Rabb Oral History (OH-309), Eisenhower Library, p. 12.
3. Gabriel Hauge to Eisenhower, November 13, 1952, Eisenhower Library, Administration Series, Box 18.
4. Jean Edward Smith, *Lucius Clay: An American Life*, New York, Henry Holt, 1990, p. 582, 588.
5. *Ibid.*, pp. 3, 13.
6. *Ibid.*, p. 585.
7. *Ibid.*, p. 607.
8. Herbert Brownell, with John P. Burke, *Advising Ike: The Memoirs of Attorney General Herbert Brownell*, Lawrence, University Press of Kansas, 1993, p. 133.
9. Smith, *Clay*, p. 581.
10. *Ibid.*, p. 294.
11. *Ibid.*, p. 612.

Chapter 2

1. Political speeches 1952, Eisenhower Library, Ann Whitman File, Political Campaign Series; Stephen E. Ambrose, *Eisenhower—Volume One: Soldier, General of the Army, President-Elect, 1890–1952*, New York, Simon & Schuster, 1983, p. 568.
2. Robert Coughlan, "Top Managers in 'Business Cabinet,'" *Life*, January 19, 1953.
3. Alsop, "The Man Ike Trusts with the Cash."
4. Smith, *Clay*, p. 611.
5. Alsop, "The Man Ike Trusts with the Cash."
6. Clifford Roberts Oral History (OH-266), Eisenhower Library, Vol. 6, August 3, 1969, p. 445.
7. John W. Sloan, *Eisenhower and the Management of Prosperity*, Lawrence, University Press of Kansas, 1991, p. 21.
8. After two consecutive losses in presidential contests, by 1952 Humphrey had begun to doubt Taft's electability and was persuaded to back Eisenhower. Herbert Brownell later recalled that Taft had suggested someone else for the Treasury job, though he professed to be satisfied with Humphrey (Brownell memo to Sherman Adams, undated, Sherman Adams Papers, ML-8 [14:16], p. 4).
9. Kim McQuaid, *Big Business and Presidential Power: From FDR to Reagan*, New York, William Morrow, 1982, p. 173.
10. "A Time for Talent," *Time*, January 26, 1953.
11. Eisenhower to Gruenther, November 26, 1952, Eisenhower Library, Ann Whitman File, Administrative Series. Also cited in Gerald Clarfield, *Security with Solvency: Dwight D. Eisen-*

hower and the Shaping of the American Military Establishment, London, Praeger, 1999, p. 98.

12. Roberts Oral History, Eisenhower Library, Vol. 7, August 3, 1969, p. 300.

13. The last Republican secretary of the treasury, Andrew Mellon (1921–1932), a former financier, was both a good and bad role model. His tax policies had contributed to the economic boom of the 1920s, but he was also blamed for President Herbert Hoover's failed efforts to combat the early stages of the Great Depression.

14. Cited in Richard H. Rovere, *Affairs of State: The Eisenhower Years*, New York, Farrar, Straus and Cudahy, 1956, p. 111.

15. Cited in John P. Burke, *The Institutional Presidency: Organizing and Managing the White House from FDR to Clinton*, Baltimore, Johns Hopkins University Press, 2000, p. 92.

16. Burke, *The Institutional Presidency*, p. 106.

Chapter 3

1. The biographic detail that follows comes mainly from several articles written at the time of Humphrey's appointment and based on many interviews. The most useful were Coughlan, "Top Managers in Business Cabinet"; "A Time for Talent"; and "George Humphrey? Of Course!" *Fortune*, January 1953.

2. Nathaniel Howard, ed., *The Basic Papers of George M. Humphrey as Secretary of the Treasury, 1953–1957*, Cleveland, Western Reserve Historical Society, 1965, p. 49.

3. Thomas Parthenakis, *George M. Humphrey, Secretary of the Treasury 1953–1957: A Political Biography*, Ph.D. Dissertation, Kent State University, December 1985, p. 43.

4. "George Humphrey? Of Course!"; Parthenakis, *George M. Humphrey*, p. 14.

5. Humphrey to Jerry Parsons, June 11, 1957, White House Correspondence, George M. Humphrey Papers, Western Reserve Historical Society (WRHS), Container 10, Folder 59.

6. Fletcher Knebel, "The Star of Ike's Team," *Look*, December 13, 1955.

7. Biographic data on Wilson was derived mainly from magazine and newspaper articles of the early Eisenhower years, which featured interviews with Wilson acquaintances. Notable among them were George Kennedy, "The New Cabinet," *Washington Evening Star*, January 12, 1953; Coughlan, "Top Managers in 'Business Cabinet'"; and Beverly Smith, "Secretary Wilson's Year of Trial," *Saturday Evening Post*, May 1, 1954.

8. A confidential memorandum prepared for Westinghouse management in 1918 painstakingly rated forty-eight of the company's engineers on a variety of measures, including potential executive ability. Wilson received the top score (Smith, "Wilson's Year of Trial").

9. The apt observation of Kim McQuaid, *Big Business and Presidential Power*, p. 52.

10. McQuaid, *Big Business and Presidential Power*, p. 30.

11. The tongue-in-cheek observation is McQuaid's (*Big Business and Presidential Power*, pp. 52–53).

12. Ralph Flanders, Henry S. Dennison, and Lincoln Filene, *Toward Full Employment*, New York, Whittlesey House, 1938; McQuaid, *Big Business and Presidential Power*, p. 67.

13. Cited in A. J. Baime, *The Arsenal of Democracy: FDR, Detroit and an Epic Quest to Arm an America at War*, New York, Houghton, Mifflin, Harcourt, 2014, p. 72.

14. Cited in John Morton Blum, *V Was for Victory: Politics and American Culture During World War II*, New York, Harcourt, Brace, Jovanovich, 1976, p. 122.

15. *Business Week*, April 1946.

16. McQuaid, *Big Business and Presidential Power*, p. 130.

17. Oral History Interview with Paul G. Hoffman, October 25, 1964, Harry S. Truman Library, p. 17. Despite his acceptability to Truman as Marshall Plan administrator, Hoffman lost no time in jumping on the Eisenhower bandwagon when it first seemed possible that the general might run for president in 1952.

18. "George Humphrey? Of Course!"

19. Ibid.

20. Ibid.

21. Baime, *Arsenal of Democracy*, p. 136.

22. *Time*, January 24, 1949.

23. According to a writer for *Look* magazine, Humphrey engaged in a running battle during the late 1940s with Ohio governor Frank Lausche, who wanted the Hanna Company to clean up a strip mining site. After fighting Lausche for years, Humphrey gave in and paid to restore the site. He later admitted that his persistence was misguided (Fletcher Knebel, "The Star of Ike's Team," *Look*, November 1955).

24. *New York Times*, July 17, 1947.

25. Coughlan, "Top Managers in 'Business Cabinet,'" *Life*, January 19, 1953. When Humphrey was appointed treasury secretary, Lewis publicly endorsed him.

26. Sidney Hyman, "The Education of George Humphrey," *The Reporter*, August 9, 1956.

27. Smith, "Wilson's Year of Trial."

28. Charles Erwin Wilson, *Dictionary of*

American Biography, Supplement 7: 1961–1965, p. 793.
29. Kennedy, "The New Cabinet."
30. Wilson, *Dictionary of American Biography, Supplement 7*, p. 794.
31. Kennedy, "The New Cabinet."
32. Coughlan, "Top Managers in 'Business Cabinet.'"
33. "George Humphrey? Of Course!"
34. Hyman, "The Education of George Humphrey."
35. "George Humphrey? Of Course!"

Chapter 4

1. Coughlan, "Top Managers in 'Business Cabinet.'"
2. *Ibid.*
3. "A Time for Talent."
4. Kennedy, "The New Cabinet."
5. Humphrey to Louis C. Cates, December 17, 1952, George M. Humphrey Papers, container 1, folder 7.
6. Coughlan, "Top Managers in 'Business Cabinet.'"
7. "Cleveland Clam," Side Lines, *Forbes*, February 1, 1953.
8. *Ibid.*
9. Coughlan, "Top Managers in 'Business Cabinet.'"
10. "George Humphrey? Of Course!"
11. Joseph R. Slevin, "Budgets and Taxes and Secretary Humphrey," *New York Times Magazine*, January 31, 1954.
12. Knebel, "Star of Ike's Team."
13. *The New Republic*, December 1, 1952.
14. *Ibid.*
15. ABC News Commentary, wire service, October 1956.
16. "George Humphrey? Of Course!"; Slevin, "Budgets, Taxes, and Secretary Humphrey."
17. Clifford Roberts Oral History (OH-266), Eisenhower Library, Vol. 10, August 3, 1969, p. 445.
18. Slevin, "Budgets and Taxes and Secretary Humphrey."
19. Roberts Oral History, Vol. 10, pp. 445–446.
20. "George Humphrey? Of Course!"
21. Herbert Brownell Oral History (OH-157), Eisenhower Library, January 25, 1967, p. 109.
22. Alsop, "The Man Ike Trusts with the Cash."
23. "George Humphrey? Of Course!"
24. Smith, "Wilson's Year of Trial."
25. *Time*, June 1, 1953.
26. *Ibid.*
27. Cited in William B. Pickett, *Eisenhower Decides to Run: Presidential Politics and Cold War Strategy*, Chicago, Ivan R. Dee, 2000, p. 136.
28. Eisenhower to Wilson, October 20, 1951, Charles E. Wilson Papers, Anderson University, Anderson, IN, Correspondence, Box 24.
29. Cited in David Halberstam, *The Best and the Brightest*, New York, Macmillan, 1972, pp. 9–10; E. Bruce Geelhoed, *Charles E. Wilson and Controversy at the Pentagon, 1953–1957*, Detroit, Wayne State University Press, 1979, p. 34.
30. The assessment of Douglas Kinnard, *President Eisenhower and Strategy Management: A Study in Defense Politics*, Washington, Pergamon-Brassey's International Defense Publishers, 1989, p. 20.
31. Smith, "Wilson's Year of Trial."
32. *Ibid.*
33. *Ibid.*
34. *Ibid.*
35. *Ibid.*
36. Kennedy, "The New Cabinet."
37. James Patterson, *Mr. Republican: A Biography of Robert A. Taft*, Boston, Houghton, Mifflin, 1972, p. 583.
38. Cited in Emmet John Hughes, *The Ordeal of Power: A Political Memoir of the Eisenhower Years*, New York, Atheneum, 1963, p. 76.
39. Wilson testimony, January 15, 1953, Senate Committee on Armed Services, Department of Defense Nominations, 1953, p. 30.
40. In later years he would flinch before using that phrase, saying: "Wait—I better watch that vice versa" (Smith, "Wilson's Year of Trial").
41. Wilson testimony, Senate Committee on Armed Services, Department of Defense Nominations, 1953, pp. 144–145.
42. *New York Post*, January 28, 1953.
43. Rovere, *Affairs of State*, p. 88.
44. Robert H. Ferrell, ed., *The Eisenhower Diaries*, New York, W.W. Norton, 1981, p. 237.
45. Cited in Piers Brendon, *Ike: His Life and Times*, New York, Harper & Row, 1986, p. 241.
46. Ellis Slater, *The Ike I Knew*, Ellis D. Slater Trust, 1980, p. 41.
47. Wilson to Lawrence P. Fisher, February 3, 1953, Wilson Papers, Box 42.
48. Humphrey Statement Before Senate Finance Committee, January 19, 1953, *Basic Papers of George Humphrey*, p. 14.
49. *Ibid.*, p. 21.
50. *Ibid.*, pp. 21, 23.
51. *Ibid.*, p. 28.
52. According to Ike friend Cliff Roberts, Democratic senator Stuart Symington had pre-

pared a "hatchet job" on Humphrey's war profiteering, alleging that he had made huge sums of money selling aluminum to the government. Humphrey countered the charge so expertly that Symington "ran for cover" (Clifford Roberts Oral History, Eisenhower Library, Vol. 10, p. 619).

Chapter 5

1. Milton Eisenhower, *The President is Calling*, Garden City, NY, Doubleday, 1974, p. 256.
2. Kinnard, *Eisenhower and Strategy Management*, p. 16.
3. Herbert Stein, *The Ford White House*, Lanham, MD, University Press of America, 1986, p. 19. See also Bradley H. Patterson, Jr., *The Ring of Power: The White House Staff and Its Expanding Role in Government*, New York, Basic Books, 1988, pp. 32–33.
4. Richard Tanner Johnson, *Managing the White House: An Intimate Study of the Presidency*, New York, Harper & Row, 1974, p. 87. Eisenhower Cabinet secretary Robert Gray held a dissenting view. He expressed surprise at the quality of ideas that sometimes came from people with no direct responsibility for the problem being considered. Robert Keith Gray, *Eighteen Acres Under Glass*, Garden City, NY, Doubleday, 1962, p. 259.
5. Cabinet meeting, January 23, 1953, Eisenhower Library, Cabinet Series.
6. Ferrell, *The Eisenhower Diaries*, p. 268.
7. Cited in Phillip G. Henderson, *Managing the Presidency: The Eisenhower Legacy—From Kennedy to Reagan*, Boulder, CO, Westview Press, 1988, p. 51.
8. Bernard Shanley Oral History (OH-348), Eisenhower Library, May 16, 1975, p. 103.
9. Ferrell, *Eisenhower Diaries*, p. 243.
10. Robert Griffith, ed., *Ike's Letters to a Friend, 1941–1958*, Lawrence, University Press of Kansas, p. 109.
11. Further developed in Geoffrey Kabaservice, *Rule and Ruin: The Downfall of Moderation and the Destruction of the Republican Party, from Eisenhower to the Tea Party*, New York, Oxford University Press, 2012, p. 15, 21–23.
12. Eisenhower to Bradford G. Chynoweth, July 13, 1954, Eisenhower Library, Ann Whitman Name Series.
13. Description by Dan Rather and Gary Paul Gates, *The Palace Guard*, New York, Harper & Row, 1974, p. 73.
14. Neil Jacoby Oral History (OH-141), Eisenhower Library, p. 48.

15. Gallup Poll, November 16, 1955.
16. Stephen Benedict Papers, Eisenhower Library, Box 14, April 27, 1954.
17. Description of James L. Sundquist, *Politics and Policy: The Eisenhower, Kennedy and Johnson Years*, Washington, D.C., The Brookings Institution, 1968, p. 419.
18. Cited in Richard Norton Smith, *Thomas E. Dewey and His Times*, New York, Simon & Schuster, 1982, p. 586.
19. Rovere, *Affairs of State*, p. 75
20. Marquis Childs, *Eisenhower: Captive Hero—A Critical Study of the General and the President*, New York, Harcourt, Brace, 1958, p. 145.
21. "Eisenhower's Advisers—and How They Rate," *Newsweek*, January 10, 1955.
22. Sherman Adams, Draft Oral History Interview, Columbia University, 1972.
23. Jean Edward Smith, *Eisenhower in War and Peace*, New York, Random House, 2012, p. 498.
24. Gabriel Hauge Oral History (OH-525), Eisenhower Library, November 22, 1968, p. 5.
25. Arthur Larson, *The President Nobody Knew*, New York, Charles Scribner's Sons, 1968, p. xii.
26. Gabriel Hauge to Humphrey, George M. Humphrey Papers, Box 19, Folder 106, April 15, 1954.
27. Stephen Benedict Oral History (OH-210), Eisenhower Library, p. 23.
28. Anderson to Eisenhower, September 19, 1957, Eisenhower Library, Ann Whitman File, Administrative Series.
29. Raymond Saulnier Oral History (OH-234), Eisenhower Library, p. 20.
30. Benedict Oral History, p. 17.
31. Douglas Dillon Oral History, Interview 2, Eisenhower Library, June 28, 1972, p. 78.
32. Cited in William Bragg Ewald, *Eisenhower the President: Crucial Days, 1951–1960*, Englewood Cliffs, NJ, Prentice-Hall, 1981, pp. 63–64.
33. *New York Times*, October 26, 1952.
34. Eisenhower to Milton Eisenhower, January 6, 1954, Eisenhower Library, Whitman File, Administrative Series.
35. McQuaid, *Big Business and Presidential Power*, p. 189.
36. Dwight D. Eisenhower, *White House Years: Waging Peace, 1956–1961*, Garden City, NY, Doubleday, 1965, p. 461.
37. *Ibid.*, p. 39.
38. Herbert Stein, *The Fiscal Revolution in America: Policy in Pursuit of Reality*, Washington, D.C., American Enterprise Institute Press, 1996, pp. 523, 580.

39. The Public Papers of the President, Dwight D. Eisenhower, National Archives and Records Service, 1959, p. 197. Also cited in Raymond J. Saulnier, *Constructive Years: The U.S. Economy Under Eisenhower*, Lanham, MD, University Press of America, 1993, p. 21.
40. Cited in Halberstam, *The Fifties*, p. 210.
41. Ann Whitman Diary File, Eisenhower Library, Box 1, September 1953.
42. Bernard Shanley Oral History (OH-141), Eisenhower Library, p. 79.
43. Ann Whitman File, Name Series (Milton Eisenhower), Eisenhower Library, Box 13, August 28, 1956.
44. Ann Whitman Diary, Eisenhower Library, Box 8, February 13, 1956.
45. Ann Whitman to Milton Eisenhower, August 1956, Eisenhower Library, DDE Diary Series, Box 17, Aug. 56 Misc. (1) file.
46. Sherman Adams, *Firsthand Report: The Story of the Eisenhower Administration*, New York, Harper, 1961, p. 74. Richard Tanner Johnson described Eisenhower's approach to his job as "organized absenteeism" (*Managing the White House: An Intimate Study of the Presidency*, New York, Harper & Row, 1974, pp. 74–119).
47. For example, he called Humphrey on the morning of January 9, 1954, and invited him to play bridge that afternoon (DDE Diary File, Eisenhower Library, Box 5).
48. Cliff Roberts Oral History (OH-266), Eisenhower Library, Vol. 10, p. 626.
49. James David Barber, *The Presidential Character: Predicting Performance in the White House*, 4th ed., New York, Pearson Longman, 2009, p. 170
50. Judgment of Rick Atkinson, *The Guns at Last Light: The War in Western Europe, 1944–1945*, New York, Henry Holt, 2013, p. 307.

leagues opined that he pontificated rather than conversed, "spelling out, in endless detail, the arid truths of economics" (Rather, *Palace Guard*, p. 65). Congress often found him overly cautious: "That boy just ducks and weaves like Joe Louis," complained one senator. But he was right much of the time, and it was to Eisenhower's credit that he could ignore matters of style and focus on content.
8. Herbert Harris, "Meet Arthur Burns: He'll Influence Your Future," *Nation's Business*, November 1953.
9. See Arthur Burns, *Prosperity Without Inflation*, New York, Fordham University Press, 1957.
10. Adams, *Firsthand Report*, p. 56.
11. Robert Cutler, *No Time for Rest*, Boston, Little, Brown, 1965, p. 402.
12. Adams, Draft Oral History, Columbia University, 1972.
13. Gabriel Hauge Oral History (OH-190), Eisenhower Library, May 31, 1967, p. 3.
14. Adams, *Firsthand Report*, p. 55.
15. Stephen Benedict Papers, Eisenhower Library, Box 14, "Reflections on the 1953–1955 Eisenhower White House," p. 31.
16. Stephen Benedict Oral History (OH-527), Eisenhower Library, April 1969, p. 24.
17. Hauge Oral History, p. 79.
18. Ann Whitman Diary File, Box 7, October 15, 1955.
19. Milton Eisenhower Oral History (OH-531), Eisenhower Library, June 19, 1969, p. 26.
20. Smith, *Lucius Clay*, p. 232.
21. Stephen Benedict Papers, Eisenhower Library, Box 14, "Reflections," p. 32.
22. Dodge to Humphrey, February 13, 1953, George M. Humphrey Papers, Case Western Reserve University, Box 7, Folder 34.

Chapter 6

1. "Straightening Out the Business Cycle," *Fortune*, December 1955, p. 102.
2. "Eisenhower's Advisers—and How they Rate."
3. Adams, *Firsthand Report*, p. 156.
4. "Republicans Need Economists Too," *Fortune*, April 1953, p. 116.
5. *Christian Science Monitor*, May 5, 1956.
6. Words of Stephen Hess, *Organizing the Presidency*, 3d ed., Washington, D.C., Brookings Institution Press, 2002, p. 63.
7. For some, Burns the economist was far more compelling than Burns the personality. No one doubted his intelligence, but some col-

Chapter 7

1. Eric Sevareid, "Secretary Humphrey a Strong Personality in Cabinet," CBS Network, May 29, 1957.
2. Merlo J. Pusey, *Eisenhower the President*, New York, Macmillan, 1956, p. 55.
3. *Time*, January 26, 1953.
4. Marion Folsom Oral History (OH-112), Eisenhower Library, p. 31.
5. *Ibid.*, pp. 58–59.
6. *Ibid.*, p. 59.
7. Slevin, "Budgets and Taxes and Secretary Humphrey."
8. Samuel Grafton, "Ike Counts on Mr. Hum," *Collier's*, May 2, 1953.

Notes—Chapter 7

9. *Ibid.*
10. Characterization of Parmet, *Eisenhower and the American Crusades*, p. 157.
11. Robert J. Donovan, *Eisenhower: The Inside Story*, New York, Harper and Brothers, 1956, p. 32.
12. Charles J.V. Murphy, "The Eisenhower Shift," *Fortune*, January 1956, p. 84.
13. Adams, *Firsthand Report*, p. 154.
14. *Ibid.*, p. 134.
15. Griffith, *Ike's Letters to a Friend*, p. 111.
16. Adams, *Firsthand Report*, p. 398.
17. Walter Lafeber, *America, Russia and the Cold War, 1945–1971*, New York, John Wiley and Sons, 1972, p. 152.
18. Douglas Dillon Oral History (OH-211), Eisenhower Library, May 2, 1972, p. 25.
19. *Ibid.*, pp. 18, 30.
20. "Treasury Secretary Humphrey: Businessman in Washington's Wonderland," *Newsweek*, March 14, 1955.
21. Humphrey interview with the author, July 2, 1969, cited in Parmet, *Eisenhower and the American Crusades*, p. 183.
22. Humphrey speech at Masonic Temple, Detroit, March 6, 1957, in Howard, *Basic Papers of George Humphrey*.
23. Adams, *Firsthand Report*, p. 163.
24. Anna K. Nelson, "The Importance of Foreign Policy Process: Eisenhower and the N.S.C.," in Gunter Bischof and Stephen E. Ambrose, *Eisenhower: A Centenary Assessment*, Baton Rouge, Louisiana State University Press, 1995, p. 120.
25. C.D. Jackson to Humphrey, April 29, 1953, Humphrey Papers, Box 10, Folder 59.
26. Hauge to Humphrey, May 25, 1953, Humphrey Papers, Box 19, Folder 106.
27. E.R. Murrow Interview, "*Person to Person*, March 10, 1954," Humphrey Papers, Box 11, Folder 65.
28. Speech to American Bankers Association, October 19, 1954, *Basic Papers of George M. Humphrey*, p. 160.
29. Alsop, "The Man Ike Trusts with the Cash."
30. According to one school of thought, the economic consequences of the lapsing excess profits tax were insignificant—the administration's main goal was to demonstrate its strong commitment to fighting inflation (Stein, p. 292).
31. Cabinet meeting, May 1, 1953, Eisenhower Library, Cabinet Series.
32. Cited in Adams, *Firsthand Report*, p. 159.
33. Folsom Oral History, Eisenhower Library, Vol. 1, p. 35.
34. Gabriel Hauge Oral History (OH-190), Eisenhower Library, p. 59.
35. Eisenhower, *Mandate for Change*, p. 202.
36. Clarence Randall Papers, Eisenhower Library, Box 1.
37. George Bookman Papers (Hauge draft autobiography), Eisenhower Library, Ch. 12, p. 5.
38. Hauge to Humphrey, May 25, 1953, George M. Humphrey Papers, Box 19, Folder 106.
39. Eisenhower to George Whitney, June 24, 1953, Eisenhower Library, Box 569, OF 115-G-1.
40. Howard, *Basic Papers of George M. Humphrey*, p. 71.
41. Humphrey Remarks to Reporters' Roundup TV Panel, June 22, 1953, Howard, *Basic Papers of George M. Humphrey*, pp. 94–97.
42. Humphrey Testimony Before House Ways and Means Committee, June 1, 1953, Howard, *Basic Papers of George M. Humphrey*, p. 74.
43. *New York Times*, July 10, 1953.
44. Cleveland *Plain Dealer*, March 6, 1953.
45. Brownell, *Advising Ike*, p. 135.
46. George Bookman Papers (Hauge draft autobiography), Eisenhower Library, Ch. 9, p. 13.
47. Department of Treasury Appointment Books, 1953–1957, Humphrey Papers.
48. Emmet John Hughes, *The Ordeal of Power: A Political Memoir of the Eisenhower Years*, New York, Atheneum, 1963, pp. 71–72.
49. Ezra Taft Benson, *Cross Fire: The Eight Years with Eisenhower*, Westport, CT, Greenwood Press, 1962, pp. 136–137.
50. Dillon Anderson Oral History (OH-165), Eisenhower Library, p. 46.
51. Kinnard, *Strategy Management*, p. 20.
52. Cutler, *No Time for Rest*, pp. 326, 359.
53. Larson, *The President Nobody Knew*, p. 26.
54. Humphrey Testimony to Senate Finance Committee, June 19–July 12, 1957, Howard, *Basic Papers of George M. Humphrey*, p. 342.
55. Humphrey Testimony to House Ways and Means Committee, June 24, 1955, Howard, *Basic Papers of George M. Humphrey*, p. 199.
56. Merlo J. Pusey, *Eisenhower the President*, New York, Macmillan, 1956, p. 212.
57. Words of John W. Sloan, *Management of Prosperity*, p. 22.
58. Eisenhower to Humphrey, October 26, 1953, Eisenhower Library, Administration Series, Box 20.
59. Ferrell, *Eisenhower Diaries*, p. 237.
60. Eisenhower to Edgar Eisenhower, February 20, 1953, Eisenhower Library, Name Series, Box 11.

61. Cited in Hughes, *Ordeal of Power*, p. 238.
62. Cited in Richard Rovere, "Eisenhower: A Trial Balance," *The Reporter*, April 21, 1955.
63. Eisenhower, *Mandate for Change*, p. 87.
64. Knebel, "The Star of Ike's Team."
65. Humphrey interview with author, July 2, 1969, Parmet, *American Crusades*, p. 175.
66. Slevin, "Budgets and Taxes and Secretary Humphrey."
67. Details on fund-raising activities in Parthenakis, *George M. Humphrey*, p. 105.
68. Humphrey to Gerald Persons, November 9, 1954, Humphrey Papers, Box 10, Folder 59.
69. Parthenakis suggests that the bond between the Eisenhowers and Humphreys may have been strengthened by the shared loss of their first-born sons at an early age (p. 95).
70. Slater, *The Ike I Knew*, p. 70.
71. Roberts Oral History, Eisenhower Library, pp. 248-249.
72. Slater, *The Ike I Knew*, p. 148.

Chapter 8

1. Family profile in *Chicago Tribune*, February 6, 1957.
2. From a confidential source, Parmet, *American Crusades*, p. 189.
3. Merlo J. Pusey, *Eisenhower the President*, New York, Macmillan, 1956, p. 60.
4. Smith, "Wilson's Year of Trial."
5. James M. Gavin, *War and Peace in the Space Age*, New York, Harper, 1958, p. 155.
6. Press conference minutes, November 20, 1953, Wilson Papers.
7. *Time*, June 1, 1953.
8. Ferrell, *Eisenhower Diaries*, p. 237.
9. Adams, *Firsthand Report*, p. 403.
10. *Ibid.*, p. 125.
11. Sherman Adams Oral History (OH-539), Eisenhower Library, March 13, 1985, p. 16.
12. Adams, *Firsthand Report*, p. 99; Geelhoed, *Controversy at the Pentagon*, p. 19.
13. Ewald, *Eisenhower the President*, p. 192; Sherman Adams Draft Oral History, p. 193.
14. Robert H. Ferrell, ed., *The Diary of James C. Hagerty: Eisenhower in Mid-Course, 1954-1955*, Bloomington, Indiana University Press, 1983, p. 3.
15. Charles J.V. Murphy, "Eisenhower's White House," *Fortune*, July 1953, p. 176.
16. Cited in Hughes, *Ordeal of Power*, p. 77.
17. Henderson, *The Eisenhower Presidency*, p. 95.
18. Dillon Anderson Oral History (OH-165), Eisenhower Library, p. 48.
19. Ewald, *Eisenhower the President*, p. 193.

20. Adams Oral History (OH-539), Eisenhower Library, March 13, 1985, p. 12.
21. The president asked Gabe Hauge to study the matter briefly and render his judgment. It will be a no-win decision for Wilson, Hauge concluded, but the facts are such that "he must have a very good reason to force the federal government to forego the 14% saving to the taxpayer that the English bid affords" (Hauge to Ike, July 6, 1955).
22. Hughes, *Ordeal of Power*, pp. 75-76. Hughes later had a serious falling-out with the administration and was regarded by several Eisenhower associates as a biased observer.
23. Account in Adams, *Firsthand Report*, p. 68.
24. Cited in Ewald, *Eisenhower the President*, p. 192.
25. *Reader's Digest*, August 1957, p. 197.
26. Hanson Baldwin, *New York Times*, May 3, 1953.
27. David Lawrence, *Washington Evening Star*, May 14, 1953.
28. According to Donovan, *The Inside Story*, p. 325.
29. Discussions of budget figures can be very confusing. There are many different kinds of budgets, and they include varying categories of expenses. The general numbers cited here and in subsequent chapters refer to the so-called administrative budget, which was the focus of political debate at the time. Precision has been sacrificed to the goal of giving the reader an overall sense of budget trends.
30. Cited in Lafeber, *America, Russia and the Cold War*, p. 140.
31. Address to Union League Club of Philadelphia, October 30, 1953, in Howard, *Basic Papers of George M. Humphrey*, p. 137.
32. Eisenhower to Wilson, October 20, 1951, Eisenhower Library; Stephen E. Ambrose, *Eisenhower: Soldier, General of the Army, President-Elect, 1890-1952*, New York, Simon & Schuster, 1983, p. 513.
33. See, for example, his address to the Investment Bankers Association, December 1, 1953, in Howard, *Basic Papers of George M. Humphrey*, p. 140.
34. Hauge to Humphrey, March 25, 1953, Eisenhower Library, "Economics 1952-3 (1)" folder, Central File, Box 558.
35. Cabinet meeting, May 22, 1953, Eisenhower Library, Cabinet Series; Morgan, *Eisenhower Versus the Spenders*, p. 52.
36. N.S.C. meeting, March 25, 1953, Eisenhower Library. Also Clarfield, *Security with Solvency*, p. 107.

37. Cabinet meeting, March 20, 1953, Eisenhower Library, Ann Whitman File, Cabinet Series.
38. *Time*, April 20, 1953.
39. James T. Patterson, *Mr. Republican: A Biography of Robert A. Taft*, Boston, Houghton, Mifflin, 1972, p. 590 (Geelhoed, p. 60).
40. Press conference minutes, March 20, 1953, Wilson Archive, Box 61; Geelhoed, *Controversy at the Pentagon*, p. 72.
41. Cited in Clarfield, *Security with Solvency*, p. 110.
42. *Newsweek*, July 6, 1953.
43. Legislative leadership meeting, May 12, 1953, Eisenhower Library, Ann Whitman File, Diary Series, Box 7; *Time*, June 1, 1953.
44. Hearings Before the Subcommittee for Defense Appropriations, 83rd Congress, 1st Session, pp. 435–438 (Geelhoed, p. 76).
45. *Time*, June 1, 1953.
46. U.S. Congress, Senate Subcommittee on Appropriations, Hearings on Defense Appropriations for 1954, 83rd Congress, 1st Session, pp. 572–578.
47. George H. Gallup, *The Gallup Poll: Public Opinion, 1935–1971*, New York, Random House, 1972, p. 1158.
48. Cabinet meeting, May 22, 1953, Eisenhower Library, Ann Whitman File.
49. Cabinet meeting, June 26, 1953, Eisenhower Library, Cabinet Series.
50. N.S.C. Session, July 14, 1953, Eisenhower Library, Ann Whitman File.

Chapter 9

1. Cabinet meeting, January 14, 1953, Eisenhower Library, Cabinet Series.
2. Hauge to Eisenhower, November 13, 1952; Sloan, *Management of Prosperity*, p. 134.
3. Adams, *Firsthand Report*, p. 162.
4. Raymond J. Saulnier, *Constructive Years: The U.S. Economy Under Eisenhower*, New York, University Press of America, 1991, p. 50.
5. Adams recalled that the "public finger was pointed at George Humphrey's attempt to tighten credit ... a little too much" (Sundquist, *Politics and Policy*, p. 16).
6. Saulnier, *Constructive Years*, p. 51, 60.
7. *Business Week*, May 9, 1953.
8. *New York Times*, September 13, 1953.
9. Arthur Burns interview in Erwin Hargrove and Samuel A. Morley, *The President and the Council of Economic Advisers: Interviews with CEA Chairmen*, Boulder, CO, Westview Press, 1984, p. 116.
10. *New York Times*, November 25, 1953.
11. Slevin, "Budgets and Taxes."
12. *Business Week*, July 18, 1953.
13. *The Nation*, November 1953.
14. *Christian Science Monitor*, May 5, 1956.
15. Burns to Eisenhower, October 13, 1953, Arthur Burns Papers, Eisenhower Library.
16. John Kenneth Galbraith, *The Affluent Society*, Boston, Houghton Mifflin, 1958, p. 227.
17. Gabriel Hauge agreed. In an October note to the president, he judged that the economy was experiencing a "moderate letdown—and that seems the best word to use as against recession or adjustment" (Hauge to Eisenhower, October 9, 1953, Eisenhower Library, Administration Series, Box 18).
18. Burns interview with author, in Flash, *Economic Advice and Presidential Leadership*, p. 115.
19. Hyman, "The Education of George Humphrey," *The Reporter*, August 9, 1956; Flash, *Economic Advice and Presidential Leadership*, 149–150.
20. Burns to Eisenhower, October 13, 1953, Arthur Burns Papers, Eisenhower Library.
21. Cited in Saul Engelbourg, "The Council of Economic Advisers and the Recession of 1953–54," *Business History Review* 54 (1980), p. 204.
22. Interview with U.S. News and World Report, June 12, 1953, in Howard, *Basic Papers of George Humphrey*, p. 83.
23. Edwin L. Dale, Jr., *Conservatives in Power: A Study in Frustration*, Garden City, NY, Doubleday, 1960, p. 127.
24. *Ibid.*, p, 85.
25. *Economic Report of the President*, Washington, D.C., Government Printing Office, January 1954, iv.
26. Joint Committee on the Economic Report, *Hearings on the January 1954 Economic Report of the President*, 83rd Congress, pp. 722–730.
27. Cabinet meeting, January 15, 1954, Eisenhower Library, Cabinet Series.
28. *Meet the Press* transcript, January 24, 1954.
29. Cabinet meeting, February 5, 1954, Eisenhower Library, Cabinet Series.
30. Hughes to Humphrey, February 4, 1954; Humphrey to Hughes, February 9, 1954, George M. Humphrey Papers, Box 7, Folder 34.
31. Knebel, "The Star of Ike's Team."
32. Related by Donovan, *The Inside Story*, p. 211.
33. Donovan, *The Inside Story*, pp. 215–216.
34. Humphrey Speech to CIO Employment

Conference, Washington, D.C., May 11, 1954, *Basic Papers of George M. Humphrey*, pp. 398–404.

35. Knebel, "The Star of Ike's Team."

36. Paul Douglas, *In the Fullness of Time: The Memoirs of Paul H. Douglas*, New York, Harcourt Brace Jovanovich, 1972, p. 457.

37. George Humphrey Testimony, *Hearings on the 1954 Economic Report*, February 2, 1954, pp. 73–77.

38. Burns interview with Edward S. Flash, cited in Flash, *Economic Advice and Presidential Leadership*, p. 149.

39. Douglas, *In the Fullness of Time*, pp. 428–448.

40. Flash, *Economic Advice and Presidential Leadership*, p. 157.

41. Cabinet meeting, March 19, 1954, Eisenhower Library, Cabinet Series.

42. According to Flash, no follow-up study was done to determine the value of budget flexibility in countering the recession.

43. Cabinet meeting, April 2, 1954, Eisenhower Library, Cabinet Series.

44. Ferrell, *The Eisenhower Diaries*, p. 278.

45. Speech to American Society of Newspaper Editors, Washington, April 15, 1954, in Howard, *Basic Papers of George Humphrey*, p. 149.

46. Eisenhower meeting with David McDonald, April 8, 1954, Eisenhower Library, Box 5 (DDE Diary Series).

47. Humphrey to Hughes, April 7, 1954, George M. Humphrey Papers, Box 7, Folder 34.

48. Ferrell, *Eisenhower Diaries*, p. 278.

49. Robert P. Bremner, *Chairman of the Fed: William McChesney Martin and the Creation of the American Financial System*, New Haven, Yale University Press, 2004, p. 101.

50. Burns to Eisenhower, April 16, 1954, in Arthur Burns Papers, Eisenhower Library, Box 103.

51. Eisenhower, *Mandate for Change*, p. 306; Sloan, *Management of Prosperity*, p. 135.

52. Donovan, *The Inside Story*, pp. 218–219; Sloan, *Management of Prosperity*, p. 135.

53. Cabinet meeting, June 4, 1954, Eisenhower Library, Cabinet Series.

54. Assessment of Edward Flash, *Economic Advice and Presidential Leadership*, p. 164.

55. George Bookman papers (Hauge draft autobiography), Eisenhower Library, Chapter 12, p. 9.

56. Cabinet meeting, June 11, 1954, Eisenhower Library, Cabinet Series.

57. Cited by Flash, *Economic Advice and Presidential Leadership*, p. 163.

58. Humphrey to Hughes, October 29, 1954, George M. Humphrey Papers, Box 7, Folder 34.

59. Humphrey Press Conference, January 15, 1957, in Howard, *Basic Papers of George Humphrey*, p. 248-249.

60. Stein, *Fiscal Revolution in America*, p. 299.

61. See Morgan, *Eisenhower Versus the Spenders*, p. 69.

62. Saulnier, *Constructive Years*, p. 74.

63. *New York Times*, October 24, 1954.

64. Raymond Moley note, October 1956, George M. Humphrey Papers, Box 19, Folder 106.

Chapter 10

1. George Humphrey with James C. Derieux, "It Looked Easier from the Outside," *Collier's*, April 2, 1954.

2. *Newsweek*, March 14, 1955.

3. "Businessman in Washington's Wonderland," *Newsweek*, March 14, 1955.

4. George H. Hall, *St. Louis Post Dispatch*, December 18, 1955.

5. Sherman Adams Oral History, Columbia University, 1972.

6. Adams, *Firsthand Report*, pp. 55–56.

7. George Bookman Papers (Hauge draft autobiography), Eisenhower Library, chapter 9, p. 11.

8. Parmet, *Eisenhower and the American Crusades*, p. 179.

9. Thomas L. Stokes, "The 'Secretary of Everything,'" *New York Herald Tribune*, April 1955.

10. See, for example, Holmes Alexander, "'Strong Man' of the Cabinet," *Washington Post*, October 1, 1956.

11. Alexander, "'Strong Man' of the Cabinet."

12. "Humphrey Becomes Secretary of Everything," *Democratic Digest*, April 1955, p. 10.

13. James Tobin, "The Eisenhower Economy and National Security," *Yale Review* 47 (March 1958), pp. 323–324.

14. Rexford Tugwell, *Off Course: From Truman to Nixon*, New York, Praeger, 1971, pp. 226–227.

15. Edwin L. Dale, Jr., "The Humphrey Theory of Economics," *New York Times Magazine*, February 1957.

16. Words of Iwan Morgan, *Eisenhower Versus the Spenders*, p. 8.

17. Judgment of John Sloan, *Management of Prosperity*, p. 23.

18. Robert Roosa Oral History Interview,

Columbia University Oral History Project, Vol. 2, November 17, 1972, pp. 59–62.
19. Hughes, *Ordeal of Power*, pp. 71–73.
20. *Ibid.*, p. 73.
21. Cited in Lubell, *Revolt of the Moderates*, p. 142.
22. Stuart Alsop, *Washington Post*, March 13, 1959.
23. *Newsweek*, January 28, 1957.
24. Stephen Benedict Papers, "Reflections on the 1952 Campaign and the 1953–1955 Eisenhower White House," Eisenhower Library, Box 14, p. 29.
25. *Christian Science Monitor*, May 5, 1956.
26. Arthur Burns letter to Edward Flash, cited in *Economic Advice and Presidential Leadership*, p. 164.
27. Neil Jacoby Oral History (OH-141), Eisenhower Library, December 5, 1970, pp. 79–81.
28. Herbert Harris, "Meet Arthur Burns: He'll Influence Your Future," *Nation's Business*, November 1953.
29. Douglas Dillon Oral History (OH-211), Eisenhower Library, interview 2, June 28, 1972, p. 81.
30. Jacoby Oral History, p. 81.
31. Erwin C. Hargrove and Samuel Morley, eds., *The President and the Council of Economic Advisers: Interviews with CEA Chairmen*, Boulder, CO, Westview Press, 1984, pp. 107–108.
32. Ewald, *Eisenhower the President*, pp. 68–69.
33. Donald F. Kettl, *Leadership at the Fed*, New Haven, Yale University Press, 1986, p. 140.
34. Eisenhower to Burns, January 14, 1955, Eisenhower Library, DDE Diary Series, Box 9.
35. Raymond J. Saulnier Oral History (OH-234), Eisenhower Library, Volume 3, pp. 58–59.
36. Eisenhower to Humphrey, October 4, 1954, Eisenhower Library, Administration Series, Box 28.
37. Eisenhower call to Humphrey, December 20, 1954, Eisenhower Library, DDE Diary Series, Box 7.
38. Eisenhower call to Humphrey, July 6, 1955, Eisenhower Library, DDE Diary Series, Box 9.
39. Hauge to Eisenhower, June 22, 1953, Gabriel Hauge Papers, Eisenhower Library, Box 1.
40. Saulnier Oral History, Volume 3, p. 57.
41. Hauge to Eisenhower, November 11, 1953, Eisenhower Library, Administration Series, Box 18.
42. According to John Sloan, Hauge delicately informed Burns early in 1955 that Humphrey was "leading a cabal" against him and the 1955 Economic Report, which the C.E.A. chairman had prepared.
43. Stephen Benedict papers, Eisenhower Library, Box 14, January 4, 1954.
44. Hauge to Humphrey, George M. Humphrey Papers, Box 10, Folder 59, July 9, 1955.
45. Hauge to Humphrey, George M. Humphrey Papers, Box 10, Folder 59, March 2, 1955.
46. Cited in Stein, *The Fiscal Revolution*, p. 297.
47. Hauge to Eisenhower, April 29, 1955, Eisenhower Library, Administration Series, Box 18.
48. Hauge to Eisenhower, December 13, 1956, Eisenhower Library, Administration Series, Box 18.
49. "Eisenhower's Advisers," *Newsweek*, January 10, 1955.
50. Slater, *The Ike I Knew*, p. 153.

Chapter 11

1. Burton I. Kaufman, *Trade and Aid: Eisenhower's Foreign Economic Policy, 1953–1961*, Baltimore, Johns Hopkins University Press, 1982, p. 14.
2. Lubell, *Revolt of the Moderates*, p. 143.
3. Speech to National Canners' Association, February 9, 1955, in Howard, *Basic Papers of George Humphrey*, p. 182.
4. Humphrey's negative attitude toward foreign spending may have helped Eisenhower make his famous decision not to intervene militarily in Vietnam to aid the French in 1954. During debate over the subject, Ike asked General Ridgway what a successful intervention would cost. His reply was $3.5 billion a year. The president then turned to Humphrey and asked what that would mean for the budget. "It'll mean a deficit, Mr. President." Someone at the meeting said the idea of intervening died then (David Halberstam, *The Best and the Brightest*, New York, Random House, 1969, p. 603).
5. H.W. Brands, Jr., *Cold Warriors: Eisenhower's Generation and American Foreign Policy*, New York, Columbia University Press, 1988, p. 39.
6. M. Eisenhower, *The President Is Calling*, p. 338.
7. Milton Eisenhower Oral History (OH-531), Eisenhower Library, p. 26, 29.
8. Milton to Dwight Eisenhower, October 1954, Eisenhower Library, Name Series, Box 12.
9. Dwight to Milton Eisenhower, November

23, 1954, Eisenhower Library, DDE Diary Series, Box 8.
10. Dwight to Milton Eisenhower, October 25, 1954, Eisenhower Library, DDE Diary Series, Box 8; Dwight Eisenhower call to Milton Eisenhower, November 9, 1954, Eisenhower Library, DDE Diary Series, Box 7.
11. McQuaid, *Big Business and Presidential Power*, p. 183.
12. Cabinet meeting, December 3, 1954, Eisenhower Library, Cabinet Series.
13. Blanche Wiesen Cook, *The Declassified Eisenhower: A Divided Legacy*, New York, Doubleday, 1981, p. 152.
14. Douglas Dillon oral history (OH-211), Eisenhower Library, interview 1, May 2, 1972, pp. 25, 30.
15. Interview with George Humphrey and Herbert Hoover, Jr., John Foster Dulles Oral History Project, Princeton University, May 5, 1964, p. 21.
16. Humphrey and Hoover interview, Dulles Oral History Project, May 5, 1964, p. 20.
17. A "confidential source" cited in Parmet, *Eisenhower and the American Crusades*, p. 192.
18. John P. Burke and Fred Greenstein, *How Presidents Test Reality: Decisions on Vietnam, 1954 and 1965*, New York, Russell Sage Foundation, 1989, p. 72.
19. Lubell, *Revolt of the Moderates*, pp. 235–236.
20. Eisenhower call to Humphrey, December 5, 1955, Eisenhower Library, DDE Diary Series, Ann Whitman File, Box 11.
21. Cited in Smith, *Eisenhower in War and Peace*, p. 690.
22. Cabinet meeting, April 20, 1956, Eisenhower Library, Cabinet Series.
23. Marquis Childs, *Washington Post*, December 24, 1954.
24. Eisenhower to Hoffman, March 27, 1957, Eisenhower Library, Ann Whitman File, Name Series, Box 13.
25. Humphrey to Eisenhower, May 8, 1957, Humphrey Office Files, National Archives of the United States, Box 10 (emphasis in original)
26. For example, Eisenhower to Humphrey, March 27, 1957, Eisenhower Library, Ann Whitman Diary Series, Box 8.

Chapter 12

1. The following paragraphs are drawn from accounts of the N.S.C. session of October 7, 1953, Eisenhower Library, Ann Whitman File, N.S.C. Series.

2. From account of N.S.C. session of October 13, 1953, Eisenhower Library, Ann Whitman File, N.S.C. Series.
3. Sloan, *Management of Prosperity*, p. 88.
4. *New York Times*, November 24, 1953.
5. *Wall Street Journal*, November 24, 1953.
6. *New York Times*, November 25, 1953.
7. Matthew B. Ridgway, *Soldier*, New York, Harper and Bros., 1956, p. 130.
8. Smith, "Secretary Wilson's Year of Trial."
9. James Hagerty Oral History (OH-91), Eisenhower Library, interview 6, p. 435.
10. Eisenhower to Wilson, November 23, 1953, Eisenhower Library, Administration Series, Box 39.
11. Larson, *The President Nobody Knew*, p. 23.
12. *Time*, June 1, 1953.
13. "Wilson Sees Defense Cuts Near Limit," *Washington Post*, September 30, 1953.
14. Ann Whitman Diary File, October 20, 1953, Eisenhower Library, Box 1.
15. Adams, *Firsthand Report*, p. 99.
16. Smith, "Secretary Wilson's Year of Trial."
17. Eisenhower to Wilson, November 2, 1953, Administration Series, Box 39.
18. Eisenhower call to Wilson, October 14, 1953, Eisenhower Library, Administration Series, Box 39.
19. Eisenhower to Wilson, November 30, 1953, Eisenhower Library, Administration Series, Box 39.
20. Eisenhower to Wilson, December 2, 1953, Eisenhower Library, Administration Series, Box 39.
21. Eisenhower to Wilson, January 27, 1954, Eisenhower Library, Administration Series, Box 39.
22. Eisenhower to Wilson, May 21, 1954 and July 21, 1954, Eisenhower Library, Administration Series, Box 39.
23. *Readers Digest*, August 1957.
24. N.S.C. session, July 15, 1953, Eisenhower Library, Ann Whitman File, N.S.C. Series.
25. Eisenhower to Wilson, November 30, 1953, Eisenhower Library, Ann Whitman File, Diary Series, Box 7.
26. Ridgway, *Soldier*, p. 311.
27. *Ibid.*, p. 289.
28. N.S.C. session, October 7, 1953, Eisenhower Library, Ann Whitman File, N.S.C. Series.
29. N.S.C. 162/2, Foreign Relations of the United States, 1952–1954, Vol. 2, p. 582; Clarfield, *Security with Solvency*, p. 134.
30. Adams, *Firsthand Report*, p. 399.
31. At this early stage in the development of

the New Look doctrine, Eisenhower seems to have harbored the belief that "cleaner" battlefield nuclear weapons producing less radioactive fallout would make their use more acceptable.

32. Speech of October 30, 1953, *Basic Papers of George Humphrey*, p. 137.
33. Speech of November 9, 1953, *Basic Papers of George Humphrey*, p. 494.
34. Humphrey transcript, Dulles Oral History Project, Princeton.
35. George H. Gallup, *The Gallup Poll: Public Opinion, 1935–1971*, New York, Random House, 1972, Vol. 2, July 24, 1953, p. 1158 and October 9, 1954, p. 1274.
36. N.S.C. session, May 20, 1954, Eisenhower Library, Ann Whitman File, N.S.C. Series.
37. *New York Times*, November 6–7, 1953.
38. Ridgway's resistance might have been fueled at least in part by personal pique. According to Sherman Adams, Ike's comments about his performance as head of N.A.T.O. were "less than glowing." (Adams, *Firsthand Report*, p. 400.)
39. Bernard Fall, *Hell in a Very Small Place: The Siege of Dien Bien Phu*, Philadelphia, J. B. Lippincott Co., 1967, p. 309.
40. N.S.C. session, May 20, 1954, Eisenhower Library, Ann Whitman File, N.S.C. Series.
41. *Ibid*.
42. N.S.C. session, June 24, 1954, Eisenhower Library, Ann Whitman File, N.S.C. Series.
43. *New York Times*, April 27, 1954.
44. Morgan, *Eisenhower Versus the Spenders*, p. 2.
45. See especially William W. Kaufman, ed., *Military Policy and National Security*, Princeton, Princeton University Press, 1956.
46. N.S.C. session, November 24, 1954, Eisenhower Library, Ann Whitman File, N.S.C. Series.
47. James Hagerty diary entry, January 4, 1955, FRUS, 1955–57, Vol. 19, pp. 5–6.
48. N.S.C. Session, December 10, 1954, Eisenhower Library, Ann Whitman File, N.S.C. Series; Clarfield, *Security with Solvency*, p. 159.
49. See, for example, "Humphrey Becomes Secretary of Everything," *Democratic Digest*, April 1955, p. 10.
50. Fletcher Knebel, "Every Time He Opens His Mouth, He Says Something," *Look*, March 19, 1955.
51. Wilson to Eisenhower, January 3, 1955; Eisenhower to Wilson, January 5, 1955, "Addresses by C. E. Wilson," 1955, p. 6. Perhaps this was a case of Eisenhower thinking issues through by writing down his thoughts (see p. 113).
52. *New York Times*, February 10, 1955.

53. Senate Appropriations Committee, Hearings on H.R. 6042, 84th Congress, 1955, pp. 1426–1428.
54. Maxwell Taylor, *An Uncertain Trumpet*, New York, Harper, 1959, p. 28.
55. Maxwell D. Taylor, *Swords and Plowshares*, New York, W.W. Norton, 1972, p. 164.
56. Cabinet meeting, August 5, 1955, Eisenhower Library, Cabinet Series.
57. *Ibid*.
58. Taylor, *Swords and Plowshares*, p. 170.
59. *Ibid*., p. 172.
60. *New York Times*, May 18, 1955.
61. Geelhoed, *Wilson and Controversy at the Pentagon*, p. 117, 120.
62. Goodpaster memo of conversation with Eisenhower, December 22, 1955, Eisenhower Library, Ann Whitman Diary, Box 7.

Chapter 13

1. Public Papers of the President, Dwight D. Eisenhower, 1954, Washington, D.C., Government Printing Office, 1962, p. 12.
2. Adams, *Firsthand Report*, p. 165.
3. Milton Eisenhower Oral History (OH-531), Eisenhower Library, June 19, 1969, p. 32.
4. Ann Whitman note, October 18, 1955, Eisenhower Library, Ann Whitman Diary File, Box 7.
5. Eisenhower note, April 15, 1954, Eisenhower Library, DDE Diary File, Box 5.
6. Whitman diary entry, May 18, 1956, Eisenhower Library, Whitman Diary, Box 8.
7. Whitman to M. Eisenhower, August 28, 1956, Eisenhower Library, DDE Diary Series, Box 17, Miscellaneous (1).
8. Transcript, "Face the Nation," October 28, 1956, Wilson Papers.
9. Ferrell, *Diary of James C. Hagerty*, p. 28.
10. Ferrell, *Eisenhower Diaries*, p. 296.
11. Eisenhower memo for the record, March 12, 1955, Eisenhower Library, Administration Series, Box 39.
12. Dulles to Eisenhower, August 8, 1956, Eisenhower Library, DDE Diary Series, Box 16, August 1956 phone calls; Eisenhower, *Waging Peace*, p. 43.
13. *Time*, June 4, 1956.
14. *New York Times Magazine*, February 14, 1954.
15. Larson, *The President Nobody Knew*, p. 77.
16. Congressional Record, 84th Congress, 2nd Session, 1956, pp. 10814–17.
17. Brownell, *Advising Ike*, pp. 135, 141.

18. Sherman Adams Oral History (OH-539), Eisenhower Library, March 13, 1985, p. 12.
19. Cutler, *No Time for Rest*, p. 337.
20. James Hagerty Oral History (OH-91), Eisenhower Library, pp. 532-533.
21. *New York Daily News*, June 26, 1956.
22. *Newsday*, July 5, 1956.
23. House Committee on Appropriations, Hearings Before Subcommittee on Defense Appropriations, 84th Congress, 2nd session, 1956, p. 64.
24. Roberts Oral History, Eisenhower Library, pp. 683, 724.
25. Matthew B. Ridgway, "Keep the Army Out of Politics," *Saturday Evening Post*, January 28, 1956.
26. *Washington Evening Star*, January 25, 1956.
27. Wilson Press Conference, January 17, 1956, Wilson Papers, Box 69.
28. Adams, *Firsthand Report*, p. 401.
29. Cited in Kinnard, *Eisenhower and Strategy Management*, p. 54.
30. *Washington Post*, August 4, 1958.
31. Eisenhower to Wilson, December 21, 1955, Eisenhower Library, Administration Series, Box 39.
32. Wilson Press Conference, February 1, 1956, Wilson Papers, Box 69.
33. Wilson Press Conference, March 6, 1956, Wilson Papers, Box 69.
34. Memorandum for the record, April 5, 1956, Eisenhower Library, DDE Diary Series, Box 15, April 1956 (Goodpaster).
35. Memorandum for the record, April 2, 1956, Eisenhower Library, DDE Diary Series, Box 13, March 1956 (Goodpaster).
36. Cabinet meeting, August 2, 1957, Eisenhower Library, Cabinet Series.
37. Taylor, *Swords and Plowshares*, pp. 170-171.
38. Eisenhower to Wilson, Eisenhower Library, Ann Whitman File, Administration Series, Box 41; Clarfield, *Security with Solvency*, p. 174-175.
39. Memorandum for the record, March 13, 1956, Eisenhower Library, Office of the Staff Secretary, Box 4; Clarfield, *Security with Solvency*, p. 174.
40. Memorandum for the record, April 5, 1956 (Goodpaster); Clarfield, *Security with Solvency*, p. 178.
41. Memorandum for the Record, March 29, 1956, Eisenhower Library, DDE Diary Series, Box 7; Morgan, *Eisenhower Versus the Spenders*, p. 78; Clarfield, *Security with Solvency*, p. 175.
42. Kenneth Condit, *A History of the Joint Chiefs of Staff*, Washington, D.C., JCS Historical Office, 1991, pp. 12-19; Clarfield, *Security with Solvency*, p. 189.
43. Goodpaster memorandum for the record, May 24, 1956, Eisenhower Library, Ann Whitman File, Diary Series, Box 31; Clarfield, *Security with Solvency*, p. 190.
44. Whitman Diary, March 22, 1956, Eisenhower Library, Ann Whitman Diary File, Box 8.
45. Wilson Address to National Press Club, March 13, 1956, Wilson Papers, "Addresses by C.E. Wilson."
46. N.S.C. session, March 22, 1956, Ann Whitman File, N.S.C. Series; Clarfield, *Security with Solvency*, p. 176.
47. Parthenakis, *George M. Humphrey*, p. 474.
48. Senate Armed Services Committee, Airpower Hearings, 84th Congress, 2nd Session, pp. 1789-90.
49. Adams, *Firsthand Report*, p. 404; Clarfield, *Security with Solvency*, p. 181.
50. Cited in Ewald, *Eisenhower the President*, p. 248.
51. *Time*, June 4, 1956.
52. Cited in Halberstam, *The Best and the Brightest*, p. 476.
53. Eisenhower memorandum of conversation, November 8, 1956, Eisenhower Library. Also, Kinnard, *Strategy Management*, p. 60.
54. *New York Times*, February 24, 1957.
55. Bernard Shanley Oral History (OH-348), Eisenhower Library, p. 88.
56. *St. Louis Post-Dispatch*, December 18, 1955.
57. Humphrey to Brundage, July 3, 1957, George M. Humphrey Papers, Box 7, Folder 34.
58. Humphrey to Wilson, July 13, 1953, and August 7, 1953, Humphrey Office Files, National Archives, Box 12.
59. *New York Times*, November 25, 1953.
60. Humphrey Speech to CIO Full Employment Conference, Washington, in Howard, *Basic Papers of George Humphrey*, p. 402.
61. "The Wilson Pentagon," *Fortune*, December 1954.
62. Roberts Oral History, Vol. 10, p. 462.
63. *Washington Post*, June 22, 1955.
64. Press Conference of October 15, 1955, in Howard, *Basic Papers of George M. Humphrey*, p. 584.
65. *New York Herald Tribune*, February 25, 1957.
66. Charles J.V. Murphy, "The Budget—and Eisenhower," *Fortune*, July 1957.
67. *New York Times*, January 29, 1957.
68. *Baltimore Sun*, January 29, 1957.

69. *Chicago Tribune*, January 30, 1957.
70. *New York Times*, January 31, 1957.
71. *Washington Post*, January 31, 1957.
72. Whitman Diary, February 1, 1957, Eisenhower Library, Ann Whitman Diary File, Box 8.
73. Eisenhower to Wilson, February 1, 1957, Eisenhower Library, DDE Diary File, Box 7.
74. Whitman Diary, January 30, 1957, Eisenhower Library, Ann Whitman Diary File, Box 8.

Chapter 14

1. Dale, *Conservatives in Power*, p. 90.
2. Marion Folsom Oral History (OH-112), Eisenhower Library, January 10, 1968.
3. Drew Pearson, *Washington Post*, February 1957.
4. Robert Merriam Oral History (OH-118), Eisenhower Library, January 13, 1969.
5. Eisenhower to Burns, January 14, 1955, Eisenhower Library, Arthur Burns Papers.
6. Cabinet meeting, May 13, 1955, Eisenhower Library, Cabinet Series.
7. Gabriel Hauge Oral History (OH-190), May 31, 1967, Eisenhower Library, p. 78.
8. Humphrey memorandum, August 16, 1955, Humphrey Papers, Box 10, Folder 59; Dale, *Conservatives in Power*, p. 72. The program still had an ancillary but significant effect on the budget, by necessitating a $2 billion increase in highway spending between 1955 and 1959.
9. Adams, *Firsthand Report*, p. 170.
10. *Ibid.*, p. 169.
11. Humphrey and Hoover interview, Dulles Oral History Project, pp. 17–18.
12. Cabinet meeting, November 4, 1955, Eisenhower Library, Cabinet Series.
13. Cabinet meeting, May 13, 1955, Eisenhower Library, Cabinet Series.
14. Adams, *Firsthand Report*, p. 171.
15. Cabinet meeting, May 13, 1955, Eisenhower Library, Cabinet Series.
16. Ewald, *Eisenhower the President*, p. 70.
17. Adams, *Firsthand Report*, p. 171. Cabinet meeting, August 5, 1955, Eisenhower Library, Cabinet Series.
18. Adams, *Firsthand Report*, p. 173.
19. Cabinet meeting, August 12, 1955, Eisenhower Library, Cabinet Series.
20. Cabinet meeting, October 21, 1955, Eisenhower Library, Cabinet Series.
21. Cabinet meeting, November 4, 1955, Eisenhower Library, Cabinet Series.
22. Cabinet meeting, December 2, 1955, Eisenhower Library, Cabinet Series.
23. Whitman Diary, December 12, 1955, Eisenhower Library, Ann Whitman Diary File, Box 8.
24. Cabinet meeting, January 16, 1956, Eisenhower Library, Cabinet Series.
25. Cabinet meeting, March 2, 1956, Eisenhower Library, Cabinet Series.
26. Humphrey to Hughes, February 1, 1956; Hughes to Humphrey, February 2, 1956, George M. Humphrey Papers, Box 7, Folder 34.
27. See especially Edwin L. Dale, Jr., *Conservatives in Power: A Study in Frustration*, New York, Doubleday, 1960, pp. 61–69.
28. *The Papers of Dwight D. Eisenhower*, Baltimore, Johns Hopkins University Press, 1989–96, Vol. 17, doc 2136, p. 2443; McClenahan, *Eisenhower and the Cold War Economy*, p. 59.
29. Rowland Hughes to Cabinet, March 30, 1956, Ann Whitman File, Eisenhower Library, DDE Diary Series, Box 14.
30. Humphrey to Eisenhower, September 7, 1956, Eisenhower Library, Ann Whitman File, Administration Series.
31. Parmet, *Eisenhower and the American Crusades*, p. 497.
32. Hauge to Humphrey, October 8, 1956, George M. Humphrey Papers, Box 19, Folder 106.
33. Eisenhower to Humphrey, July 22, 1958, Eisenhower Library, Ann Whitman File, Administration Series.
34. Cabinet meeting, March 4, 1955, Eisenhower Library, Cabinet Series.
35. William McChesney Martin, "A Five-Year Balancing Act," *Business Week*, February 12, 1956, p. 150.
36. Martin testimony to the U.S. Congress, *Hearings on the Economic Report of 1956*, 84th Congress, 2nd Session, 1956, p. 302.
37. *Christian Science Monitor*, May 5, 1956.
38. Humphrey to Martin, April 24, 1956, Humphrey Papers, Box 6, Folder 37.
39. Bremner, *Chairman of the Fed*, p. 117.
40. Humphrey to Eisenhower, June 21, 1956, Eisenhower Library, Ann Whitman File, Administration Series.

Chapter 15

1. Larson, *The President Nobody Knew*, p. 40.
2. Eisenhower, *Waging Peace*, p. 7.
3. Childs, *Captive Hero*, p. 223.
4. Memo of conversation, Eisenhower and Adams, October 10, 1955, Eisenhower Library, Ann Whitman Diary File, Box 7.
5. Ann Whitman notes, Adams conference with Eisenhower, October 10, 1955, Eisenhower

Library, Ann Whitman file, DDE Diary Series, Box 9.
6. Ewald, *Eisenhower the President*, p. 181.
7. "Humphrey Liked for President," *Pittsburgh Press*, July 17, 1955.
8. See, for example, "Humphrey: Businessmen," *Newsweek*, March 14, 1955.
9. For example, Walter Kerr in *New York Herald Tribune*, October 23, 1955.
10. Childs, "Humphrey Dark Horse?" *Boston Herald*, October 11, 1955.
11. Howard, *Basic Papers of George Humphrey*, p. 593.
12. Hall, *St. Louis Post Dispatch*, December 18, 1955.
13. Howard, *Basic Papers of George Humphrey*, p. 593.
14. Slater, *The Ike I Knew*, p. 148.
15. Whitman Diary, May 21, 1957, Eisenhower Library, Ann Whitman Diary File, Box 8.

Chapter 16

1. Humphrey to Eisenhower, December 6, 1956, Eisenhower Library, Administration Series, Box 21.
2. *Ibid.*
3. Humphrey interview with *U.S. News and World Report*, February 5, 1957, in Howard, *Basic Papers of George Humphrey*, p. 273.
4. Cabinet meeting, January 9, 1957, Eisenhower Library, Cabinet Series.
5. Brundage to Wilson, December 5, 1956, Charles Wilson Papers, Correspondence File, Box 24.
6. Roberts Oral History, Eisenhower Library, Volume 10, pp. 623-624.
7. Murphy, "The Budget and Eisenhower."
8. Roberts Oral History, Eisenhower Library, Volume 10, p. 624.
9. Adams, *Firsthand Report*, p. 360.
10. The letter went through several drafts, the first of which contained many more specific suggestions for cuts. Eisenhower rejected this version.
11. Cabinet meeting, January 9, 1957, Eisenhower Library, Cabinet Series; Sloan, *Management of Prosperity*, p. 100.
12. Roberts Oral History, Eisenhower Library, Volume 10, p. 624.
13. Adams, *Firsthand Report*, p. 366.
14. Humphrey Press Conference, January 15, 1957, in Howard, *Basic Papers of George M. Humphrey*, p. 246.
15. Slater, *The Ike I Knew*, p. 150.
16. Adams, *Firsthand Report*, p. 367.
17. Eisenhower, *Waging Peace*, p. 130.
18. Milton Eisenhower, *The President is Calling*, p. 371.
19. The Eisenhower White House Oral History (OH-508), Eisenhower Library, June 11, 1980, p. 9.
20. Adams, *Firsthand Report*, p. 367.
21. Cabinet meeting, February 27, 1957, Eisenhower Library, Cabinet Series.
22. Legislative leaders meeting, March 5, 1957, Eisenhower Library, Legislative Meeting Series, Box 4.
23. Cabinet meeting, March 11, 1957, Eisenhower Library, Cabinet Series.
24. Eisenhower to Humphrey, April 8, 1957, Eisenhower Library, Ann Whitman File, Administration Series, Box 23.
25. Speech to Iowa Republican Leaders, Des Moines, May 7, 1957, Howard, *Basic Papers of George Humphrey*, pp. 286-292.
26. Adams, *Firsthand Report*, p. 380.
27. Larson, *The President Nobody Knew*, p. 26.
28. Whitman Diary, May 21, 1957, Eisenhower Library, Ann Whitman Diary File, Box 8.
29. Cabinet meeting, June 3, 1957, Eisenhower Library, Cabinet Series..
30. Cabinet meeting, June 21, 1957, Eisenhower Library, Cabinet Series.
31. Stein, *Fiscal Revolution in America*, p. 317.
32. Memorandum of discussion of meetings of the Federal Open Market Committee, Board of Governors, Federal Reserve System, Washington, April 16, 1957, p. 37.
33. Whitman Diary, July 29, 1957, Eisenhower Library, Ann Whitman Diary File, Box 8.
34. Saulnier Oral History (OH-234), Eisenhower Library, Vol. 3, p. 58.
35. Bremner, *Chairman of the Fed*, p, 125.
36. Dillon Oral History (OH-211), Eisenhower Library, Vol. 1, p. 35.
37. Bremner, *Chairman of the Fed*, p. 130.
38. Stevenson to Cyrus Eaton, February 14, 1958, in Walter Johnson, ed., *The Papers of Adlai Stevenson*, Boston, Little, Brown, 1977, p. 166.
39. M. Stephen Weatherford, "The President and the Political Business Cycle," in James P. Pfiffner, ed., *The President and Economic Policy*, Philadelphia, Institute for the Study of Human Issues, 1986, p. 45.
40. Weatherford, "The President and the Political Business Cycle," p. 45.
41. Cabinet meeting, November 15, 1957, Eisenhower Library, Cabinet Series.
42. Burns to Eisenhower, March 10, 1958, Eisenhower Library, Ann Whitman File, Admin. Series.
43. Eisenhower to Burns, March 12, 1958,

Eisenhower Library, Ann Whitman File, Admin, Series.

44. Weatherford, "Political Business Cycle," p. 47.

45. Others believe, however, that Eisenhower was convinced his fight against inflation would be politically popular.

46. Eisenhower, *Waging Peace*, pp. 305–306; Stein, *The Fiscal Revolution in America*, p. 324.

47. Weatherford, "Political Business Cycle," p. 50.

48. Morgan, *Eisenhower Versus the Spenders*, p. 160.

49. Cited in C.L. Sulzberger, *The Last of the Giants*, New York, Macmillan, 1970, p. 321.

Chapter 17

1. *Washington Post*, May 30, 1957.

2. Eric Sevareid, "Secretary Humphrey a Strong Personality in Cabinet," CBS Network, May 29, 1957.

3. M. Eisenhower, *The President Is Calling*, p. 256.

4. Pach and Richardson, *The Presidency of Dwight Eisenhower*, p. 34.

5. Humphrey and Radford transcripts, Dulles Oral History Project, Princeton University Library; Kinnard, *Strategy Management*, p. 27.

6. Hauge to Humphrey, March 25, 1953, George M. Humphrey papers, Box 10, Folder 59.

7. George Bookman Papers (Hauge draft autobiography), Eisenhower Library, ch. 9, p. 11.

8. Bookman Papers, Eisenhower Library, ch. 9, p. 14.

9. Douglas Dillon Oral History (OH-211), Eisenhower Library, Interview 2, June 28, 1972, p. 79.

10. Herbert Stein, *The Fiscal Revolution in America: Policy in Pursuit of Reality*, 2d rev. ed., Washington, D.C., American Enterprise Institute Press, 1996, p. 283.

11. A good example was Ike's constant suspicion (with little evidence) that an attack on waste in government would save millions of dollars annually.

12. Flash, *Economic Advice and Presidential Leadership*, p. 303.

13. James Desmond, *Nelson Rockefeller: A Political Biography*, New York, Macmillan, 1964, p. 144.

14. Rovere, *Affairs of State*, p. 350.

15. Patrick Anderson, *The President's Men: White House Assistants of Franklin D. Roosevelt, Harry S. Truman, Dwight D. Eisenhower, John F. Kennedy and Lyndon Johnson*, Garden City, NY, Doubleday, 1968, p. 156.

16. As James Ledbetter and others have written, contradiction and paradox were common elements of Eisenhower's actions and belief system (James Ledbetter, *Unwarranted Influence: Dwight D. Eisenhower and the Military-Industrial Complex*, New Haven, Yale University Press, 2011, p. 126).

17. Andrew Goodpaster, Ann Whitman, Raymond Saulnier, Elmer Staats, Arthur Burns, Gordon Gray, Joint Oral History (OH-508), Eisenhower Library, June 1980, pp. 7, 10.

18. Ledbetter, *Unwarranted Influence*, p. 98.

19. Humphrey to McElroy, November 21, 1958, Eisenhower Library, Administration Series, Box 21.

20. Eisenhower to Humphrey, November 28, 1958, Eisenhower Library, Administration Series, Box 21.

21. Slater, *The Ike I Knew*, p. 150.

22. Cited in Ewald, *Eisenhower the President*, p. 181.

23. Adams, *Firsthand Report*, p. 164.

24. Words of John W. Sloan, *Management of Prosperity*, p. 155.

25. For example, see *New York Times*, May 1 and May 7, 1960.

26. Nixon to Father John Cronin, August 21, 1958, cited in Stephen Ambrose, *Nixon: The Education of a Politician, 1913–1962*, London, Simon & Schuster, 1987, p. 486.

27. Smith, *Lucius D. Clay*, p. 611.

28. *U.S. News and World Report*, October 18, 1957.

29. James J. Gavin, *War and Peace in the Space Age*, New York, Harper and Bros., 1958, p. 155.

30. Ridgway, *Soldier*, p. 283.

31. Duncan Norton-Taylor, "The Wilson Pentagon," *Fortune*, December 1954.

32. Eric Sevareid, "Secretary Humphrey: A Strong Personality in Cabinet," CBS Network, May 29, 1957.

33. Later, Ike's thinking evolved until he saw nuclear weapons as a moral issue (Ledbetter, *Unwarranted Influence*, 80). By the end of his administration, he had become a believer in arms control and a test ban treaty (Led, 125).

34. Wilson testimony at Senate Subcommittee on Defense Appropriations, 1957, quote in Richard A. Aliano, *American Defense Policy from Eisenhower to Kennedy*, Athens, Ohio University Press, 1975, p. 104.

35. Deborah Shapley, *Promise and Power: The Life and Times of Robert McNamara*, Boston, Little, Brown, 1993, p. 232, 238.

36. Eisenhower to Wilson, August 4, 1958, Eisenhower Library, DDE Diary Series, Box 7.

Bibliography

Manuscript and Archival Materials

Eisenhower Library, Abilene, KS

Collections

George Bookman Papers
Arthur Burns Papers
Gabriel Hauge Papers
C.D. Jackson Papers
Clarence Randall Papers

Papers as President of the United States (Ann Whitman File)

Administration Series
Ann Whitman Diary Series
Cabinet Series
DDE Diary Series
Name Series
NSC Series

Oral Histories

Sherman Adams
Dillon Anderson
Stephen Benedict
Herbert Brownell
Percival Brundage
Arthur Burns
Douglas Dillon
Robert J. Donovan
Dwight Eisenhower
Milton Eisenhower
Marion Folsom
Andrew J. Goodpaster
James Hagerty
Gabriel Hauge
Neil Jacoby
Wilton Persons
Maxwell Rabb
Clifford Roberts
Richard Rovere
Raymond Saulnier
Bernard Shanley

Sherman Adams Papers, Hanover, NH

Boxes 7, 8, 14, 18
Box 39 (scrapbook)

George M. Humphrey Papers, Cleveland, OH

Boxes 7, 10, 19
Clippings File

Charles E. Wilson Papers, Anderson, IN

Correspondence File
Clippings File

Dissertations

Parthenakis, Thomas, *George M. Humphrey, Secretary of the Treasury, 1953–1957: A Political Biography.* Ph.D. Dissertation, Kent State University, December 1985.

Published Sources

BOOKS

Adams, Sherman, *Firsthand Report: The Story of the Eisenhower Administration.* New York: Harper and Brothers, 1961.

Aliano, Richard A., *American Defense Policy from Eisenhower to Kennedy*. Athens: Ohio University Press, 1975.

Ambrose, Stephen E., *Eisenhower—Volume One: Soldier, General of the Army, President-Elect, 1890-1952*. New York: Simon & Schuster, 1983.

———, *Eisenhower—Volume Two: The President*. New York: Simon & Schuster, 1984.

Anderson, J.W., *Eisenhower, Brownell, and the Congress—The Tangled Origins of the Civil Rights Bill of 1956-1957*. The Inter-University Case Study Program, University of Alabama, 1964.

Anderson, Patrick, *The President's Men: White House Assistants of Franklin D. Roosevelt, Harry S. Truman, Dwight D. Eisenhower, John F. Kennedy and Lyndon Johnson*. Garden City, NY: Doubleday, 1968.

Arnold, William A., *Back When It All Began: The Early Nixon Years*. New York: Vantage Press, 1975.

Atkinson, Rick *The Guns at Last Light: The War in Western Europe, 1944-1945*. New York: Henry Holt, 2013.

Baime, A.J., *The Arsenal of Democracy: FDR, Detroit and An Epic Quest to Arm an America at War*. New York: Houghton, Mifflin, Harcourt, 2014.

Barber, James David, *The Presidential Character: Predicting Performance in the White House*, 4th ed. New York: Pearson Longman, 2009.

Benson, Ezra Taft, *Cross Fire: The Eight Years with Eisenhower*. Westport, CT: Greenwood Press, 1962.

Bischof, Gunter, and Ambrose, Stephen E., *Eisenhower: A Centenary Assessment*. Baton Rouge: Louisiana State University Press, 1995.

Bowie, Robert R. and Immerman, Richard H., *Waging Peace: How Eisenhower Shaped an Enduring Cold War Strategy*. New York: Oxford University Press, 1998.

Brands, H.W., Jr., *Cold Warriors: Eisenhower's Generation and American Foreign Policy*. New York: Columbia University Press, 1988.

Bremner, Robert P., *Chairman of the Fed: William McChesney Martin, Jr., and the Creation of the American Financial System*. New Haven: Yale University Press, 2004.

Brendon, Piers, *Ike: His Life and Times*. New York: Harper & Row, 1986.

Brownell, Herbert, with Blake, John P., *Advising Ike: The Memoirs of Attorney General Herbert Brownell*. Lawrence: University Press of Kansas, 1993.

Burke, John P., *The Institutional Presidency: Organizing and Managing the White House from FDR to Clinton*. Baltimore: Johns Hopkins University Press, 2000.

Burke, John P., and Greenstein, Fred, *How Presidents Test Reality: Decisions on Vietnam, 1954 and 1965*. New York: Russell Sage Foundation, 1989.

Childs, Marquis, *Eisenhower: Captive Hero—A Critical Study of the General and the President*. New York: Harcourt, Brace, 1958.

Clarfield, Gerald, *Security with Solvency: Dwight D. Eisenhower and the Shaping of the American Military Establishment*. London: Praeger, 1999.

Condit, Kenneth, *A History of the Joint Chiefs of Staff*. Washington, D.C.: JCS Historical Office, 1991.

Cook, Blanche Wiesen, *The Declassified Eisenhower: A Divided Legacy*. New York: Doubleday, 1981.

Cutler, Robert, *No Time for Rest*. Boston: Little, Brown, 1965.

Dale, Edwin L., Jr., *Conservatives in Power: A Study in Frustration*. Garden City, NY: Doubleday, 1960.

Desmond, James, *Nelson Rockefeller: A Political Biography*. New York: Macmillan, 1964.

Dockrill, Saki, *Eisenhower's New Look National Security Policy, 1953-1961*. New York: Palgrave Macmillan, 1996.

Donovan, Robert J., *Eisenhower: The Inside Story*. New York: Harper and Brothers, 1956.

Eisenhower, Dwight D., *White House Years: Waging Peace, 1956-1961*. Garden City, NY: Doubleday, 1965.

Eisenhower, Milton, *The President is Calling*. Garden City, NY: Doubleday, 1974.

Ewald, William Bragg, *Eisenhower the President: Crucial Days, 1951-1960*. Englewood Cliffs, NJ: Prentice-Hall, 1981.

Fenno, Richard F., *The President's Cabinet: An Analysis in the Period from Wilson to Eisenhower*. Cambridge: Harvard University Press, 1959.

Ferrell, Robert H., ed., *The Diary of James C. Hagerty: Eisenhower in Mid-Course, 1954-1955*. Bloomington: Indiana University Press, 1983.

———, ed., *The Eisenhower Diaries*. New York: W.W. Norton, 1981.

Flash, Edward S., Jr., *Economic Advice and Presidential Leadership: The Council of Economic Advisers*. New York: Columbia University Press, 1965.

Frier, David A., *Conflict of Interest in the Eisenhower Administration*. Baltimore: Penguin Books, 1969.

Gallup, George H., *The Gallup Poll: Public Opin-*

ion, 1935-1971. New York: Random House, 1972.

Gavin, James, *War and Peace in the Space Age.* New York: Harper and Brothers, 1958.

Geelhoed, E. Bruce, *Charles E. Wilson and Controversy at the Pentagon. 1953-1957.* Detroit: Wayne State Press, 1979.

Gilder, George F., and Chapman, Bruce K., *The Party That Lost Its Head.* New York: Alfred A. Knopf, 1966.

Gray, Robert Keith, *Eighteen Acres Under Glass.* Garden City, NY: Doubleday, 1962.

Greenstein, Fred I., *The Hidden-Hand Presidency: Eisenhower as Leader.* New York: Basic Books, 1982.

Griffith, Robert, ed., *Ike's Letters to a Friend, 1941-1958.* Lawrence: University Press of Kansas, 1984.

Halberstam, David, *The Best and the Brightest.* New York: Random House, 1969.

———, *The Fifties.* New York: Villard Books, 1993.

Hammond, Paul Y., *Organizing for Defense: The American Military Establishment in the Twentieth Century.* Princeton: Princeton University Press, 1961.

Henderson, Phillip G., *Managing the Presidency: The Eisenhower Legacy—From Kennedy to Reagan.* Boulder, CO: Westview Press, 1988.

Hess, Stephen, *Organizing the Presidency*, 3rd ed. Washington, D.C.: Brookings Institution Press, 2002.

Hoopes, Townsend, *The Devil and John Foster Dulles.* Boston: Little, Brown, 1973.

Howard, Nathaniel, ed., *The Basic Papers of George M. Humphrey as Secretary of the Treasury, 1953-1957.* Cleveland: Western Reserve Historical Society, 1965.

Hughes, Emmet John, *The Ordeal of Power: A Political Memoir of the Eisenhower Years.* New York: Atheneum, 1963.

Johnson, Richard Tanner, *Managing the White House: An Intimate Study of the Presidency.* New York: Harper & Row, 1974.

Johnson, Walter, ed., *The Papers of Adlai Stevenson.* Boston: Little, Brown, 1977.

Kabaservice, Geoffrey, *Rule and Ruin: The Downfall of Moderation and the Destruction of the Republican Party, from Eisenhower to the Tea Party.* New York: Oxford University Press, 2012.

Kaufman, Burton I., *Trade and Aid: Eisenhower's Foreign Economic Policy, 1953-1961.* Baltimore: Johns Hopkins University Press, 1982.

Kaufman, William W., ed., *Military Policy and National Security.* Princeton: Princeton University Press, 1956.

Kettl, Donald F., *Leadership at the Fed.* New Haven: Yale University Press, 1986.

Killian, James R., Jr., *Sputnik, Scientists and Eisenhower: A Memoir of the First Special Assistant to the President for Science and Technology.* Cambridge: MIT Press, 1977.

Kinnard, Douglas, *President Eisenhower and Strategy Management: A Study in Defense Politics.* Washington, D.C.: International Defense Publishers, 1989.

Krieg, Joann, ed., *Dwight D. Eisenhower: Soldier, President, Statesman.* New York: Greenwood Press, 1987.

Lafeber, Walter, *America, Russia and the Cold War, 1945-1971.* New York: John Wiley and Sons, 1972.

Larson, Arthur, *The President Nobody Knew.* New York: Charles Scribner's Sons, 1968.

Ledbetter, James, *Unwarranted Influence: Dwight D. Eisenhower and the Military-Industrial Complex.* New Haven: Yale University Press, 2011.

Lewis, Wilfred, Jr., *Federal Fiscal Policy in the Postwar Recessions.* Washington, D.C.: The Brookings Institution, 1962.

Lodge, Henry Cabot, *As It Was: An Inside View of Politics and Power in the '50s and '60s.* New York: W.W. Norton, 1976.

Longstreet, Stephen, *A Century on Wheels: The Story of Studebaker, A History, 1852-1932.* New York: Henry Holt, 1952.

Lubell, Samuel, *Revolt of the Moderates.* New York: Harper, 1956.

Mayer, George H., *The Republican Party, 1854-1966.* New York: Oxford University Press, 1967.

McClenahan, William M., Jr., and Becker, William H., *Eisenhower and the Cold War Economy.* Baltimore: Johns Hopkins University Press, 2011.

McQuaid, Kim, *Big Business and Presidential Power: From FDR to Reagan.* New York: William Morrow, 1982.

Mitchell, George C., *Matthew B. Ridgway: Soldier, Statesman, Scholar, Citizen.* Mechanicsburg, PA: Stackpole Books, 2002.

Morgan, Iwan, *Eisenhower Versus the Spenders.* New York: St. Martin's Press, 1990.

Myers, Linfield, *As I Recall…: The Wilson-Morrison Years.* Anderson, IN: Anderson College Press, 1973.

Pach, Chester J., Jr., and Richardson, Elmo, *The Presidency of Dwight Eisenhower.* Lawrence: University Press of Kansas, 1991.

Parmet, Herbert S., *Eisenhower and the American Crusades.* New York: Macmillan, 1972.

Patterson, Bradley H., Jr., *The Ring of Power: The*

White House Staff and Its Expanding Role in Government. New York: Basic Books, 1988.

Patterson, James T., *Mr. Republican: A Biography of Robert A. Taft*. Boston: Houghton Mifflin, 1972.

Perrett, Geoffrey, *A Dream of Greatness: The American People, 1945–1963*. New York: Coward, McCann & Geoghegen, 1979.

Pfiffner, James P., *The Strategic Presidency: Hitting the Ground Running*. Chicago: The Dorsey Press, 1988.

_____, ed., *The President and Economic Policy*. Philadelphia: Institute for the Study of Human Issues, 1986.

Pickett, William B., *Eisenhower Decides to Run: Presidential Politics and Cold War Strategy*. Chicago: Ivan R. Dee, 2000.

Pusey, Merlo J., *Eisenhower the President*. New York: Macmillan, 1956.

Rae, Nicol C., *The Decline of Liberal Republicanism: From 1952 to the Present*. New York: Oxford University Press, 1989.

Rather, Dan, and Gates, Gary Paul, *The Palace Guard*. New York: Harper & Row, 1974.

Reichard, Gary W., *The Reaffirmation of Republicanism: Eisenhower and the Eighty-third Congress*. Knoxville: University of Tennessee Press, 1975.

Ridgway, Matthew B., *Soldier*. New York: Harper and Bros., 1956.

Rovere, Richard H., *Affairs of State: The Eisenhower Years*. New York: Farrar, Straus and Cudahy, 1956.

Satin, Joseph, ed., *The 1950s: America's "Placid" Decade*. Boston: Houghton Mifflin, 1960.

Saulnier, Raymond J., *Constructive Years: The US Economy Under Eisenhower*. Lanham, MD: University Press of America, 1993.

Schlesinger, Arthur M., Jr., *Journals—1952–2000*. New York: Penguin, 2007.

Shapley, Deborah, *Promise and Power: The Life and Times of Robert McNamara*. Boston: Little, Brown, 1993.

Slater, Ellis, *The Ike I Knew*. Ellis D. Slater Trust, 1980.

Sloan, John W., *Eisenhower and the Management of Prosperity*. Lawrence: University Press of Kansas, 1991.

Sloan, Alfred, Jr., *My Years with General Motors*. New York: Doubleday, 1963.

Smith, Jean Edward, *Eisenhower in War and Peace*. New York: Random House, 2012.

_____, *Lucius Clay: An American Life*. New York: Henry Holt, 1990.

Smith, Richard Norton, *Thomas E. Dewey And His Times*. New York: Simon & Schuster, 1982.

Sobel, Robert, *The Age of Giant Corporations: A Microeconomic History of American Business, 1914–1992*. London: Praeger, 1993.

Stebenne, David L., *Modern Republicanism: Arthur Larson and the Eisenhower Years*. Bloomington: Indiana University Press, 2006.

Stein, Herbert, *The Fiscal Revolution in America: Policy in Pursuit of Reality*, 2d rev. ed. Washington, D.C.: The American Enterprise Institute Press, 1996.

_____, *Presidential Economics: The Making of Economic Policy from Roosevelt to Reagan and Beyond*. New York: Simon & Schuster, 1984.

Sulzberger, C. L., *The Last of the Giants*. New York: Macmillan, 1970.

_____, *Seven Continents and Forty Years: A Concentration of Memoirs*. New York: Quadrangle, 1977.

Sundquist, James L., *Politics and Policy: The Eisenhower, Kennedy and Johnson Years*. Washington, D.C.: The Brookings Institution, 1968.

Taylor, Maxwell D., *Swords and Plowshares*. New York: W.W. Norton, 1972.

_____, *An Uncertain Trumpet*. New York: Harper, 1959.

Tugwell, Rexford, *Off Course: From Truman to Nixon*. New York: Praeger, 1971.

Tugwell, Rexford G., *How They Became President: Thirty-Five Ways to the White House*. New York: Simon & Schuster, 1964.

Vatter, Harold G., *The U.S. Economy in the 1950s: An Economic History*. New York: W.W. Norton, 1963.

Wagner, Steven, *Eisenhower Republicanism: Pursuing the Middle Way*. DeKalb: Northern Illinois University Press, 2006.

Warshaw, Shirley Anne, *Powersharing: White House-Cabinet Relations in the Modern Presidency*. Albany: State University of New York Press, 1996.

Ziparo, Jessica, and Galambos, Louis, *Dwight David Eisenhower: Annotated Bibliography of Selected Publications, 1991–2010*. The Eisenhower Institute, 2011.

Articles

Alexander, Holmes, "'Strong Man' of the Cabinet." *Washington Post*, October 1, 1956.

Alsop, Joseph. *The Washington Post*, June 22, 1955.

Alsop, Joseph, and Stewart Alsop. "The Man Ike Trusts With the Cash." *Saturday Evening Post*, May 28, 1953.

Alsop, Stewart, "Humphrey Proves Return to Low Tax Era is Impossible." *New York Herald Tribune*, July 1957.

Bibliography

Berle, A.A., "Businessmen in Government: The New Administration." *The Reporter,* February 3, 1953.

"Businessman in Washington's Wonderland." *Newsweek,* March 14, 1955.

Childs, Marquis, "Humphrey Dark Horse?" *Boston Herald,* October 11, 1955.

"Cleveland Clam." Side Lines, *Forbes,* February 1, 1953.

Collins, Frederic W., "The Education of a Cabinet." *The Reporter,* May 12, 1953.

Coughlan, Robert, "Top Managers in 'Business Cabinet.'" *Life,* January 19, 1953.

Dale, Edwin L., Jr., "The Humphrey Theory of Economics." *New York Times Magazine,* February 1957.

____, "Can We Afford to Keep Strong?" *The Reporter,* June 23, 1953.

Egan, Charles E., "Balanced Budget Possible in 1956, Humphrey Says." *New York Times,* August 26, 1955.

"Eisenhower's Advisers—and How They Rate." *Newsweek,* January 10, 1955.

"Four-and-a-half Years of George Humphrey." *Washington Post,* May 30, 1957.

"George Humphrey? Of Course!" *Fortune,* January 1953.

Gilpatric, Roswell L., "Retreat in Air Power." *The Reporter,* June 23, 1953.

Gladwell, Malcolm, "The Uses of Adversity." *The New Yorker,* November 10, 2008.

Grafton, Samuel, "Ike Counts on Mr. Hum." *Collier's,* May 2, 1953.

Gregory, Nicholas P., "Foreign Aid Policy Humphrey Victory." *Philadelphia Inquirer,* January 3, 1957.

Griffith, Robert, "Dwight D. Eisenhower and the Corporate Commonwealth." *American Historical Review* 87, no. 1 (February 1982), pp. 87–122.

Harris, Douglas B., "Dwight Eisenhower and the New Deal: The Politics of Preemption." *Presidential Studies Quarterly* 27, no. 2 (Spring 1997), pp. 333–342.

Harris, Herbert, "Meet Arthur Burns: He'll Influence Your Future." *Nation's Business,* November 1953.

Harsch, Joseph C., "Eisenhower's First Hundred Days." *The Reporter,* May 12, 1953.

"He's Watching for Trouble." *Business Week,* July 18, 1953.

Hessler, William H., "George Humphrey, New Name on the Dollar." *The Reporter,* February 17, 1953.

Hobbs, Edward H., "The President and Administration: Eisenhower." *Public Administration Review* 8, no. 4 (Autumn 1958), pp. 306–313.

Howard, Nathaniel, "George M. Humphrey." *Ohioana Quarterly,* Summer 1974.

Humphrey, George, with Derieux, James C., "It Looked Easier from the Outside." *Collier's,* April 2, 1954.

"Humphrey at Treasury." *Business Week,* February 28, 1953.

"Humphrey Becomes Secretary of Everything." *Democratic Digest,* April 1955, p. 10.

Hyman, Sidney, "The Education of George Humphrey." *The Reporter,* August 9, 1956.

"Index Man" (Arthur Burns). *Newsweek,* February 8, 1954.

Jacoby, Sanford M., "Employers and the Welfare State: The Role of Marion B. Folsom." *Journal of American History* 80, no. 2 (September 1993), pp. 525–556.

Kennedy, George, "The New Cabinet." *Washington Evening Star,* January 12, 1953.

Knebel, Fletcher, "Every Time He Opens His Mouth, He Says Something." *Look,* March 19, 1955.

____, "The Star of Ike's Team." *Look,* November 1955.

Lindley, Ernest K., "Businessmen in Government." *Newsweek,* March 14, 1955.

Martin, William McChesney, "A Five-Year Balancing Act." *Business Week,* February 12, 1956.

Moley, Raymond, "A Credit to the Cabinet." *Los Angeles Times,* May 3, 1957.

Murphy, Charles J.V., "The Budget and Eisenhower." *Fortune,* July 1957.

Norton-Taylor, Duncan, "The Wilson Pentagon." *Fortune,* December 1954.

Preston, Rick, "Humphrey Liked for President." *Pittsburgh Press,* July 17, 1955.

"Republicans Need Economists Too." *Fortune,* April 1953.

Rovere, Richard, "Eisenhower: A Trial Balance." *The Reporter,* April 21, 1955.

"Seaway Seen as Certain by Humphrey." *Cleveland Plain Dealer,* March 6, 1951.

Sevareid, Eric, "Secretary Humphrey A Strong Personality in Cabinet." CBS Network, May 29, 1957.

Slevin, Joseph R., "Budgets and Taxes and Secretary Humphrey." *New York Times Magazine,* January 31, 1954.

____, "Rise in Arms Spending Blocks Economy Drive." *New York Herald Tribune,* February 25, 1957.

Smith, Beverly, "Secretary Wilson's Year of Trial." *Saturday Evening Post,* May 1, 1954.

Stokes, Herman L., "The 'Secretary of Everything.'" *New York Herald Tribune,* April 1955.

"Straightening Out the Business Cycle." *Fortune*, December 1955.

"Thomasville: Another White House?" *US News and World Report*, March 2, 1956.

"A Time for Talent." *Time*, January 26, 1953.

Tobin, James, "The Eisenhower Economy and National Security." *Yale Review* 47 (March 1958,) pp. 323–324.

"The Wilson Pentagon." *Fortune*, December 1954.

NEWSPAPERS

The Baltimore Sun
The Chicago Tribune
Christian Science Monitor
The New York Times
St. Louis Post-Dispatch
The Wall Street Journal
The Washington Post
The Washington Star

Index

Numbers in **bold italics** indicate pages with illustrations

Adams, Sherman 59–61, 64–65, 67, 69, 70–71, 81, 87, 96–97, 111, 130, ***136***, 165, 168, 170, 188–192, 201, 209–211, 223, 226
Alsop, Joseph 44, 82, 95, 161, 170, 179
Alsop, Stewart 44, 82, 220
American Banker's Association 73, 82
American Red Cross 38
American Society of Newspaper Editors 122
Anderson, Dillon 89
Anderson, Robert 60–61, 178–179, 200, 213–215, 224
Aswan Dam 144

Barber, James David 65
Benedict, Steven 61, 71, 132
Benson, Ezra 89, 190, 194
Bevin, Ernest 34
Bradley, Omar ***108***
Brownell, Herbert 11, 12, 13, 19, 44, 87–88, 168, 201, 208, 237*n*8
Brundage, Percival 61, 171, 178, 181, 205–206, 208, 211, 215
budgets: FY-1954 78–79, 83–84, 99–100, 103–107, 186; FY-1955 107, 146, 153–155, 157, 164, 186; FY-1956 158, 159, 161–164, 172, 188–190, 193–195; FY-1957 158, 164, 169, 174–175, 177, 189, 191–193, 195–196, 211–212; FY-1958 173, 175–176, 181, 204–213, 224; FY-1959 215–216; FY-2015 budget 2
Bureau of the Budget 57, 67, 71, 73, 121, 141
Burns, Arthur 60, ***72***, 112–113, 130, ***136***, 176, 187–189, 191, 193, 196, 204, 209, 223–224, 241*n*7; appointment to C.E.A. 68–69; economic views 68–70, 113, 116, 120, 134, 191; and Humphrey 69, 112, 115–116, 120, 133–135, 187, 192, 222, 246*n*42; and recession of 1953–54 112–118, 120–128, 221; and recession of 1957–58 216
Bush, Prescott 43
Business Advisory Council 14, 15, 16, 17, 29–35, 44, 77, 227
Business Week 71, 87, 111, 113
Byrd, Harry 9
Byrnes, James 12

Cabinet: collective personality 9, 19; recruitment 11–13
Carnegie, Andrew 15
Carnegie Tech 27, 37
Carney, Robert 158, 162
Castro, Fidel 141
Childs, Marquis 59, 201–202
Christian Science Monitor 133
Chrysler Corporation 18–19, 37
Churchill, Winston 55
Cities Service Company 14
Clay, Lucius 9, 11, 13–14, 16–19, 33–34, 40, 48, 60, 73, 201, 226–227, 229; personality and style 11–12, 34, 229
Coca-Cola Company 14
Collier's magazine 129
Committee for Economic Development 14, 31–32, 77
Communist China 10
Council of Economic Advisers 61–62, 67–69, 71, 73, 111–113, 115, 125, 131, 133–134, 204, 214
Cutler, Robert 71, 89, 103, 146, 168

De Gaulle, Charles 55
Delco-Remy Co. 28–29
Dewey, Thomas E. 5, 6, 7, 12, 19, 58–59, 71, 199
Dillon, Douglas 61, 80, 142, 214
Dodge, Joseph 9, 73, 78–79, 83, 100–101, 103–105, 115, 118, 142, 148, 152–154, 206
Donovan, Robert 118, 128
Douglas, Paul 117, 120, 131
Drucker, Peter 45
Dulles, John F. 9, 10, 16, 42, 55, 71, 105, 118, 140–141, 151, 153, 157, 160; and Eisenhower 64, 223, 225–226; and Humphrey 79–80, 103, 109, 142–145, 147–149, 156, 159, 193, 208, 219, 222, 225; and Wilson 95, 167, ***179***, ***232***
Durkin, Martin 97

Eastman Kodak Co. 30, 76–77
Economic Cooperation Administration 33
Economic Report of the President 116–117, 134, 187
Eisenhower, Dwight D.: 1, ***100***, ***108***, 164, ***182***, 223, 227, ***232***, 234–235; and balance of pay-

259

ments 216; on budget issues 56, 61, 63, 78–79, 85, 99–100, 106–107, 147, 162–163, 170–172, 177, 186–187, 190–192, 194–196, 198, 204–206, 209, 211–217, 221, 227–228; and Burns 68–69, 112, 115, 122–123, 126–127, 134; on Cabinet government 54–56; dealing with Congress 106–107, 195, 209–212; on defense issues 18, 46, 79, 94, 96, 98–105, 108, 146, 148–151, 154–160, 162, 165, 167, 171, 173, 175, 177–180, 220, 222, 225, 227, 230, 233; evaluation of 234–235; farewell speech 224–225; and Federal Reserve 74, 123, 197; on foreign economic assistance 80, 108–109, 139–140, 142–145, 187; on general economic issues 60–63, 116, 123, 147–148, 163, 205, 211, 221–222, 224, 226; general policy views 2, 6, 8, 57–59, 187; health 65, 166, 191–193, 199, 201–202, 215, 227; and Humphrey 75–76, 90–93, 106, 108–109, 115, 119, 130, 132, 135, 141–145, 178–179, 187–188, 201–202, 209–211, 213, 220–224, *225*, 226, 243*n*69; leisure activities 5, 92; as military leader 16, 151; personality and style 6, 11, 13, 20, 29, 54, 64–66, 144–145, 161; as presidential candidate 6, 7, 9, 71; on presidential succession 199–202; and recession of 1953–54 110, 112–119, 121–128, 215; on St. Lawrence Seaway 87–88; on tax cuts 83–85, 107, 115, 120, 188–194, 196, 216; and Wilson 46, 48, 50–51, 96–98, 101, 104, 108, 151–154, 161–163, 165–167, 169, 172–174, 176, 182–184, 211, 229–230, 232, 234, *235*
Eisenhower, Edgar 65, 91
Eisenhower, Mamie 92–93, *232*
elections: (1944) 5; (1948) 5, 6; (1952) 6–9, 17; (1954) 128, 177; (1956) 169, 171, 174, 181, 185, 191, 195, 197–199, 204, 205–206; (1958) 3, 216, 228; (1960) 3, 217, 227–228
Employment Act of 1946 62
Ervin, Sam 174
Ewald, William 97, 134, 189
Export-Import Bank 60, 74, 140

Face the Nation 166
Fair Deal 58
Federal Reserve 67, 70, 73, 74, 90, 110, 112–114, 123, 125, 127, 132, 194–197, 212–214
Flash, Edward 222
flexible response doctrine 173
Folsom, Marion 30–31, 76–77, 84, 186–187, 207, 210, 212
Forbes magazine 25
Ford, Edsel *37*
Ford, Gerald 55, 169
Ford, Henry 15, 30
Ford Motor Co. 37, 229, 233–234
Forrestal, James 19
Fortune magazine 34, 42, 43, 178
Friedman, Milton 217

Galbraith, John Kenneth 31, 114
Gallup Poll 58, 107, 128, 157, 202
Gardner, Trevor 170

Gates, Thomas 231
Gavin, James 95
General Electric 16, 30
General Motors 15, 16, 18, 27–29, 31, 34, 36–38, 45, 48–50, 95, 99, 229–230
George, Walter 120
Godfrey, Arthur 41, 95
Goldman, Sachs 17
Goldwater, Barry 205, 209
Grant, Richard 22
Great Depression 2, 10, 15, 25, 26, 29–30, 43, 44, 62, 70, 82, 118, 125, 128
Gruenther, Albert 201

Hagerty, James 97, 151, 168, 225
Hanna, Howard 23
Hanna, Mark 43
Harriman, Averill 30, 33
Harris, Seymour 131
Hauge, Gabriel 11, 59–61, 68, *72*, 74, 78–79, 84, 136–137, 201, 214; appointment as assistant to the president 70–71; and Eisenhower 73, 135–137, 224; and Humphrey 81, 84–85, 88, 103, 110, 130, 134–137, 188, 195, 220–221, 226; personality and style 71, 135; and recession of 1953–54 110–111, 125–126, 244*n*17
Hazlett, Swede 65, 175
Hoffman, Paul 14, 15, 17, 19, 31, 33–35, 145, 238*n*17
Hoover, Herbert 5, 10, 24, 26, 61, 70, 117, 128, 147
Hoover, Herbert III 80
Hughes, Emmet 88, 97, 132
Hughes, Rowland 73, 118, 122, 127, 158, 160, 173–174, 187, 191–195, 206
Humphrey, George M. 2, 4, 9, *24*, 29, 30, 38, 75, 80, *82*, *93*, *100*, 152, 157, 167, 218–226, 228; on budgets, deficits and inflation 78–81, 83, 89, 93, 115, 158, 185–198, 204–208, 211, 215, 219, 221–222, 227; and Burns 69, 112–113, 115–116, 118, 132–134, 246*n*42; confirmation hearings 49, 51–52, 239–240*n*52; and Congress 40, 84–86, 88–90, 109, 111, 131, 190, 206, 208, 210, 219; criticism of 130–133, 163, 170, 211; on defense spending 79, 81, 100–105, 107–109, 146–151, 154–156, 158–161, 163, 170–172, 174, 177–178, 180, 189, 205, 219–220, 225–226, 233; early life and career 21–26; and Eisenhower 73, 75–77, 91–93, 101, 105–106, 113, 130, 133, 135, 142–144, 178–179, 187, 201–202, 204–210, 219, 221–224, *225*, 226, 229, 237*n*8, 243*n*69; and Federal Reserve 74, 196–197, 213; on foreign economic assistance 80, 108–109, 139–145, 219, 223, 225, 246*n*4; general economic views 2, 32, 44–45, 52–53, 59, 61, 70, 80, 82, 91, 93, 116, 118, 127, 129, 131–132, 134–135, 147–148, 163, 195, 220–221; leisure activities 40–42, 65, 92; at M.A. Hanna 23–26, 39, 218; personality and style 2, 17–18, 23, 25, 33–34, 39, 41, 42–44, 49, 56, 76–78, 88–91, 93, 112, 130–137, 141, 202, 213–214, 219–220, 223, 225–227;

and recession of 1953–54 110–119, 121–128, 131, 215; recruitment as treasury secretary 2–3, 16–20, 226–227; as Republican activist 25–26, 92, 130, 132, 177, 199, 203; resignation 213–215, 217; on St. Lawrence Seaway 86–88; on taxes 81, 83–86, 107, 112, 115–116, 119–120, 185, 188–189, 191–194, 205–206, 211, 219, 223; on wage and price controls 76, 78; and Wilson 101, 109, 177–180, 187, 192, 206, 222, 228, 232; World War II and after 31, 33–36
Humphrey, Hubert 119, 157
Humphrey, Pamela S. 17, 22, 81, 92

Internal Revenue Act of 1954 77, 119–121, 127, 212
Interstate highway system 188, 202, 250*n*8
Iron Ore Company of Canada 39–40

Jackson, C.D. 81
Jackson, Henry 168, 174
Jacoby, Neal 126, 133–134
Johnson, Lyndon 157, 163, 217

Kefauver, Estes 170
Keller, K.T. *37*
Kennedy, John F. 3, 157, 228, 230, 233
Keynes, John Maynard 31, 62
Keynesian economics 61–62, 133
Keyserling, Leon 68
Kissinger, Henry 113, 159
Knowland, William 164, 200, 202, 209
Knudsen, William S. 29, 31, 36, 48
Korean War 2, 7, 8, 9, 10, 46, 63, 75, 76, 78–79, 83, 97, 99–101, 105, 107, 111, 146, 158, 173, 181, 188
Krock, Arthur 81
Kyes, Roger 94, 124

Landon, Alf 26
Larson, Arthur 63, 89, 152, 199–200, 214
Lausche, Frank 238*n*23
Lend-Lease program 74
Lewis, John L. 35–36, 38
Life magazine 39
Lodge, Henry Cabot 12, 78, 201
Long, Russell 52
Look magazine 170
Lovett, Robert 12, 19, 46, 98

M.A. Hanna Co. 16, 22–26, 27, 39, 42, 52, 78, 86, 90, 208, 210, 218
MacArthur, Douglas 12, 73, 151
Malone, George 89–90
Marshall, George 7, 32–33
Marshall Plan 32–33
Martin, William McChesney 74, 89–90, 111, 114, 123, 196–197, 213–214
McCarthy, Joe 166
McDonald, David 122
McElroy, Neil 215, 224–225
McKinley, William 22–23, 26, 43, 124

McNamara, Robert 229–230, 233–234
Meet the Press 81, 117
Mellon, Andrew 25, 52, 238*n*13
Michigan Central Railroad 22
Michigan Heart Association 38
Mills, Wilbur 86
Mitchell, James 55, 97, 124
Mitchell, Wesley 68
Modern Republicanism 57–58, 70–72, 135, 137, 187, 200, 205, 209, 214, 223, 226
Moley, Raymond 128
Montgomery, Bernard 55
Morgenthau, Henry 18
Morse, Wayne 43, 117, 181
Murrow, Edward R. 81

Nasser, Gamal 144
The Nation magazine 113
National Bureau of Economic Research 68, 204
National City Bank of Cleveland 25
National Grange Convention 89
National Labor Relations Board 26
National Security Act of 1947 46
National Steel 24
Nehru, Jawaharlal 143
Nelson, Donald 48
New Deal 8, 26, 30, 32, 35, 38, 58, 69, 81, 118, 209
New Look 3, 153–165, 169–170, 174, 181, 185, 220–221, 233
New York *Daily News* 168
New York Federal Reserve Bank 123
New York *Herald Tribune* 14, 180
New York Stock Exchange 74
New York Times 42, 81, 91, 111, 112, 150, 159, 167, 173, 206
Newsday 169
Newsweek magazine 45, 59, 129, 130
Nixon, Richard 3, 7, 57, 121, 128, 187, 191–193, 200, 202, 216–217, 228, ***232***
North Atlantic Treaty Organization (NATO) 7
NSC-68 99
Nuclear Weapons and Foreign Policy 159

Paarlberg, Don 214
Parmet, Herbert 130
Patton, George 55
Pearson, Drew 112, 178, 211
Person to Person 81
Persons, Wilton 97
Pittsburgh Consolidated 25
Pittsburgh Press 202
Project Solarium 147

Radford, Adm. Arthur 9, 99, ***108***, 147, 149, 154–155, 160, 171–173, 175
recession: of 1953–54 2, 110–128, 185, 196, 212, 215, 223; of 1957–58 212–217, 228
Reed, Dan 83–86, 89, 110
Remy Electric Co. 27–28
Republican party 1, 3, 5–8

Index

Reuther, Walter 36–38, 117, 124, 166
Ridgway, Matthew 151, 155–156, 158–159, 161–162, 165, 169–170, 173, 230, 246n4, 248n38
Roberts, Clifford 18–19, 43, 65, 92, 169, 178, 206, 208, 223
Rockefeller, John D. 25
Rockefeller, Nelson 98, 143–144, 222
Roosevelt, Franklin D. 2, 5, 12, 13, 15, 21, 26, 29–30, 57–58, 62, 74, 75, 82
Roosevelt, Theodore 21
Rose, H. Chapman 77
Rovere, Richard 51, 59
Russell, Richard 50, 168

St. Lawrence Seaway 40, 52, 86–87
St. Louis Post Dispatch 130
Saturday Evening Post 169
Saulnier, Raymond 61, 111, 127, 134–135, **136**, 176, 204, 212–213, 224
Schlesinger, Arthur, Jr. 43, 51
Shanley, Bernard 64, 177
Slater, Ellis 92–93, 202, 208, 225
Sloan, Alfred 15, 27, 28–30, 48
Smith, Margaret Chase 106
Snyder, John 18
Social Security 30, 77, 186
Sproul, Allan 123
Sputnik 215, 228
Stassen, Harold 78, 103, 114–115, 121, 141, 143, 145, 193, 207
Stein, Herbert 55, 63, 212
Stennis, John 164
Stettinius, Edward 19
Stevens, John 155
Stevenson, Adlai E. 8, 215
Stimson, Henry L. 31
Studebaker Motors 14, 19
Suez crisis 167
Swope, Gerard 30
Symington, Stuart 106, 157, 162–164, 170–172, 174, 239–240n52

Taft, Robert 7, 12, 15, 17, 19, 23, 26, 33, 46, 49, 59, 62, 90, 99, 104–105, 200, 237n8
Taft, William Howard 21
Taft-Hartley Act 32
Taylor, Maxwell 162–163, 172–173
Thomasville, GA 26, 65, 88, 92–93, 201, 215
Time magazine 16, 45, 96, 104, 106, 117, 152, 167, 175
Tobin, James 131
Toward Full Employment 31
Truman, Harry S. 5, 6, 13, 32–33, 46, 57–58, 63, 73, 74, 75–76, 86, 101, 106, 107, 124, 132
Tugwell, Rexford 131
Twining, Nathan 172

Union Bank of Commerce 25
United Auto Workers 36, 38, 166
United Fund 38
United Mine Workers 35–36

U.S. Chamber of Commerce 140
U.S. Congress 2, 3, 8, 56, 137, 183; on defense cuts 104–106, 157; House Armed Services Committee 165; House Ways and Means Committee 83–86, 90, 131; Senate Appropriations Committee 157; Senate Armed Services Committee 49–53; Senate Finance Committee 51–53, 90
U.S. News and World Report 80
United Steel Workers 122
University of Michigan 22, 24
U.S. Steel Co. 36
U.S.S.R. 3, 7, 10; Cold War with 94, 99, 106, 139, 144, 148–149, 156, 159, 163, 228; weapons development 10, 101, 158, 163, 169–171, 174

Vietnam 158
Vinson, Fred 18

Wake Island 1, 9
Wall Street Journal 150
Warren, Earl 199–200, 202
Washington Post 152, 183, 218
Weeks, Sinclair 88
Weinberg, Sidney 17
Weir, Ernest 210
Westinghouse Electric Co. 27
Whitman, Ann 64–65, 166, 173, 183–184, 202, 213
Wilson, Charles E. (GE) 19, 48
Wilson, Charles E. (GM): 2, 9, 33, 42, 55, 93–94, **102**, **108**, 117, 130, **179**, **181**, **182**, 186, **232**; appraisal of performance 228–234; confirmation hearings 49–51, 106, 239n40; and Congress 96–97, 106–107, 174, 181, 183, 210; criticism of 50–51, 95–98, 151–153, 162–163, 165–170, 177, 181–182, 234; and defense budget 2, 81, 94, 101, 103–105, 108, 115, 146–147, 149–150, 152, 154–155, 157, 159–164, 166, 170–176, 178, 180–181, 189, 193, 195, 206, 210–211, 222, 224, 228, 230–233; early life and career 21, 26–29; and Eisenhower 95–98, 123–124, 151–154, 160–162, 164–167, 172, 176, 182–184, 193, 225, 231, **235**; at General Motors 16, 18, 29, 33, 35–36, **37**, 38; health problems 27, 29, 35, 38, 161, 180–181; and Humphrey 109, 161, 177–180, 206, 222, 226, 231–232; leisure activities 38, 41; management of Defense Department 94–96, 98–99, 101, 104, 106, 146, 150–153, 159, 161, 163, 165, 168–169, 175–177, 179, 222, 230–232, 234; and National Guard 181–184; and the New Look 154–157, 159–165, 170; personality and style 2, 36, 41, 45, 47–48, 50, 95–97, 101, 102, 151–153, 165–169, 177, 184, 229–231; political views 45; recruitment as defense secretary 2, 3, 16, 18–20, 46–47, 53, 229; resignation 213–215, 218, 228
Wilson, Jessie 47, **182**–183
World Bank 140
World War II 2, 10